D0065447

THE DIVINE AVERAGE

Also by William G. Mc Collom:
Tragedy (1957)

THE
DIVINE AVERAGE

A View of Comedy

WILLIAM G. MC COLLOM

1971
The Press of Case Western Reserve University
Cleveland/London

PHILLIPS MEMORIAL
LIBRARY
PROVIDENCE COLLEGE

To Cathleen and Mimsie

Preface

EVERYONE TAKES PLEASURE IN COMEDY, but not everyone respects it. The unthinking spectator turns to it for entertainment and looks for nothing else. The intellectual reader often has an uneasy feeling that, instead of celebrating life, comedy ought to look unblinkingly at suffering and derangement; the superiority of *Twelfth Night* to *Measure for Measure* in form and finish does not affect his suspicion that the dark comedy is the greater because it probes evil more relentlessly. Shelley would seem to have been almost correct: our most important if not our sweetest songs are those that tell of saddest thought.

But as L. C. Knights has insisted, comedy is a serious activity. It is serious, first of all, in the degree that it realizes the aesthetic possibilities of its premises and perceptions. The object of its seriousness differs, of course, from that of tragedy and other forms: the seriousness of Molière is not that of Swift or Spenser. In contrast to tragedy, comedy directs itself toward those levels of mind and feeling concerned not with perilous moral choices made in isolation from others but with the steps or leaps taken, the adjustments made, the routines rehearsed, and the chances encountered in an endless variety of social settings from family to committee room to carnival. The advanced drama of the fifties and sixties has reminded us that even farce can be serious. It has often been so. Most great comedy includes farce; the war veterans in Aristophanes, the gaping heirs in Jonson, the anguished cuckolds in Molière are alternately hilarious and troubling, even though they do not encourage the idea that man is a hopeless alien in the universe.

The laughter of both farce and comedy can be serious. In much farce, laughter issues from a drastically penetrating look into disproportion and injustice. In the upper ranges of social comedy, laughter is both laughter at and laughter with, a two-sidedness reflecting the balance of an art supported by ironic insight and humane sentiment. This balance goes with a tendency to step back from the spectacle, so that it may be clearly seen and coolly evaluated. High comedy is seriously impartial.

The early chapters of this book seek to define comedy, to indicate its reach, and to see how its nature manifests itself in structure, characterization, and language. The later chapters examine significant examples of comedy from Aristophanes to the twentieth century. I have not limited my gallery to works that would most easily support the ideas developed in Chapter One. *Tartuffe*, for example, challenges them; but I believe that current readings of this play make it look too much like an expression of our century, which is notable in the drama for what I call dialectical tragicomedy.

The names of some eminent writers on comedy appear fairly frequently in these pages. Others might have been invoked more often. Among recent writers on the subject from whom I have learned much, even when I learned to disagree, are James K. Feibleman, Albert Cook, Susanne Langer, and Northrop Frye.

In the desire to reach those interested in Greek and French drama but lacking special linguistic equipment, I have quoted Aristophanes and French dramatists other than Molière in English. Molière is usually quoted in both French and English, since many readers will want to have his words before them. Unless acknowledged, translations are my own.

Unless otherwise specified, citations from Shakespeare are to *The Complete Plays and Poems of William Shakespeare*, edited by William Allan Neilson and Charles Jarvis Hill. For Molière and Marivaux, I refer to the volumes in the Bibliothèque de la Pléiade, edited by Maurice Rat and Marcel Arland respectively. For Shaw's plays, I cite *The Complete Plays of Bernard Shaw* (London: Odhams Press Limited, 1934). Other editions are cited in the notes.

Acknowledgments

Chapter 1 originally appeared, in somewhat different form, in *Drama Survey*, Spring-Summer 1963. Chapter 7 originally appeared, in somewhat different form, in *Shakespeare Quarterly*, Spring 1968, and is here reprinted by permission.

The author is indebted to the following for quotations of copyrighted material:

Harcourt, Brace & World, Inc.: Dudley Fitts, trans., *Ladies' Day*.
Oxford University Press: Christopher Fry, *A Phoenix Too Frequent*.
The Society of Authors, for the Bernard Shaw Estate: *The Complete Plays of Bernard Shaw, Prefaces, Our Theatres in the Nineties*.

Contents

PART ONE: THEME

1. Form and Attitude in Comedy   5
2. The Area of Comedy   31
3. Types of Comic Structure   52
4. Character   75
5. Speech   97

PART TWO: VARIATIONS

6. The Ambiguities of *The Birds*   125
7. The Role of Wit in *Much Ado About Nothing*   139
8. On the Edge of Comedy: Jonson's *Bartholomew Fair*   153
9. *Tartuffe*: The Victory of Light   165
10. Marivaux: The Nuances of Love and the Balance of Comedy   180
11. Shaw's Comedy and *Major Barbara*   198

    Postscript   213
    Bibliography   220
    Index   227

THE DIVINE AVERAGE

PART ONE

THEME

and critics have found it valuable. With this in mind, I should like to offer the following definition: *Comedy is an amusing, relatively discontinuous action concerning success and failure in social relations and culminating in a judgment whereby the "divine average" triumphs over the exceptional or peculiar. The movements toward success and failure are arranged in a pattern of inevitability and chance: the freedom of the will is not stressed. The total work, therefore, presents life as a product of natural law and erratic fortune.*

This is the form with which a playwright who wishes to write a comedy may be said to start. The particular comedy at which he finally arrives is a product of this basic form, or norm, and his individual aims, attitudes, and finally, vision. The comedy is not wholly his, though what matters most in a work of art is the particular imprint which the artist places upon his material. In Aristophanes, in the comedies of Shakespeare, in Molière, and even in Shaw, who called himself a classical dramatist, we are always aware of the form with which the playwright began, and it is still discernible in the finished work. Sometimes we can sense little conflict between the artist's hand and his material; the writer seems happily ensconced in the patterns given him and in the social attitudes they recall; he does not so much remake his material as improve its articulation and conviction. But ironically, the greatest comedies often develop attitudes which not merely qualify but transform the structure which tradition has presented to them. *The Misanthrope* is a comedy and not an anti-comedy à la Ionesco, but it so persistently questions the way of life which it must have been expected to celebrate that it strains the form almost beyond what it can bear. Much the same has been said of Falstaff in relation to his Lancastrian world. Of course, no great example of art can merely express what the tradition of the form would lead one to expect. In great comedy the product of form and attitude is a profound vision, a vision which either penetrates to a new and vivid justification of common sense and "public policy" or affirms this consensus while intimating ways in which it may be reinterpreted and transcended. But a great play which unequivocally rejects the common sense of mankind can hardly be classed as comedy, however merrily it recommends a world hitherto unrealized. This is not to rule out "radical" or "insane" action but merely to insist that such action must imply some rationally conceivable norm. Nor does the restriction deny that a play recommending a new kind of irrationalism might be of great value.

From this point of view, it is not so much the mood of the play as its manipulation of the form and attitude which marks it as comic or otherwise. When Ernst Cassirer asserts that great comedy is "often filled with great bitterness," he makes an overstatement; but he is surely right when he adds, "Comic art possesses in the highest degree that faculty shared by all art, sympathetic vision."[2] Such vision must include at least a measure of agreement with what has been generally thought and felt.

The pages which follow will be a series of annotations on the definition offered above. After clarifying the various parts of the definition and showing their relevance to recognized examples of comic art, I shall attempt to show how all the parts of the definition, when seen together in one play, can make up the inner nature of a particular comedy. The precise way in which a given example fulfills the definition is unique, but even in a great play, part of the artist's genius is in realizing the possibilities and implications of the form he adopts.

My definition began by stating that comedy is an amusing action. The statement recognizes that the art has traditionally been, among other things, a machine for producing laughter. Sir Philip Sidney was unwilling to admit this truth; Bergson in effect asserted it, but the reflection may only have strengthened his belief that comedy is a relatively crude form of art, if indeed it is art at all. If an entire audience, Bergson might have asked, can respond as one man to the dramatist's depiction of absurdity, must not the picture be rather crudely drawn? In response one might inquire, how effective would the comic dramatist be if his jokes and witticisms appealed to his auditors just one at a time? The man who laughed would be asserting not his solidarity with the group but his superiority to it, that is, its failure to grasp the intelligent idea that he and the writer held in common. Whereas tragedy celebrates and speaks to the individual, as auditor or reader, comedy not only rehearses and re-creates the rituals of social life but depends upon *agrément*, a word indicating not only agreement but pleasure in a shared activity.

The notion that "effective" comedy must necessarily be crude may be answered in several ways. First of all, such writers as Molière, Congreve, Shaw, and Giraudoux either found or developed audiences capable of subtlety. Wilde thought that instead of art coming down to the level of the people, the people must come up to the level of art, and *The Importance of Being Earnest* is a triumphant vindication of that thesis. The work of Wilde and Shaw was educational in the best sense. Audiences learned to laugh at Shaw's radical but not despairing wit, though they sometimes succeeded in doing so only after concluding that the writer was a privileged clown not to be taken seriously. Yet the laughter awakened by Shaw's plays proved to be a subtle kind of sub-version finally issuing in liberation.

Conservative laughter can be as subtle and as liberating as liberal or radical laughter. The laughter in Molière supports the morally eman-cipated, yet absolutist, codes of Louis XIV and his court. The codes themselves were not necessarily very enlightened, but in the comic art and technique of Molière, the *honnête homme* for whom he wrote could find a handsome justification of what he wanted to believe. In the eighteenth century, even the enlightened Voltaire could say that the speeches of Cleante in *Tartuffe* were "the best sermons in our lan-guage." Molière's raisonneurs do not always speak very subtly, but much of what they say needed to be said. Nor was the need merely social in the obvious sense of that word. When Philinte says to Alceste, "In this world you need a manageable virtue,"[3] his demand for moral pliancy demonstrates both common sense and a valuable comic and artistic ambiguity. Philinte's pithy sentence points to the half-admirable, half-ridiculous rigidity of Alceste, to the shoddy, inevitable, accept-able, and amusing slipperiness of social life, and to the controlled tol-erance of Molière himself, watching the struggle from a position above it but by no means indifferent to it. Perhaps no other statement in the play says so much as this or lingers in the mind as long.

The great comedians are subtle, but they are not afraid of farce. Molière's raisonneurs get the support of the Dorines and the Toinettes, who mercilessly ridicule the hydra-headed nonsense which is always in need of decapitation. If the point of view represented by Dorine is crude, the world needs more crudity. In Molière's comedies, intellectual and visceral laughter converge on the same object.

Although some great comic writers have leaned toward preciosity—among them are Marivaux, Musset, Giraudoux, Shakespeare in *Love's Labour's Lost*, and at moments even Molière himself—the masters of comedy have been strongest when they have joined forces with the popular tradition of masculine farce. One thinks of Cervantes in the scene featuring Maritornes the Asturian, Chaucer and his Wife of Bath, Falstaff with Doll Tearsheet on his knee, Molière's Sganarelle, plan-ning a marriage at the age of fifty: "Is there a man of thirty who looks fresher and more vigorous than me? Don't I have all the movements of my body as good as ever; do I need a carriage or a chair to go down the street? Aren't my teeth still the best in the world? (*He shows his teeth.*) Don't I masticate my four meals a day as well as ever? And have you ever seen a stronger stomach than mine? (*He coughs.*) What have you got to say to that?" (*The Forced Marriage*, i). A Molière will throw more lights on a farcical scene than will a street-entertainer like Tabarin, but he has one eye on the gross facts and calls for as loud a laughter.

Molière speaks as a pragmatist, condemning late marriages for the reason that they won't work (though he may have made the same mistake himself in his own life). Yet one cannot imagine him reaching his conclusions on the basis of statistics and questionnaires. When asked, during a TV symposium, for his "position" on censorship of television comedy, Steve Allen replied: "Well, my feet are dangling from this stool." The reply was at once an acknowledgment of the limitations of sponsored comedy, for which he is well known, and a good-natured thrust at solemn interviewers. Mr. Allen was expressing an attitude not unlike that of a Molière, who also worked for a sponsor.

Fortunately, the laughter in comedy will often be far more ambiguous than the sponsor will ever understand. A good joke is as rich in overtones as a good metaphor and puts up as much resistance to simple interpretation. One cannot read Freud's "reductions" of his jokes, in *Jokes and Their Relation to the Unconscious*,[4] without frequently realizing that the paraphrases are truly reductions. Often an explanation given by Freud is merely one of a number of meanings which form the penumbra of the joke. Freud himself knows, of course, that a laughable remark which at first seems merely stupid or ridiculous may contain a sharp criticism of a class or an institution. His stories concerning the European *Schadchen* (marriage-broker), for example, show that a broker may become unwittingly ridiculous in his eagerness to make a sale but may at other times use his technique to attack his clients at the cost of a deal. Sometimes the climax of the joke may be a Pyrrhic victory of honesty over the sales instinct.

The *Schadchen* stories are on the way to becoming little comedies, for the protagonist begins to take on the complexities of a dramatic character. But a witty comedy has the controlled overtones of good poetry and is far more than a connected series of jokes. *The School for Wives* is, at first glance, a practical joke on Arnolphe. The play conforms well enough with the Idols of the Tribe—well enough, that is, to satisfy the tribe. Arnolphe thinks that, unlike most men, he is too good to be a cuckold, he treats Agnès as if she were a potential maker of cuckolds, and he is at last publicly shamed and cast out before he can make her his wife. The modest common sense of his friend Chrysalde contrasts with Arnolphe's comic hybris. When Arnolphe ridicules the deceived husbands he knows and insists that he will never be among them, Chrysalde replies that it is best to avoid such satire, for one can never know what his own wife will do. He continues:

... quant à mon front, par un sort qui tout mène,
Il serait arrivé quelque disgrâce humaine,
Après mon procédé, je suis presque certain
Qu'on se contentera de s'en rire sous main.
Et peut-être qu'encor j'aurai cet avantage
Que quelque bons gens diront que c'est dommage.

[I,i]

If, by the fate to which we all must bow,
I find disgrace descending on my brow,
After the fact, the town will, I believe,
Content itself with laughing up its sleeve.
I'll have that solace; and I make this claim:
Some kindly folks will say that it's a shame.

Where could be found a saner rejection of the pride which not only goes before a fall but makes it unbearably painful? Even if Chrysalde's wife should give him horns, he will never become a scapegoat driven into the wilderness; some friendly citizens will always be ready to take him in. He is a model of the well-adjusted man in an age of conformity. Yet he is so lacking in pride, so resigned, so passive in his conservatism that he can hardly be the mouthpiece of the author. Without following those French critics who find in the contrasted Arnolphe a picture of the sexual anxieties of Molière, we can see that the fatalism of Chrysalde reflects some sober thought on the part of a writer professionally devoted to laughing at sexual jealousy and, what is more important to the analysis of comedy itself, enriches the statement of the play. For a moment the Deceived Husband ceases to be a signal for laughter and is seen from the inside. The crowd in the auditorium has suddenly become a collection of exposed individuals—an event they could hardly have expected.

I have said that the amusing action of comedy is a discontinuous, interrupted, and often jagged movement from frustration to satisfaction of desire. This discontinuousness is, indeed, insured by the frequent laughter of the audience; for laughter in the theatre not only stops the dramatic action but throws it in and out of focus, as would the movement of a bifocal lens. In farce the movement is radically discontinuous; in mannerly comedy there may be an approach to the continuity of drama and tragedy. The two kinds of comic movement may be illustrated by Aristophanes' *The Women of Thesmophoria* and Marivaux's *The Surprise of Love.*

The Women of Thesmophoria, effectively translated by Dudley Fitts as *Ladies' Day,* presents a tricky Euripides attempting to escape the wrath of the women of Athens, whom he has so often insulted in his plays. The festival of the Thesmophoroi, Demeter and Persephone, is in progress, and Euripides expects the assembled women to take a dire revenge upon him. He attempts to find a man who will attend the festival in a woman's clothing and plead his case. Mnesilochus, a relative, agrees to do so. Euripides exits hastily as the assembly begins. Instead of soothing the women, Mnesilochus delivers a diatribe against them, whereupon they seize him and discover his sex. Tied to a post, he invokes the aid of Euripides in speeches drawn from his plays. When Euripides arrives, the two men try to pass off Mnesilochus as Helen of Troy, then Andromeda—both captive women in dramas of Euripides. These tricks fail, but Euripides manages to distract the attention of Mnesilochus' Scythian guard, and the two clowns escape after getting the rather casual acquiescence of the choral leader. The Chorus ends the comedy by asking the blessing of Demeter and Persephone.

The play is the jeopardy and the escape of Euripides, but before escaping, both he and Mnesilochus are "ritually" abused and roughly handled. The revenge on the tragic poet has been a practical and relatively harmless joke, but not without frightening overtones. Although Euripides has made his getaway, it is really the festival spirit, serious, mystical, unpredictable, but fundamentally cheerful, which has triumphed.

The tone of Aristophanes, so difficult for us to grasp today, embraces brutal attack and benign acceptance. The play is the voice of a basically strong and confident tribal consciousness, quite capable of punishing laughter which does not so much express ingrained hatred of the perverse individual as good-natured contempt—contempt that may issue in a terrible but unresentful violence. Whether Euripides is released or torn to pieces, the women at the festival will quickly forget him. One gets no such feeling at the end of Euripides' great tragedy *The Bacchae,* in which Maenads destroy one who has insulted Dionysus and his cult.

Although Aristophanes' play expresses a social consciousness seemingly confident of its unity, the aesthetic surface of the work is radically broken and discontinuous. At one moment the women are howling at Mnesilochus; at the next they are singing religious songs. (These are often very beautiful and moving in Mr. Fitts' translation.) The songs themselves shift without warning from piety to sarcasm or shrewishness, sometimes in the middle of a sentence:

> Sing for the gods
> Olympian deathless Sing
> Timeless hours in the lyric rage of the dance
>
> No woman's tongue
> Contrive in this ritual
> A word of hate for any hateful man....[5]

This kind of reversal, which is entirely characteristic of Aristophanes, jolts the audience into an awareness of the two poles of its existence, the divine and the all too human.

The plot of this comedy is less episodic than is usual in Aristophanes, but the scenes continually produce electrifying surprises. The sudden decision to use Mnesilochus as advocate for Euripides, the former's sudden abandonment of his plan to soothe the women, the choral leader's last-minute decision to make peace with Euripides—these and other turning points increase the feeling of unpredictability and deliberately reduce the impression of a continuous and inward mental life. The scene based on the *Andromeda* is an especially dazzling specimen of the technique. Mnesilochus, now tied to the post and in the custody of the Scythian, tells the audience that Euripides has just appeared in the costume of Perseus (perhaps there had just occurred a hasty, whispered conference within view of the audience) and instructed him to take on the role of Andromeda bound to a rock in the sea. The next lines apparently go to Mnesilochus: as Andromeda, he laments his plight and yearns to go back—to his "spouse." But the last word must refer to the wife of Mnesilochus! As the lament continues, we hear Echo, another character in Euripides' play. The voice, from offstage, is that of the tragic dramatist himself, dressed as Perseus but speaking in treble for the feminine Echo. Euripides plays this role with such enthusiasm and persistence that he irritates both Mnesilochus and the Scythian. A moment later Euripides appears as Perseus the rescuer, speaking lines from the *Andromeda*. As Mr. Fitts suggests, he may have entered on a machine.

The transformations of Euripides are as astounding as the kaleidoscopic reversals of character in Ionesco's *Victims of Duty*. In neither play does one find that evolution of character associated with drama and tragedy. Euripides is a preternaturally clever and indefatigable puppet. He is *panourgos*—ready to do anything, especially if it is shady. If a machine could think, it would think as he does.

Marivaux's *The Surprise of Love* (1722), the first of his two brilliant plays bearing this title, is at the opposite extreme of comedy from

Aristophanes' play. Where Aristophanes is tough, Marivaux is gentle; the Aristophanic action moves like a bouncing car in an amusement park; Marivaux's play flows like water on a slight downgrade. To change the figure, a laugh in Aristophanes is like a brick wall in the way of forward movement; a smile in Marivaux is a veil through which one looks attentively to see what follows. Marivaux's view of man is far more conducive to the presentation of character seen from within; he therefore comes much closer to the line separating comedy from the *drame*, a dramatic mode in which the alterations in tone and mood are not so sharp as in most tragicomedy. And since he handles character sympathetically, his action is far more continuous than that in Aristophanes. Marivaux respects his people sufficiently to follow their thinking closely.

Théophile Gautier thought *The Surprise of Love* the best of Marivaux's comedies because it produced purely through shades of feeling all the reversals usually accomplished by external incidents. The observation is shrewd. To illustrate Gautier's point, the progressing love affair between the Countess and Lélio constantly turns on each character's anxious interpretation of the other's cautious periphrases. If she sends him a note declaring that "it would be rather useless for us to see each other; I foresee that it would disturb you . . . and I should be sorry to constrain you," his vanity will interpret her words as a seductive insult perpetrated against one doing his best to stay out of love. If he says to her, "Madame, you do not love me, I am convinced of it; and I swear to you that this conviction is absolutely necessary to me," the Countess will need an entire scene with Columbine to penetrate the implications of Lélio's sentence.[6]

Every misgiving of these sensitive lovers is followed with delighted attention, yet Lélio and the Countess are always laughable or on the edge of being so. For this reason, the audience is not completely involved in their mental processes, and as a consequence the action preserves the discontinuity always found in comedy. But as if realizing that he had moved to the very limit of comedy, Marivaux interrupts his aristocratic dialogues with scenes presenting two peasants, then two servants in love. In each of the three plots, love has to contend with *amour-propre*, but the demurrers of Jacqueline, the *paysanne*, are very modest indeed compared with those of the Countess, and in resisting Columbine, Arlequin is merely imitating the psychic action of his master. The "low" plots not only prevent the comedy from becoming etiolated but allow aristocratic delicacy to be seen from a healthy perspective.

In the second scene of Act One, a brief exchange between Arlequin and Lélio suggests the kind of comic discontinuity which Marivaux so well illustrates. Both men have been jilted, and as they walk in Lélio's garden, they compare notes on their feelings. Arlequin reveals that he doesn't feel well, but when questioned, he admits that he can "drink marvellously, eat the same way, and sleep like a squirrel." Yet he feels a "laziness in the limbs; I yawn without reason; I have no enthusiasm except at meals; everything displeases me." Lélio interprets all this as "un peu d'ennui."

ARLEQUIN. Monsieur, with your permission, I will pass to the other side.
LÉLIO. Why? What ceremony is this?
ARLEQUIN. It's so I won't see those two little affectionate birds on that
    tree; that torments me. I have sworn never to make love again;
    but when I see them, I almost want to break my vow, I become rec-
    onciled with those plaguy women. And then it's as hard as the
    devil to get angry with them again.
LÉLIO. Ah, my dear Arlequin, do you think I am more free than you
    from these little inquietudes? I recall that there are women in the
    world, that they are lovable, and this memory does not return with-
    out some stirrings of the heart; but these very emotions render me
    inflexible in my resolution to see women no more.

                                                            [I,ii]

Arlequin is an excellent comic character in his own right, but when his speeches are placed in opposition to Lélio's, they significantly alter the sense of the gentleman's statements and even block the sympathy we might otherwise be expected to feel for them. Reading only these lines, we can see the action of the play shifting from the refusal to love (*aimer*) to the refusal to make love (*faire l'amour*). Each stance is the more comic, the more liberating to the audience, because it is set against the other. Lélio is comic because of his excessive refinement, Arlequin because of his bumbling attempts to refine away his natural earthiness. The consciousness of neither character preoccupies us for very long.

In tragedy we follow the movement of the purposive, evolving consciousness on its journey through suffering to victory in defeat. The consciousness we observe is primarily that of the tragic hero, though his intense awareness can be partially shared by other characters. Because of the dominance of the tragic hero, an Edmund Kean or a Charles Macready could almost carry a tragedy on his shoulders. On the other hand, the star system is unnecessary or confusing in comedy. If the star is playing the leading role, he is likely to seem more impressive than the character he is playing. If he takes a secondary role, the play becomes unbalanced, even if he acts as modestly as he can, for the audience will confer importance upon him by recalling his eminence in his profession. Ordinarily we can closely follow and strongly respond to the consciousness of only one character in a play. By comparison with the mind of Macbeth, for example, that of Lady Macbeth is at a remove from us. In her opening scene, she calls on infernal spirits:

> Make thick my blood;
> Stop up th'access and passage to remorse,
> That no compunctious visiting of nature
> Shake my fell purpose. . . .[7]

Though we hear her with horrified fascination, she has already moved further than Macbeth will ever do into the realm of the inhuman forces to which she appeals. Hers is not the consciousness to which we most fully respond.

The deeply thoughtful and human consciousness of a Macbeth is not found in comedy. Comic action tends to be as Bergson described it, physical or purblind instead of highly conscious. Similarly, the great comic actor specializes in the presentation of mental obtuseness. One of the most vivid accounts of comic acting ever written appears in Charles Lamb's description of the style of Dodd: "In expressing slowness of apprehension, this actor surpassed all others. You could see the first dawn of an idea stealing slowly over his countenance, climbing up by little and little, with a painful process, till it cleared up at last to the fullness of a twilight conception—its highest meridian. He seemed to keep back his intellect, as some have had the power to retard their pulsation."[8] It must have been as if the thoughts leading to overt action slowly forced themselves upon him, so that a character played by Dodd would be an object of action rather than an instigator of conscious activity.

The amusing, discontinuous action of comedy presents successes and failures in social relations, but it is not so much the individual that succeeds as life itself, in spite of all its blunders and sometimes because of them. The playwright conducts his happy lovers—happy because life and the playwright control them—to their "green felicity." He may also conduct clowns and rogues and gentlemen to success. In Aristophanes, the energetic vulgarian Peithetaerus becomes the master of the Olympian gods; in Jonson, a Dauphine or a Quarlous, each a gentlemanly rogue, wins a handsome fortune. If the successful are a bit unsavory as individuals, as is Quarlous, we may yet feel that they adequately represent forces larger and better than themselves.

Although we approve the success of the young and innocent and merry, we take keener pleasure in casting out or ridiculing the failures. We are glad that Maugham's "constant wife" achieves justice in the end, but there is a greater joy in seeing her husband get what is coming to him. When Argan's daughter succeeds in marrying the right man, we give her our blessing; but we experience active enjoyment in the failure of Argan, the imaginary invalid. We think it right that the Venetian court should clear Bonario and Celia, but these innocents appear in a play named *Volpone*. Success in itself is not, in fact, comic but romantic or heroic or shrewd, unless the successful man has the good grace to trip over himself now and then, as do Benedick, Beatrice, Viola, Rosalind, and some other comic heroes of the same playwright. Shakespeare seems to be almost alone among the great comic playwrights in making the successful man at once successful, comic, and admirable.

Life succeeds, and the desires of the audience. To a degree the desires of the playwright and his audience must be at one if *he* is to succeed, and this creates a problem for a Ben Jonson or a T. S. Eliot. A good comedy will include a superior kind of wish-fulfillment, satisfying the desire for laughter and for pleasure in victory over everything in the play that opposes us. But the finer the comedy, the more completely does it transcend what is implied in so repellent an expression as "wish-fulfillment." In Giraudoux's *Intermezzo* (*The Enchanted*), one of the great comedies of the twentieth century, the easy laughter at the expense of bureaucratic thinking allows a very modestly enlightened audience to congratulate itself upon its superior perceptiveness, but this fact in no way reduces the strength of Giraudoux's insight into the relation between literal-mindedness and mysticism, flesh and spirit, fact and value, nor does the laughter raise any question about his ability to comprehend all these opposites within his genial embrace. The play is slyly dialectical in structure. The Inspector, representing the government in Paris, is the archetype of the official, literal-minded mentality; when he sees further than the end of his nose, he concludes that what he sees is not worth seeing. Isabel, the *jeune fille* as schoolteacher, is in absolute contrast with the Inspector; for her, no fact has value unless it is part of the universal poem of life —life extending beyond the knowable into the wonderful realm of death and ghosts and spirit. The Inspector's knowledge is abstract in the sense that it is cut off from a living and breathing reality. Isabel appreciates the concrete, but what she most values in it is its adumbration of the realm of spirit. So attractive does this realm become for her that toward the end of the play she is ready to leave the world of the here and now.

At this point, enter the synthesis, a good-looking young Supervisor of Weights and Measures who can domesticate the spirit in the seemingly narrow world of a provincial civil-service worker. With the aid of a doctor who believes in universal harmony, the Supervisor succeeds in bringing Isabel back to the life she had been ready to forsake. The play is an amusing and moving victory for philosophic monism. One of Giraudoux's happiest productions, *Intermezzo* proves that comedy can transcend malice in a generosity born of wisdom. It is one of those rare comedies in which laughter achieves a genuine catharsis of scorn and divisiveness.

We have said that in comedy the "divine average" triumphs over the exceptional or peculiar. This is a tendency within the form itself, and the playwright who elects comedy will be likely to use this tendency as a working principle. Naturally, as the artistic creation begins to take on a life and a logic of its own, the writer may begin to find that he is writing something other than comedy, perhaps romance or satire. If he decides and is able to remain within comedy, he may discover that he is writing what amounts to a justification and, above all, an enhancement of the average, as we can say of Giraudoux's Supervisor. If the play is very successful, it will not only testify to but extend the wisdom of the race. On the other hand, he may develop an ambiguous, almost inscrutable work of art, one that will allow the audience only a very qualified self-congratulation. The life in time of such a play will more often increase than lessen its ambiguity, for its audience will have changed. Shakespeare's *Henry IV* takes Prince Hal on a journey from the world of Falstaff to the world of the Lancastrian dynasty. This is the road he must take, and after much argument, criticism has again accepted the rejection of Falstaff. Yet there is in the play a judgment that this rejection as worked out involves the sacrifice of values which the play itself has established. For the modern reader, the sacrifice is greater than it would have seemed to a loyal Elizabethan. The new life of the play had its seed in the text as first conceived and understood, but today the play cannot mean quite what it meant to its early audiences. Or rather its meaning in the twentieth century is an accumulation of many (not all) of the meanings it has acquired in the last three hundred years.

Henry IV does not remain within the category of comedy, but it illustrates the principle that the work of art is a product of basic norms and individual attitudes. Where these are in a state of tension not amounting to flat contradiction, the result will be a play which implicitly endorses the assumptions of the form while indicating that there is a good deal more to be said than the données reveal. Ramon Fernandez has spoken of the double vision in comedy, whereby the writer offers one view of a dramatic moment and then immediately presents a sharply contrasted view. The girls in *Les Précieuses ridicules,* for example, set forth a plausible case for preciosity, whereupon Mascarille reduces the attitude to absurdity, and the audience laughs. A play which is, in part, "written for laughs" will therefore by its very nature shift back and forth between opposing appraisals of social behavior. But the oppositions need not completely destroy each other; indeed, if the play is to retain interest, the playwright will have to keep alive both halves of the vision. It does not follow that he or his work is confused. He can, if he chooses, make the best of both worlds while indicating that one is better than the other. In great comedy, such a procedure will issue in a unifying, though perhaps very complex, vision.

The action of a play includes the strivings of all the characters. It involves or seems to involve a measure of free activity, however shortsighted. But since the comic character is usually seen from the outside, there is little stress on freely chosen alternatives. The character in the inevitable grasp of his humor is a proper comic subject; for this reason, the comic action is deeply marked by inevitability. But the comic plot will often impose a life of chance balancing the inevitability created by the "humors" of character. Comedy thrives in an atmosphere of moral holiday; on such a day anything can happen, and we hope it will. Yet it regularly happens to predictable characters, for the inflexible or obsessed man is more subject to external chance than the one who can adapt to changing conditions.

The term "inevitability" is more often associated with tragedy than with comedy, but if the tragic character is freer than the comic, his errors are more avoidable. It is tragic that a hero could have avoided catastrophic error but did not; it is comic that a fool cannot help being a fool. Whereas tragedy commits the dramatist to a belief in freedom, comedy requires no such commitment. Nor does it anxiously inquire into the freedom of the will. That would be to consider too solemnly.

Not all characters in comedy are fools, but all comic characters are more or less foolish. The inevitable foolishness of men is therefore a preeminent comic theme. In dealing out rewards and punishments, comedy chooses not between the wicked and the just or even the foolish and the wise, but among the foolish, and its election lights on the healthy, the normal, the "divine average" of foolishness. Walt

Whitman might well disapprove of this use of his phrase, which is lofty
(in his poems) but also comic. In a mood of democratic enthusiasm,
the phrase can be taken in good earnest, for democratic theory tells
us that all men are equal in a universe responsive to an all-wise divinity.
But the phrase can also be used in a Pickwickian sense. When the occasion is comic, the man chosen for victory is not an ideal conception of ourselves which we recognize as a faint possibility at best, but
one who can apotheosize, raise to a higher power, the common reality
in which we know we belong. Few men are tragic, but all have their
comic seasons. No man is a hero to his valet, as a long line of French
comedies from Molière to Beaumarchais demonstrates, and of course
the valet appears in the cast because he is a comic character.

The victor in a comic action may now be described as a symbol of
what is desirably or acceptably foolish. Comedy chooses the healthy,
idle Duke of Illyria over the unhealthy, busy Malvolio, the
"blessed," volatile Benedick over the somber Claudio, the frivolous
Celimène over the sour, upright Alceste. As these examples suggest,
the comic benediction cannot always be equated with material and
obvious rewards. Claudio, like Benedick, wins the girl of his choice,
but in the process loses the esteem of the audience. The last act of
The Misanthrope leads even the outright fools among Celimène's suitors to reject her; in the eyes of the world created by the playwright,
she is now as badly off as her misanthropic lover, Alceste; yet this
"scandal-mongering coquette," as a seventeenth-century critic called
her, has demonstrated sufficient vitality to convince us that it will not
be long before she recovers from the reversals she has just encountered.
Her ability to sustain her own point of view until the end is in itself a
not unacceptable victory; she has been foolish, but she will not admit it, and we can see that her kind of foolishness will not bring her
too much pain. Though *The Misanthrope* violates the tradition of the
happy ending, it clearly shows that the roads to happiness are open
to the Celimènes, if not to the Alcestes, of the world.

A fine comedy, then, means far more than its assignments of reward
and punishment might lead one to believe. Indeed, it may not only
distinguish among the successful but may judge the successful more
severely than the unsuccessful. Where this is true, the writer's nu-
anced sense of life becomes more important than the movement of his
plot. In many an Elizabethan comedy, for example, the wicked suddenly reform and win happiness in the last act. However perfunctory
the development may be as plotting, it need not affect the fundamental
vision of the playwright. If the writer wishes to affirm the values of love

effect of the finest plays within the group. Without denying
dy shades into romance, satire, and drama or tragicomedy
es, and while recognizing that it covers a larger part of the
spectrum than does tragedy, an especially restricted form,
ed to show that there is a definite kind of play which is prop-
d "comedy" and to demonstrate that a play conforming to this
art of the definition can be a superior work of art. It has not
shown that a particular comedy can illustrate the complete
n and yet remain a distinguished work. This should be at-
, since one function of genius is to recapture and revivify tra-

definition has emphasized the amusing, unpredictable, and yet
ely inevitable movement of comedy toward a conclusion sup-
g and supported by the natural desires of man as a social being.
Molière the "natural" and the "social" are absolutely indistin-
ble; the man who behaves with a civilized regard for others is
ing naturally. In the works of this writer, comedy is an expression
urban society. In those of Shakespeare, who is closer than
re to a feudal and rural way of life, comedy is not so clearly lim-
by a given milieu. Indeed one might feel that applying such a
se as "success and failure in social relations" to Shakespeare un-
narrows his comedies and turns him into a citified rival of Jonson
Middleton. George Gordon, thinking especially of Meredith's fa-
s essay, once remarked that Shakespeare has always been a source
embarrassment to comic theory. It is true that Meredith's Comic
rit, with "her town clothes intact," as Gordon sardonically de-
ibed her, is more genteel than a Beatrice or a Rosalind, yet even
en Shakespeare moves his action outside polite society, he is con-
ntly aware of man as a social being. The comic successes and fail-
es in the "desert" of Arden, for example, are as socially meaningful
those taking place in Celimène's house or St. James' Park.
As You Like It is both a witty play, an extended comment on the wit
nd wisdom of folly, and a tribute to folly as a form of natural piety.
oth wit and folly are natural endowments, and in that they are natural,
hey are desirable. Nature and Fortune are contrasted in the key dia-
ogue which opens Act One, Scene Two, but the scene hints that he
who is favored by Nature will ride with the blows of Fortune and ultimately achieve the good fortune—here the inheritance—to which his
nature entitles him. Soon we see that in repairing to the Forest of Arden,
Duke Senior, Rosalind, and Touchstone gain a perspective on society

and friendship, let us say, and
from the general happiness, why
wrong he has been? The happy can
if he can join the consensus, so mu
sensus. His unsociability has already
no effect on that judgment.

Comedy is often said to be more re
is both true and false. Comedy stays
external behavior from moment to mo.
of class, to his gestures, his characteri.
and exaggerating the chances of life, it
Fortune is a "right whore," says an El
the phrase is bitter, it has comic overton
and ludicrous deity. She has served as p
comedy, but the tragedies inspired by her
Aristotle's remark, "It is probable that r
contrary to probability," is more helpful t
to the tragic.[9] The comic writer is repeate
by the odd fact that although men behave
reers develop just as unpredictably. When th
cause insuperable wonder and awe, the effec
a medieval and Renaissance tale; where they
gruity recognized and welcomed as such, the
comic truth and feigning are concerned, the.
first a feeling of verisimilitude, then a series
and at last a sense that these shocks occurrin
true, not so much to the ordinary, quotidian
to an order of desire recognized by the commor
related to the way things very frequently fall out
sion: "The course of true love was absurdly impr
end was what we should have expected anyhow."
Nothing, after Friar Francis tells Claudio that
dead, he adds:

> . . . let wonder seem famil
> And to the chapel let us presently.

The road to the chapel was wonderful, but where else
go?

A definition of comedy would be most satisfactory i
describe the species without falsifying or grossly under:

and custom which prepares for the basic reversal in the play, the restoration to society of health and strength. Even before the unnatural villains renounce their evil ways, a new and better society has been created in the forest. Jaques and Touchstone have laughed at the folly of cultivating the pastoral mood, but Jaques finally decides to abjure court life, and Touchstone marries a country wench, thereby negating their criticism of the natural life.

As the play begins, Nature and Fortune are rival deities. Both Orlando and Rosalind, well endowed in the "lineaments of Nature" (I,ii, 45), are "out of suits with Fortune" (I,ii,258). Orlando has been left a thousand pounds, but his elder brother refuses him the money; Rosalind's father, Duke Senior, has been driven into banishment by his brother, Duke Frederick; and Rosalind herself will soon be expelled from the court. At the opening of Act One, Scene Two, in an attempt to conquer grief, Celia gives Rosalind this advice: "Let us sit and mock the good housewife Fortune from her wheel, that her gifts may henceforth be bestowed more equally" (ll. 34–36). Rosalind responds so quickly and brilliantly, we doubt she will ever be seriously injured by ill fortune. For the present, however, the girls proceed to "reason of [the] goddesses" (l. 55). When Touchstone enters, Fortune seems to be triumphing over Nature, for "though Nature hath given us wit to flout at Fortune, hath not Fortune sent in this fool to cut off the argument?" (ll. 48–50). Fortune is making "Nature's natural [Touchstone] the cutter-off of Nature's wit" (ll. 52–53). But then Celia reflects that the entrance of the "natural" may be the work of a kindly Nature after all, in an attempt to sharpen their wits on Touchstone's folly.

On a superficial reading the passage is one more tiresome example of Elizabethan logic-chopping. When read with attention, however, the dialectic is seen as basic to the whole play, for Rosalind will use folly, including Touchstone's, as a means toward strengthening Nature in her struggle with Fortune. By an extralogical movement of mind, the girls are already able to conclude that a seemingly fortuitous entrance can be transformed into the work of Nature. Nature can destroy Fortune and appropriate her powers.

Inevitably the word "fool" occurs a prodigious number of times throughout the play. An essay could be written on the attitudes toward folly taken by almost all the characters and on what these attitudes reveal as to the characters' wisdom and folly. The "humorous" but humorless Duke Frederick is merely angered by what he takes to be folly; when Celia, for example, defends Rosalind against criticism, Fred-

erick simply dismisses Celia as a "fool." Jaques, the fashionable mal-
content of 1599, both patronizes the fool Touchstone and gushes over
his cleverness:

> When I did hear
> The motley fool thus moral on the time,
> My lungs began to crow like chanticleer,
> That fools should be so deep-contemplative;
> And I did laugh sans intermission
> An hour by his dial.
>
> [II,vii,28–33]

Jaques would like to use folly as a means toward biting satire in the
manner just then being developed by Ben Jonson. Duke Senior, on the
other hand, appreciates Touchstone for what he is and sees that "he
uses his folly like a stalking-horse and under the presentation of that
he shoots his wit" (V,iv,111–12). But the Duke has no sympathy with
folly as an excuse for bitter satire. He rightly banishes satire from the
world of *As You Like It*.

If Jaques patronizes Touchstone, the fool patronizes Corin, Audrey,
and William. The limitations of Touchstone's wisdom-folly are nowhere better shown than in the scene (V,i) where his cleverness wins
an easy victory over the simplicity of William. In catechizing this country fellow, Touchstone traps him into asserting that he has a "pretty
wit." This innocent remark gives Touchstone the opportunity to quote
the saying, "The fool doth think he is wise, but the wise man knows
himself to be a fool" (ll. 34–35). The epigram is good, but in Touchstone's mouth it is now merely a means of self-congratulation. Indeed
his encounter with the rustics proves unsettling to him. In the court
his jokes could unmask many a solemn pretension, but in the Forest
his cleverness goes to his head, and his wise folly develops into pseudo-
wisdom.

Soon after the arrival in Arden this significant dialogue occurs:

TOUCHSTONE. . . . as all is mortal in nature, so is all nature mortal in
    folly.
ROSALIND. Thou speak'st wiser than thou art ware of.
TOUCHSTONE. Nay, I shall ne'er be ware of mine own wit till I break
    my shins against it.

> [II,iv,55–60]

At this moment, one may feel that Rosalind should have given Touchstone credit for the wisdom of his sentence, but we later find that

when he does become definitely conscious of his wit, it begins to evap-
orate. Rosalind has judged him rightly. He is wise only so long as he is
unself-conscious. As Celia points out, he is useful primarily as a whet-
stone. Without Falstaff's brilliance, he is, like Sir John, "the cause
that wit is in other men." Rosalind uses him to remind herself of the
folly constant in human life, including her own. If Duke Frederick had
called Touchstone a "dull fool," the insult would have criticized him
rather than the fool, but Rosalind has the right to use the phrase and
does, though only under provocation. Perhaps no other character in
Shakespearian comedy can equal her balanced perceptions or her understanding of herself. Self-consciousness rarely sits well on the comic
character. This heroine has that double vision ordinarily reserved for
the playwright and his audience. She is fully aware of the absurdities
into which her love can drive her, without loving any the less. She can
smile at the amorous excesses of Silvius, while recognizing their kin-
ship with her own. Half-seriously, half-mockingly, she sets out to cure
Orlando of his love for her, reminds herself and him of the brevity of
love, and goes so far as to slander both her sex and herself. One could
almost think that she does not believe in love. Instead, she sees it more
clearly than any other passionate heroine in comedy.

In her attitude toward love, Rosalind may be said to represent the
divine average, for although she is superbly clear-sighted, her emotions keep her safely in the world of men. She is admirably placed between the pastoral naiveté of Silvius and the gross realism of Touchstone, but she is not merely the happy medium between these extremes;
the breadth of her humanity can grasp both the purity of Silvius' feelings—

> Jove, Jove! this shepherd's passion
> Is much upon my fashion
>
> [II,iv,61–62]

—and the earthiness of Touchstone's desires. It is she who most justifies the words in Hymen's marriage ritual:

> Then is there mirth in heaven
> When earthly things made even
> Atone together.
>
> [V,iv,114–16]

Orlando's marriage with Rosalind will be an approach to divine comedy.
Very far from being an ingénue, she regularly speaks in an idiom
closer to Touchstone's than to Silvius' or even Orlando's. Her criticism

of Orlando's love poetry is not very different from the fool's. In the love-game which occupies Act Four, Scene One, it is she who introduces and appreciates the typically Shakespearian double-entendres, as in her suggestion that "for lovers lacking—God warn us!—matter, the cleanliest shift is to kiss" (ll. 76–78). The innocent Orlando seems not to understand the jokes at all. Though her witticisms are subtler than Touchstone's, they are not always more chaste. In her company, even the "heavenly" Celia can speak of putting "a man in your belly" (III,ii, 215). The chief difference, of course, between Touchstone's sensuality and Rosalind's is that for him sex exists for itself, for her it is a means toward marriage and a family. Touchstone despises Audrey and tells her, "We must be married or we must live in bawdry" (III,iii, 99); he would clearly prefer the latter. But when Rosalind first confesses her love to Celia, she is already thinking of Orlando as her "child's father." And so it is right that in the last scene Hymen should say of Rosalind and Orlando, "You and you no cross shall part," but of Touchstone and Audrey,

> You and you are sure together,
> As the winter to foul weather.
>
> [V,iv,141–42]

The plot of *As You Like It* brings not only Rosalind, Orlando, and Duke Senior but also Celia, Silvius, and even Touchstone, Oliver, and Duke Frederick to success. So positive is the mood of the play that failure is merely the inability to remain unpleasant and antisocial. At the beginning of the play the situation is clearly abnormal and pretty clearly destined to change for the better. Though the "good" characters criticize the state of the world, we cannot believe that conditions are quite so bad as they look. For one thing the pleasant critics greatly outnumber those who are criticized. Celia regrets her father's silencing of "the little wit that fools have" (I,ii,95). Le Beau informs Orlando that Frederick has suddenly become angry at the young man, advises Orlando to leave the court, and concludes:

> Hereafter, in a better world than this,
> I shall desire more love and knowledge of you.
>
> [I,ii,296–97]

Nobody seems to think well of either Frederick or Oliver. Even in the first scene news comes that young gentlemen are flocking to Arden every day. Both Frederick and Oliver know they are far less popular than their brothers, and this realization is the chief reason for their hatred of Duke Senior and Orlando. Learning of Oliver's plot to kill Orlando, old Adam cries:

> O, what a world is this, when what is comely
> Envenoms him that bears it!
>
> [II,ii,14–15]

When he offers to devote himself and his life's savings to Orlando, the hero sees him as a symbol of the "antique world,"

> When service sweat for duty, not for meed!
> Thou art not for the fashion of these times,
> When none will sweat but for promotion. . . .
>
> [II,iii,58–60]

Since the times are bad, Duke Senior and his friends are far happier in exile than in the "envious court." But all this criticism creates the feeling that a reversal will come before long. When affairs are so generally known to be bad, they cannot be so bad as they seem.

The position of Orlando and Duke Senior resembles that of Hamlet and Prospero, but here the atmosphere is neither tragic nor tragicomic, for the victims are far simpler than either Hamlet or Prospero, far more able to find books in the running brooks. Success comes easily to men with their talent for living and their modest demands. In moving to the Forest, they can take the good society with them.

The retreat to Arden not only enables Shakespeare to regenerate society but to widen its embrace. The courtiers see that just as they have been driven from court, so are they driving the deer, those "dappled fools," from their proper home. In Jaques the thought inspires a deal of artificial moralizing, but Duke Senior's sympathy is more genuine. In Act Four, Scene Two, the slaying of a deer permits a ritualistic identification of beast and man. The successful hunter puts on the deer's horns, and a song follows:

> Take thou no scorn to wear the horn;
> It was a crest ere thou wast born;
>   Thy father's father wore it,
>   And thy father bore it.
>
> [IV,ii,14–17]

In these lines, horns signify more than cuckoldry. They envisage man and beast, hunter and hunted, as part of that greater society which is nature. At other points, the puns suggested by the forest life—"heart" and "hart," "deer" and "dear"—support the feeling that man is part of a society larger than human. In his own way, Touchstone is cementing the bond between man and beast. Like the forester in the song, Touchstone reflects that horns are necessary and that "the noblest deer hath them as huge as the rascal" (III,iii,57–58)—one meaning of "rascal" being "lean deer." He looks upon wedlock as a kind of "nibbling." Though he reproaches Corin for supporting himself by the "copulation of cattle" (III,i,84), he describes his last entrance with Audrey as a pressing in "amongst the rest of the country copulatives" (V,iv,57–58). Jaques, in fact, sees Touchstone and Audrey as "a pair of very strange beasts, which in all tongues are called fools" (V,iv,36–38). If fools are beasts and if folly is as widespread as we have seen, the cast of characters will be securely placed in the animal kingdom.

The many references to the gods, the name "Celia," and the poetic deification of Rosalind all serve, of course, to balance the downward extension of society indicated in the preceding paragraph. In Act Three, Scene Two, the matching poems of Orlando and Touchstone, both inspired by Rosalind, present her, first, as an aerial spirit and then as an animal. For Orlando her worth is "mounted on the wind"; but she reminds Touchstone that "the cat will after kind" (ll. 95, 109). The fool's reply to Orlando's verse is mainly a burlesque of bad poetry, but it has another purpose. Without denying the rare virtue sung by Orlando, Touchstone's couplets point to the very ordinary, uncomplicated basis of Rosalind's attraction to Orlando. Both heavenly and earthy accounts of Rosalind are plausible, so balanced yet versatile is this comic heroine.

In *As You Like It*, the good, the "open" society succeeds not by plotting against evil but through a process of absorption. One hardly needs to document the assertion that Nature and Fortune, inevitability and chance, control the movement of the play more fully than do the deliberate choices of the particular characters. Oliver and Frederick are as they are and suddenly become something else. Touchstone, Orlando, and Phoebe illustrate the saw, "Whoever loved that lov'd not at first sight?" Rosalind is able to observe and judge (though not to limit) her feelings. Her insight helps to preserve the play from an excessive romanticism, but it has little effect on the overall movement of the action itself.

Similarly, there is no difficulty in demonstrating that *As You Like It* illustrates the relative discontinuity of the comic form. Elizabethan drama, with its double and triple plots, always tended toward discontinuity, but the method worked better in comedy than in tragedy. Of Shakespeare's great tragedies, only *King Lear* gave much attention to subplot. Marlowe used parallel actions in *Doctor Faustus*, but with dubious results. Webster's two famous tragedies are more nearly single in movement. Middleton and Rowley's best-known tragedy, *The Changeling*, very strikingly exemplifies the Elizabethan fondness for the double plot, and William Empson's now classic essay in *Some Versions of Pastoral* shows what strange effects the authors were able to get from their duplicity. But however interesting the cross references in *The Changeling* are, they are not so much tragic as ironic and satiric. The whole tendency of the action is to limit, indeed to degrade, the consciousness of the heroine, Beatrice, so that she emerges not as a developed tragic figure but as one actor in a spectacle of human vileness.

A parallel subplot both turns the audience's attention from a central character and renders him less remarkable than he might have been. The effect will probably injure tragedy but not comedy. Unconcerned with the unique individual, comedy studies the species and its varieties. In *As You Like It*, despite the commanding charm of Rosalind, the dramatis personae are carefully balanced, group against group, and character against character. Group follows group across the stage; one constellation breaks up, and its members gravitate into new spaces and take on a variety of new traits depending on the particular direction taken. The relationships of the individual are more important than the individual himself. The cast can be classified according to differing systems—for example, villains and victims or lovers and inamoratas—and anyone can move, like a dancer, from one progressive pattern into another, changing his style as he goes. Orlando has one voice for Oliver-as-villain, at least two for Rosalind-Ganymede, and another for Jaques, with whom he can bandy insults with surprising agility. The Oliver of Acts Four and Five less resembles the Oliver of Act One than the latter resembles Duke Frederick, since both villains were motivated in exactly the same way. The new Oliver is a function of the magical situation developing in Arden, where beasts behave as if in a medieval bestiary, Rosalind asserts without contradiction that she is a magician, and a Roman god manages the final scene. Viewed as a whole, the patterns of the play are a clear yet intricate and ever-changing dance of life.

What is continuous in the play is the design, not any personal mode of consciousness. Rosalind is the only character who approaches that kind of continuous mental life we find in Shakespearian tragedy. She is most herself in her prose scenes, and there are moments when her vividness threatens to overpower the play. But as if to subdue her a bit, Shakespeare sometimes makes her speak blank verse. Significantly, in the final scene, which reveals her identity to Orlando and her father, she speaks a purely functional iambic pentameter. Once she has clarified the situation, she says no more. The last seventy lines go to minor characters. Although she makes a final "personal appearance," it is outside the play, in the Epilogue.

In many comedies failure is as striking as success. In *As You Like It*, possibly the happiest of Shakespeare's plays, the art of the playwright praises the art of living, an art which comes naturally to such as Duke Senior and his daughter. Their dramatic action carries Shakespeare's vision of life lived as it ought to be, can be, and sometimes is. It would be easy to dismiss such a play as too serenely presenting life "as you like it," but to do so would be to deny that life can sometimes take the form our desires would create.

NOTES

1. *The Principles of Art* (Oxford, 1955), p. 280.

2. *An Essay on Man* (Garden City, N.Y., 1953), p. 192.

3. My translation from *Le Misanthrope*, I,i, in Molière, *Oeuvres Complètes*, ed. Maurice Rat, Bibliothèque de la Pléiade, Nos. 8 and 9, 2 vols. (n.p., 1956). Citations from Molière will be to this edition. Unless otherwise acknowledged, all translations are my own.

4. *Jokes and Their Relation to the Unconscious*, trans. James Strachey (New York, 1960).

5. Aristophanes, *Ladies' Day*, trans. Dudley Fitts (New York, 1959), lines 960–65.

6. *The Surprise of Love*, II,ii; II,viii, in Marivaux, *Théâtre Complet*, ed. Marcel Arland, Bibliothèque de la Pléiade, No. 79 (n.p., 1949). Citations from Marivaux will be to this edition.

7. *Macbeth*, I,v, 44–47, in *The Complete Plays and Poems of William Shakespeare*, ed. William Allan Neilson and Charles Jarvis Hill (Boston, 1942). Unless otherwise specified, citations from Shakespeare will be to this edition.

8. "On Some of the Old Actors," in *The Complete Works and Letters of Charles Lamb* (New York, 1935), p. 121.

9. *Poetics*, trans. S. H. Butcher, XVIII, 6. Aristotle is quoting Agathon's defense of odd happenings in the drama and may not agree. G. F. Else thinks that Agathon was making a sophistical defense of one of his satyr plays. See *Aristotle's Poetics: The Argument* (Cambridge, Mass., 1957), p. 551.

CHAPTER TWO

The Area of Comedy

THE DEFINITION OF ANY ART FORM obviously depends upon the sampling used to define it. However confident one is of intuiting the tragic or the comic, the intuition cannot in itself determine for all time the exact membership of the class held in mind. But comedy has at least a norm providing a center of attraction for a considerable number of plays. To the phrase "center of attraction" we should now add "or repulsion," for the breakthrough in drama since 1945 has produced a genre that may well be called anti-comedy, comedy turned inside out —not tragedy, but drama which consistently reverses comic assumptions. So hypnotic is the new form that it makes comedy of the past look different from itself: a recent critic has written a plausible existentialist interpretation of Molière.

Even before this unsettling advance in the drama, the difficulty in establishing the frontiers of comedy was apparent. One has only to mention *As You Like It, The Birds, The Alchemist,* and *Tartuffe* to remember that the form can accommodate romance, ironic fantasy, hard-headed realism approaching cynicism, and even fright at the spectacle of human wickedness. If one adds *The Tempest* at one extreme and *The Wild Duck* or *The Sea Gull* at the other, one extends the range beyond the limits of visibility.

The many variations within comedy are connected with the many causes of laughter; for although not all laughter is comic laughter, the reasons for laughing at the comic or the ludicrous are famously varied and ambiguous. Consequently, it is impossible to deny that there is often a comic element in what at first seems merely grim, frightening, ironic, or aggressive, or to deny that comedy can find a place for each of these moods. We are not especially concerned here with the laughable or the comic detached from comedy, but realization of the many causes of laughter can do something to widen over-restricted definitions of what Goldsmith called laughing comedy.

Laughter can give voice to happy companionship (largely or completely devoid of feelings of superiority), friendly greeting, playfulness, surprise, shock, tension or fear followed by relief, sudden deflation of expectation (or the reverse of this—sudden inflation), sudden awareness of incongruity, the clash of independent patterns of thought (Arthur Koestler's "bisociation"), release of inhibition, Hobbes' "sudden glory," ironic feeling, bitterness, and if Edmund Bergler is right, the effective masking from oneself of psychic masochism. Indeed, for Bergler, this unconscious maneuver is the key to laughter. The list is not, of course, complete. There is nothing inconsistent between most of these items and the action of comedy; but while happy companionship, let us say, is certainly a staple, it could hardly be the essence of comedy, which like all other kinds of drama thrives on conflict. In *The Nature of Laughter*, J. C. Gregory roughly groups laughters into the delighted, the scornful, and the amused, though admitting that the classes often overlap. So far as comedy is concerned, the first and the second would be useless without a mixture of the third, and the third alone would be trivial. Even in merry comedy there must be an interplay of lighter and darker colors.

Comic laughter is most distinctive as we hover about the middle of the list I have given above. Tension-relief, sudden deflation, and incongruity are dramatic by nature and encourage the idea that comic laughter is the laughter of conflict, which is not equal to saying that comedy is laughable conflict. We do not expect to laugh or even to smile at every contretemps in comedy; and when we do laugh, it is not merely at the particular words or action extractable from the whole as especially ludicrous. The laughter, to adapt a valuable insight of Susanne Langer's, is a response to a momentarily heightened quality in the total work of art. If comedy were merely a succession of jokes, there would be a basis for the suspicion of Schopenhauer, Bergson, and Koestler that comedy is either no art or bad art.

By contrast with this notion, Marie Swabey's *Comic Laughter* (1961) is attractive partially because she insists that great comedy testifies to the reality of logic and value and is indeed the work of rational minds. She rejects sick jokes and irrational literature as not truly comic or laughable. Though excellently reasoned, her book has a somewhat lonely position, coming as it does in the wake of an intellectual revolution that denigrates the power of mind. The Freudian and post-Freudian explanations of laughter and comedy have combined with the intellectual climate of the twentieth century to affect recent students of comedy strangely. Under the influence of Freudian thinking one prominent critic, Eric Bentley, discusses comedy in terms more pessimistic than Schopenhauer's. For where Schopenhauer declares that comedy holds life to be good, though adding that to a deeply reflective spectator the comic action arouses pessimistic misgivings, Bentley asserts that misery is the "basis of comedy."[1] The familiar view that comedy presents experience as more happy than unhappy he tags as conventional. Certainly the picture of great comedy as fundamentally miserable is unconventional, though quite in tune with the age. The attribution of conventionality can in fact be a sword cutting two ways. It is all a matter of whose conventions you are talking about.

Apart from the question whose side one would rather be on, we can distinguish three areas of disagreement. (1) Great comedy—meaning the work of Aristophanes, Shakespeare, Jonson, Molière, Congreve, Marivaux, and perhaps Shaw and Giraudoux—is or is not pessimistic. (2) If it is not, it ought or ought not to be. Ought Congreve, for example, to be more like Swift than is the case? (3) Now that we have passed through two-thirds of a dark century, critics and stage directors should or should not interpret these dramatists more darkly than they have been interpreted in the past. Obviously, the first problem cannot be handled, let alone settled, without some detailed consideration of the playwrights mentioned. This will be one concern of later chapters in this book. But if the ritualistic critics are even half right, comedy cannot possibly be pessimistic, since it is closely associated, in form and hence in spirit, with the rites of spring, rebirth, and renewed vigor. (I believe that the ritualists *are* about half right, more right than they are about tragedy, which, because of its strong emphasis on individuality, challenges ritualistic thinking.) The second question can be rephrased: Is negative drama necessarily more profound, or better art, than positive? This is not equivalent to asking whether tragedy is superior to comedy, for the effect of tragedy cannot be described as simply negative. The statement that life is an endless alternation of sorrow and happiness will hardly come as a revelation, and no one can answer for others the question whether life is on the whole good. Comedy ignores the most paralyzing sorrows; tragedy ignores most of the world's merriment. A work of art is not required to ask every question or canvas every possibility. The artist consciously restricts himself to questions appropriate to the form in which he has chosen to work. In an age of sadness, it may require an effort of mind and imagination to attend seriously to great comedy; its sanity and balance may seem inappropriate to the time. If such is the verdict of the age, the age has more to lose than has the art form. The third question can be answered more ambiguously. In a sense, every great drama of the past belongs to the creative critic or stage director of the present and to those who admire his work. For even if he is fundamentally mistaken in his interpretation of an old play, which had a historical life and meaning in its own time, his talent, if not his reasoning, can have a validity and beauty if it finds in the work of art and makes resonant certain chords and themes that have not previously been appreciated. No one who saw the production of *Julius Caesar* by the young Orson Welles can deny that, however far it deviated from the first meanings of the play, it was strikingly "right" for the moment, the day in which fascism was sweeping to its early victories. Such interpretations are often criticized by the occupational pedantry of those buried by the weight of their information. Unhistorical interpretations do not disfigure the work. One can always go back to the book and read it in a well-printed edition.

Psychoanalytic explanations of laughter do much to confirm pessimistic readings of comedy. It is possible that the still undeveloped science of psychoanalysis will one day prove conclusively that we always have the saddest reasons for enjoying comedy and wit. Meanwhile, when one expert explains a joke as an attempt by the id to outwit that "inner Frankenstein," the superego, and another maintains that the ego is winning a momentary triumph, what is the dramatic critic to do but reread the plays with which he is concerned and determine his conscious response to them?

As I have said earlier, most one-way attempts to explain a witticism must fail to convince all or most of those who laugh at it. One of the most closely reasoned essays of this kind is Ludwig Eidelberg's analysis[2] of a joke involving Mae West. Eidelberg divides the joke into three parts: "(A) Mae West returns home and finds ten sailors in her bedroom. She says: (B) 'I am tired. (C) Two must go.'"

Attempting to determine why people laugh at this joke (and they do), Eidelberg found by experiment that, although the wording may vary somewhat, all three parts are necessary; if the narrator tells only the first two parts, nobody laughs! Before giving his own analysis, he rejects four others. (1) People do not laugh simply because Mae West decides to keep eight sailors in the bedroom, for if her reply is "Eight can stay," the joke is unsuccessful. (2) The laughter does not result from our pleasure in suddenly solving the puzzle; for the solution is much too easy to permit "joy." (3) Laughter does not follow the sequence: sexual stimulation in A, frustration or disappointment in B, and reappearance of sexual pleasure in C. The listener who laughs has broken off all identification with the actors, whereas the sailors presumably do not laugh, for stimulation remains strong. (4) Laughter is not the result of a bribe offering pleasure in laughter for pleasure in sex: "Pleasure which is being described as a result of laughter cannot at the same time be named its cause." Since these explanations have failed, Eidelberg examines the unconscious of the listener. In submitting to the authority of the narrator, the listener must regress to the infantile level. Part A creates an inspectionistic pleasure in the id. Part B inhibits this instinct, whereupon the instinct and aggressive feeling are built up. When the listener hears Part C and understands it, he acquires (a) a feeling of infantile omnipotence because the infantile superego is deceived, (b) a similar feeling because of his ego's easy triumph over the id (which receives, however, exhibitionistic instead of inspectionistic pleasure), and (c) exhibitionistic and aggressive pleasure from instinctual satisfaction in laughter. The laughter means that the listener is interested not in inspection but in penetrating the joke and enjoying his success. The infantile, unconscious part of the superego has been deceived partially because of the seeming innocence of the narrator and partially because of the formulation of the joke.

Eidelberg has valiantly sought to compartmentalize the feelings we experience on hearing this joke, but it appears that after rejecting certain motivations as irrelevant, he reintroduces them under new guises. Conscious pleasure in quickly solving the puzzle is thrown out, but unconscious pleasure of an almost identical kind is then allowed as part of a hidden warfare within the unconscious: for example, I, the ego, enjoy my superior penetration and enjoy my enjoyment at the expense of the superego. Furthermore, although it is true that the result of laughter cannot be its cause, it is not at all clear in the fourth rejected explanation that the pleasure following laughter is to be equated with the *immediate* response to a bribe. Why could not the order be: annoyance at frustration in B, bribe, acceptance, laughter, pleasure in laughter? One could accept the bribe because of the perception that Mae West's astonishing vigor appears even in her sly pretense of being less than superhuman—a deception that fools no one, except for a split second.

If one reads the joke as part of a dramatic action starring the famous actress, one's laughter and pleasure are increased by visualizing the earthy and humorous Mae West, a symbol of sex valued but placed as an element in a comical scheme of things. Perhaps the weakest part of Eidelberg's analysis is his paraphrase of "Two must go." According to the analyst, "It is as if she were to say, 'My instincts want sexual intercourse, my superego is against it. I solve the conflict by withdrawing

my libido from these two parts of my personality.'" One wonders if
Eidelberg had ever seen Mae West. In the joke, she has no moral conflict whatever. She admits to physical weakness and then implies her
vast superiority to ordinary frailty. Compare Falstaff's "They hate us
youth." The joke essentially celebrates a triumph of pseudo-modest energy and is thoroughly comic. Our laughter involves pleasure in vigor
and our pleasure in the ability to have this pleasure, as well as enjoyment in seeing the point and amusement over the evasion of morality.
This explanation is undoubtedly not exhaustive. One could mention,
for example, the incongruity of the heroine's tiredness with her extraordinary availability, or the suggestion that *her* weariness equals anyone else's maximum strength.

Does one need to introduce dreadful motivations like "regression to
the infantile" or "narcissistic humiliation" in order to explain such wit?
No doubt these technical terms awaken less dread in the professional
analyst than in the laity, yet it is the laity writing about comedy that
proceeds from terrible terms to fearful interpretations of the comic.
If all dramatic critics were psychoanalysts, probably the interpretations
of comedy would not be so pessimistic as those of literary men influ-
enced by psychoanalysis.

Laughter is sometimes ironic. Some listeners might find in the Mae
West story an ironic criticism of the average, unheroic man or woman;
if there, this element would be an overtone, not the basis of the laughter.
The suspicion of irony might result in something like a double-take.
Mae's pseudo-modesty resembles the stance of the Greek ironist exem-
plified both in Socrates and in some of Aristophanes' buffoons. But
whereas the ironist used his modesty mainly for attack, Mae seems to
be interested mainly in getting a laugh.

In comedy as elsewhere irony takes many shapes. Although it often
gives amusement a serious, even painful, turn, the movement may create
little more than a ripple of seriousness. At the beginning of the first
proposal scene in *The Importance of Being Earnest,* we get the following exchange:

JACK (*nervously*). Miss Fairfax, ever since I met you, I have admired
   you more than any girl . . . I have ever met since . . . I met you.
GWENDOLEN. Yes, I am quite well aware of the fact. And I often wish
   that in public, at any rate, you had been more demonstrative. For
   me you have always had an irresistible fascination. Even before
   I met you I was far from indifferent to you. (*Jack looks at her in
   amazement.*) We live, as I hope you know, Mr. Worthing, in an
   age of ideals. The fact is constantly mentioned in the more expen-

sive monthly magazines, and has reached the provincial pulpits, I am told. . . .[3]

Few critics find any seriousness in this play, which Wilde himself subtitled: "A trivial comedy for serious people." (Is it rather a serious comedy for trivial people?) In which of the many current senses of the word is this passage ironic? In what senses is it serious? Jack's situation is ironic since he supposes that he must persuade Gwendolen to marry, whereas she is determined to have him; but no one would call this irony serious. Not only is he ignorant of her feelings, but she is fully informed of his; the great disparity in knowledge and perhaps in character gives her an ironic advantage which she fully exploits. She can play with him as a Greek god plays with a hero. Similarly, the contrast between Jack's and Gwendolen's style can be called ironic since a romantically tongue-tied young man has every right to expect his beloved to be equally timid. Jack's speech in itself is not ironic unless it be contrasted with the social hypocrisy, the Bunburying, he has previously revealed to Algernon—a duplicity he himself seems largely unaware of. Gwendolen's speech is clearly ironic. Her preternatural glibness creates a contrast not only with Jack's inarticulateness but with the emotion which the audience may have been inclined to attribute to her and which she attributes to herself. Yet she wants affection not in private but in public, where it will impress others. Wilde apparently alludes here to Millamant's request, in *The Way of the World*, that Mirabell refrain from public demonstrations of affection after they are married; the Victorian Gwendolen oddly emerges as more affected than the coquettish Restoration heroine. The lines quoted from Gwendolen's speech make extensive ironic commentary on the age. Wilde obliquely criticizes Victorian hypocrisy, the cheapness of idealism in the rich, the backwardness of the rural ministry, and the snobbery of the urban aristocrat speaking of the country ("I am told"). To summarize, the ironies I have first mentioned are not serious; the satiric meaning of Gwendolen's speech is. But Wilde has so dehumanized his characters that most audiences and readers have failed to take him seriously and in the process have failed to realize his achievement, almost unparalleled in English.

This brief exchange has revealed irony of situation, structure, character, theme, and language. The theatre as an art form encompasses other kinds of irony. Dramatic dialogue itself tends toward irony, since every speaker fails to anticipate exactly what will next be said (and done) and often alludes consciously or unconsciously to what has been

said. A dramatic character frequently emerges in contradictory facets
or phases, provoking ironic reflections, and his estimate of himself regularly goes wrong or proves hopelessly unattainable. "Oneself is what
oneself would be known as if one knew oneself," said Leo Stein; but
since we rarely know ourselves, we and our image are seldom one.
Stage groupings frequently become ironic tableaux: one may think of
the mock-trial in *King Lear*, the ball in *The Cherry Orchard*, or the
brilliantly shifting ironies in the long dialogue which makes up Ghelderode's *Escurial*. Aristophanes waxed ironic over Euripides' fondness
for putting kings in rags, but the device was itself ironic. Even a stage
director's casting may be ironic, for he can decide that the actor should
play "against" the role in order to make a critical comment on the play.
This heterogeneous list suggests that irony may appear almost any-
where as a diversifying element in the drama. Whenever a contrast
forces us to think harder about the limitations of men and their language, irony appears, especially if we find ourselves inhibiting a smile.

Comedy is ironic, but comedy is not irony. Comedy says, "He is a
fool, but . . ."; irony says, "He is a remarkable man, but. . . ." In each
sentence, the climax comes in the second clause. To expand the comic
sentence: "He is a fool, but he is no different in that from other men, and
foolishness is by no means unbearable. Suppose we distinguish between
foolishness and folly. Foolishness has no vast pretensions; folly does.
When Erasmus floated his ship of fools, he embraced the foolishness
of man but despised the folly of infatuated lawyers, theologians, and
doctors. In Shakespeare the most colossal folly does not appear in his
comedies; his modest fool can learn. Nor is it true that all Molière's
fools are hopelessly sunk in folly. Orgon has to hide under a table to
learn the truth, but he learns it. That learned lady, Philaminte, has her
eyes opened at last, if not to the vanity of 'philosophy,' then to the falsity
of her most admired professor. Even Aristophanes' fools can make correct decisions."

At the very center of the comic area stands Molière's *The Learned
Ladies*. Though often ironic, it avoids both the darkness of *Tartuffe*
and the sentimental pallor of some love scenes in Molière. The pedant
Trissotin, base as he is, creates far less discomfort than the *faux dévot*;
and far from being too sweet, the young girl in love, Henriette, is
sharply ironic, even a bit sour, in her best scenes. The play is unusual
in selecting for the chief antagonist not a heavy father but the *savante*
mother, Philaminte, who has chosen Trissotin for Henriette. The father,
Chrysale, approves the quite normal love of Henriette and Clitandre
while opposing feminine learning. Aristophanes had misrepresented

Socrates in *The Clouds*; Molière misrepresents the Abbé Cotin in the person of Trissotin. In attacking pseudo-learning, the play is at the center of the comic tradition and almost commits itself to anti-intellectualism. At least Chrysale thoroughly approves the servant Martine's dictum that marriage and books do not go together, and Martine's simplicity is clearly more "right" than the pretensions of the ladies. The play makes a good deal of the Cartesian dualism of mind and matter, the *savantes* being for pure mind or *la substance qui pense*, Chrysale for matter ("My body is myself"), and the *honnête homme* Clitandre for the claims of both mind and matter; Clitandre carefully points out that the admired Trissotin (thrice a fool) is a fraud who deceives no one outside the Philaminte circle. But though his intellect may tell him that Clitandre is the soundest speaker in the play, Molière's comic impulse strikes with more force in the speeches of Martine. It is she who, apart from the ladies themselves, makes the *savantes* look most ridiculous. The play is characteristically comic in its willingness to risk anti-intellectualism before intellectual pretensions.

The alignment of the varied stresses within the play at once keeps *The Learned Ladies* entirely comic and preserves it from becoming a *pièce à thèse*. Farcical elements include the absurd tirades of the illiterate Martine and the ladies' mad adulation of Trissotin's poems, as at the point where Philaminte keeps parroting his phrase "Quoi qu'on die" as if it were immortal. Chrysale himself can be foolish enough, especially in his *galop oratoire* against learning (II,viii), as Alfred Simon calls it. Molière allows him some effective though elementary satire when he asserts that if he had his way, he would throw out all the ladies' books except for a large Plutarch, which he could use for pressing his collars. But what of his complaint that Philaminte, Armande, and Bélise know too much about astronomy, which is "not my affair"? Obviously he is not speaking for Molière. Clitandre, on the other hand, has all the discrimination and address of the raisonneur. But Molière avoids making him a disembodied voice from above telling us exactly what to think. Trissotin arouses his "distress," "torments" him; the ladies' esteem for the scoundrel "enrages" him (I,iii). By giving Clitandre mock-tragic diction at such a moment, Molière forces the audience to smile at him and thus gives him a vitality denied the typical sage.

If the "content" of the play is for common sense, the subtlety of the writing drives toward an enlightened average, a happy marriage of *sens* and *esprit*. Henriette is especially useful to Molière as a center of comic-ironic gravity. In the opening scene, with Armande, Henriette quietly demolishes her learned sister's arguments for an exclusively intellectual life. When Armande objects to her "festive" plans and asks whether the vulgar notion of marriage can excite her, she simply replies, "Yes, my sister." For Armande, marriage presents a "dirty prospect" that makes one shiver. Suggesting gross appetites, it lowers one to the beast. Speaking of her mother, Henriette replies:

> Et bien vous prend, ma soeur, que son noble génie
> N'ait pas vaqué toujours à la philosophie.
> De grâce, souffrez-moi, par un peu de bonté,
> Des bassesses à qui vous devez la clarté;
> Et ne supprimez point, voulant qu'on vous seconde,
> Quelque petit savant qui veut venir au monde.
>
>   [I, i]

> Her noble genius, Sister, as you see,
> Did not cling always to philosophy.
> Do, please, allow me, if you'll be so kind,
> That lowness which permitted you your mind.
> And don't suppress, hoping I'll share your scorn,
> Some little savant wishing to be born.

The tone is cool, lightly and justifiably malicious. Henriette's sharp-shooting continues in the later acts. In her scene with Trissotin, one senses more definitely than at any other moment Molière's anger and spite in the face of pious and triumphant cunning. Trissotin is confident that he will be able to marry Henriette. When she implies that he wants her money, he protests in standard vocabulary that her charms alone have attracted him. When she apologetically declares that she prefers Clitandre to him, he answers that she will come to love him after their marriage. To a direct appeal that he give his love to another, he protests his inability to do so; her "celestial" beauty is too great. Urged to keep this "galimatias" for his love poems, he neatly replies: those were the issue of my wit; this love is from the heart. He expects formidable aid from Philaminte, and if he can win Henriette, he does not care how. This baring of the fangs stimulates Henriette's harshest insinuation—delicately introduced.

> Mais savez-vous qu'on risque un peu plus qu'on ne pense
> A vouloir sur un coeur user de violence?
> Qu'il ne fait pas bien sûr, à vous le trancher net,
> D'épouser une fille en dépit qu'elle en ait,

Et qu'elle peut aller, en se voyant contraindre,
A des ressentiments que le mari doit craindre?

[V,i]

But I believe you err, thinking that force
In love will triumph in due course.
To speak out plainly, if you use constraints
Upon a girl, ignoring her complaints,
The more she thinks of this, the more she'll veer
Toward feelings that a husband ought to fear.

To this threat—a more polished version of Dorine's warning to Orgon in *Tartuffe*—Trissotin opposes the stoicism of the sage! Henriette can do little more than repeat that she will not have him. Words alone have failed to solve the dramatic problem, but they have explored a comic range of feeling while stopping short of real fright or pathos. Trissotin is a dangerously adroit antagonist in this scene, but Henriette is uncowed, and the forces opposed to the marriage have already been shown as strong.

The passage illustrates a crucial point in Molière's high comedy: while preserving the "decorums" of his age and the class that concerns him, this master comedian can be as tough and relentless as those who scorn understatement. There are glints of steel in this mannerly scene.

The Learned Ladies is less festive than *The Bourgeois Gentleman* or *The Imaginary Invalid*, whose characters are frequently ready to break into song and dance. The expulsion of Trissotin, whose venality even Philaminte finally sees, does not develop into a scene of resounding, let alone brassy, laughter. Meredith's silvery laugh, Donneau de Visé's *rire dans l'âme*, finally prevails. When Armande, formerly engaged to Clitandre, asks if she is to be sacrificed to the lovers' vows, Philaminte replies:

It won't be you that's sacrificed by me,
And you'll have comfort in philosophy.

[V,iv]

She may imply that she is sacrificing her own intellectual arrogance along with the braggart Trissotin. The ritual pattern is suggested. At any rate Henriette and Clitandre will *faire fête* (I,i) in their restrained way.

The comic celebration of life cannot avoid attacking the life-denying forces that would prevent little savants from coming into the world. Festivity attacks: drama would not otherwise be possible. But the balance is tipped toward celebration. Whatever the origin of Harlequin's baton, the blows in Italian and French farce express vivacity more than lust for blood. In the late medieval *Farce du Cuvier*, a stupid husband is dominated by a noisy wife during most of the action, but when she slips and falls into a washtub, he gets his revenge by allowing her to shriek helplessly in the boiling water; for pulling her out is not down on the list of duties she has assigned him. To an educated audience this would look like merely brutal destructiveness, yet the point is not that the wife is destroyed or permanently maimed but that the battle of life has taken a sharp turn for the refreshment of the audience.

The festive spirit of comedy precludes elaborate psychology. The characters do not evolve notably during the dramatic action, though they may be shown in changing lights or may change their minds. Our estimate of what they were before the enlightenment does not vary much thereafter; we are happy to believe, if we can, that the great revelation will have permanent effect. In *The Learned Ladies*, for example, each dramatic person is immediately stamped as ridiculous, ironic, kindly, domineering, or whatever. One speculates whether Chrysale will summon enough courage to oppose his wife's folly, but we soon see that he will need a great deal of help if he is to do so. He gets so much assistance that his final decision does not make him look very different from what he was, a peaceful bourgeois. In his essential changelessness, he is typically comic. The characters of the Restoration comedies, considerably longer than Molière's plays, are drawn in greater detail than figures like Armande or Henriette. When the English characters are hard to interpret, however, it is not because of their complexity, but because they are hard to judge from a twentieth-century point of view. Is Horner, in *The Country Wife*, an accomplished gentleman or a monster of iniquity? Is Dorimant, in *The Man of Mode*, capable of love or not? We do not see these wits veering between virtue and vice, love and cynicism, responsibility and irresponsibility. Some rakes reform, but the change is expedient, not moral. In Elizabethan comedy, a comic character—Orsino or Olivia in *Twelfth Night* or Sir Politic Would-Be in *Volpone*—will sometimes emerge from self-hypnosis, driven "out of his humor," but one may feel that his true self has been waiting in the wings or that his awakening cannot really improve him. In *As You Like It*, Oliver's conversion from villainy to brotherly love is pure romance.

Most of the characters I have just touched upon could not be con-

sidered problematical, nor are their plays problem plays. For some critics this is their deficiency. In his fresh and searching book, *The Dark
Comedy*, J. L. Styan sees high comedy and low farce as providing
patterns of easy success by selecting characters for ridicule or admiration. Thoughtful comedy is dark. This kind of comedy, Mr. Styan points
out, disturbs the spectator, embarrasses him, upsets his preconceptions,
forces him to review his own life, shunts his sympathies between opposed points of view, makes him an advocate now of society, and now
of the individual, thrusts him alternately into subjective and objective
responses to the characters, forbids him to be complacent about himself, constantly forces him into uncertainty about judgments of character, and makes him yearn for release from a very uncomfortable experience. Chekhov, Pirandello, and Anouilh are chosen as the modern
masters of dark comedy, which is also studied in such writers as
Beckett, Ionesco, and Osborne. These dramatists, Styan suggests, have
an affinity with the ambivalences of the medieval mystery play, the
grotesquerie of *King Lear*, the ironies of *The Misanthrope*, but not with
Molière's farces or, presumably, with that high comedy, *The Learned
Ladies*. Restoration comedy is outmoded. "A renaissance today of the
comedy of Congreve and his contemporaries, or the confident comedy
of Goldsmith, Sheridan, and Wilde, would be an affront to the dignity
of the atomic-age audience."[4]

Could this be excessive pride in the modern lack of confidence? For
Mr. Styan dark comedy is impressive because it makes us think. About
what? Life—and the uncertainties of character. But there are other
things to think about. A positive comedy presenting a coherent and
stable view of life is not necessarily less thoughtful than one that constantly darts into dark corners and mental confusion. Its theme may
have to do with questions difficult enough: what is the ideal stance
between sentimentality and cynicism? when is social tradition healthy
and when not? how can one be an *honnête homme* in a society crowded
with pretenses? Such questions are more social and less moral than
Styan's, but they lend themselves as well to dramatic development.

Inevitably the question arises, how dark can comedy become while
remaining comedy? The question is important if there is a possibility
that "traditional" comedy is going to be judged by its ability to approximate dark comedy, as if darkness were the measure of artistic maturity.

Recently, various writers, including Styan, have discussed Chekhov's
major plays as comedy. The classification gets some support from Chekhov himself, but his remarks were stimulated by dissatisfaction with

what he considered the over-solemn productions of Stanislavsky, who frankly admitted that his early productions of Chekhov were far from perfection. But it should be said bluntly that to describe Chekhov's major work as comedy is perverse. In each of the plays hope recedes further as the action unfolds, though Sonya, Nina, Mme. Ranevsky, and the Three Sisters reach for happiness with heart-breaking intensity. The sensitive and promising Treplev commits suicide. The admirable Tusenbach is killed by a morbid dandy. Vanya shoots at Serebryakov but misses (a development that many audiences are able to laugh at). The central figures in the plays are often foolish or given to folly, but it is difficult to dissociate oneself from them long enough to describe them as comic. It would be special pleading to speak of them, except perhaps for Gaev, as "clowns." The characters of Sonya and Olga are saintly; Sonya's great, last speech is a deeply moving prayer. In his *Letters* Chekhov called Varya a crybaby, but what actress would play her that way? The dialogue of the plays is a recurring blend of humor and pathos, but "dark comedy" seems hardly the label, for although we can fully understand the characters' limitations, the dominant response is one of love. If the only way to avoid the charge of reading Chekhov sentimentally is to categorize his work as comedy, one should be ready to be called sentimental. On the other hand, much as one may admire Chekhov, one must refuse to use him as a stick with which to beat Congreve, Sheridan, Goldsmith, and Wilde.

Dramatic theory must constantly seek some accommodation between an inadequate terminology and a protean subject matter. Two observations are relevant. (1) While traditional forms do not cease to exist or to retain their value, they are always being supplemented or shown in a new light; consequently, one may need new terms to account for strikingly original work like *The Cherry Orchard*, or one may adapt traditional definitions as slighter changes occur. (2) A particular work may remain within one area of drama or may move freely across boundaries, inevitably hazy at best. To return to the first point, Northrop Frye's establishment of irony and satire as an intermediate form between tragedy and comedy made a positive contribution to the understanding of literature. It opens up valuable approaches to writing that critics have simply been unable to handle. It is helpful, for example, to see Webster's powerful play, *The White Devil*, as a tragic satire instead of the defective tragedy it is often taken to be. The same term fits *Troilus and Cressida* very well; "comicall satyre" in the mode of Jonson and Marston is much less apt, and comedy impossible. In other instances, the attempt to fit a play into *one* category is hopeless. Certain plays move so widely from area to area that no one specification can contain them. The critic, who must use words, has the choice of tracing the modulations in the work or ignoring "what" it is.

Keeping in mind Frye's arrangement of tragedy, irony/satire, comedy, and romance along an imaginary circle, one could slightly elaborate the figure as in this illustration.

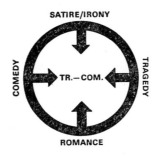

To further elaborate the picture of drama (or literature) would be to take one's ideographs too seriously. Any detailed map of the dramatic landscape will be contradicted by the fact that any genre can replace any other in a particular play, although the two genres are not adjacent on the map. Sentimentality and cynicism are as far apart as Australia and Greenland, yet an Anouilh passes, sometimes imperceptibly, from one to the other.

Despite its association in English with Beaumont and Fletcher, the term "tragicomedy" is perhaps as useful as any to indicate the variety of plays one thinks of as "between" tragedy and comedy. Even in Fletcher's time, two theories of tragicomedy were current. Today we can distinguish four kinds. (1) Alternating. This is the kind Fletcher rejected in his preface to *The Faithful Shepherdess*; his play was *not* to be a succession of scenes about people "sometimes laughing together, and sometimes killing one another." Dryden's *The Spanish Friar* is alternating tragicomedy. (2) Mixed. This is the variety favored by Fletcher, following Guarini. Nothing is very tragic, and nothing is very comic. If the result is rather sweet and bland, we have such a play as Tasso's *Aminta*. When the result is harsher and less "pastoral" we have such a play as Ibsen's *A Doll's House*. (3) Dialectical. Here a tragic moment explodes into laughter, and the comic awakens tears. Beckett's *Waiting for Godot* brilliantly exemplifies this sub-genre. *Troilus and Cressida*, which I have just called a tragic satire, impinges upon this recently developed species. One could almost say that Beckett aids in the placing of Shakespeare's play. (4) Regenerative. Here the play moves from guilt and suffering through revengefulness to forgiveness and peace. Laughter is by no means excluded. Shakespeare's *The Winter's Tale* is a good illustration of this mode. Frye places this drama in the area of romantic comedy, but this mode, like tragic satire, can easily shade into tragicomedy.

The three frontiers of comedy are tragicomedy, romance, and satire or irony. *Much Ado About Nothing* approaches the first frontier, Marivaux's *Arlequin poli par l'amour* the second, and Jonson's and Middleton's comedies the third. In *Much Ado*, the villainous plot against Hero and Claudio almost succeeds, but apart from the quick apprehension of the tool villains, the opening acts firmly establish the comic tone. Marivaux's play has the supernaturalism and good-evil opposition associated with romance,[5] but the treatment of plot, character, and dialogue is consistently comic. Jonson's and Middleton's comedies are, of course, strongly ironic and satiric, but usually the movement of the play follows the comic pattern, and the conclusion does not completely frustrate common desires. In general, all three groups make explicit or clearly imply widely accepted social standards.

It would hardly be profitable to seek the exact point at which comedy becomes a variety of tragicomedy, but it is necessary to explain how romantic comedy and ironic comedy, so far apart in tone and movement, can both be comedy.

I have mentioned *Arlequin* as an example of romantic comedy. In this play the scene alternates between the garden of the Fairy, betrothed to Merlin but in love with Arlequin, and a meadow where the shepherdess Silvia first appears—the two settings standing for the realm of the magical and the natural, or the decadent and the unspoiled. In the garden we learn that the Fairy, infatuated with the handsome but clownish Arlequin, has carried him off to her estate, where she woos him incessantly. She plies him with dancing lessons and love songs, but he responds only to the offer of food. As he is playing battledore alone, he meets Silvia; they immediately fall in love. After separating the lovers by touching them with her wand, the Fairy warns Silvia to break off her *amitié* with Arlequin lest he be put to death. Silvia's attempt to renounce Arlequin succeeds only until he draws a knife as if to kill himself. Trivelin, a servant of the Fairy, appears. He advises Arlequin to pretend fondness for the Fairy and, as if in play, to get possession of her wand. This trick provides the solution. Casting a spell on the Fairy and her goblins, Arlequin calls for a divertissement, pardons the Fairy, and announces, "Afterwards, we will go make us king somewhere."

Although the supernatural can constrain the lovers, it is the magic of unaffected love that converts Arlequin from doltishness to that delicacy of feeling the Fairy has vainly tried to teach him on her estate. He had been a poor student of dancing, had failed to understand that in receiving a gift from a lady, one brings one's hand to his own mouth instead of seizing the lady's hand and greedily kissing it. When the Fairy had awakened him, he had yawned, stretched, and slept again, his steady "baritone snore" forcing her to withdraw. His vocabulary had been largely confined to "low" expressions like *oui-da, dame,* and *si fait.* How could he respond to the penchant of this creature who must have learned to speak in a *précieuse* academy? But once he has met Silvia, he can bow and dance beautifully, manage a handkerchief and an elegant social phrase. The Fairy recognizes that she has not been responsible for the transformation. When she demands the name of his teacher, he pretends not to understand, but she warns him not to "affect a stupidity that is no longer yours" (xiv). He promises to "be as witty" as she could wish. Actually the change in him is more in manner than in substance. The asinine Italian Arlecchino has acquired the air of the French rococo, the clumsy dancer has become graceful.

Though "polished," he retains his fundamental innocence. This eventuality keeps the play within romantic comedy, a world wherein evil can be controlled by a wand one need not learn to manage. We appreciate the sincerity of the lovers while remarking the ease with which they acquire without cost the idiom of affectation. One does not sight a fallen world so clearly as in Marivaux's later play *La Double Inconstance.* Since Arlequin and Silvia are immune to the risks of sophistication, we cannot take them with full seriousness, yet a play which so effectively criticizes preciosity is something more than escapist entertainment.

Marivaux's handling of comic innocence—innocence which must be seen both from within and from without—is especially successful in Scene Eleven. Silvia's cousin has warned her to avoid confessing her love and to "severely" withhold her hand when Arlequin wants to kiss it. Arlequin appears, sees Silvia, leaps for pleasure, and performs a dance-pantomime around her. Then we have this exchange:

ARLEQUIN. So there you are, my heart.
SILVIA (*laughing*). Yes, my lover.
ARLEQUIN. Are you happy to see me?
SILVIA. Enough.
ARLEQUIN (*repeating*). Enough! That is not enough.
SILVIA. Oh, plenty! No more is necessary.

[xi]

Though critical comedy is usually ironic, this is romantic criticism of social insincerity. Attempting to satisfy both nature and propriety, Silvia later suggests a bargain, and again Marivaux is using naiveté for social criticism. "Every time," she says, "you ask me if I have much friendship for you, I will reply that I have scarcely any, but that will not be true, and when you want to kiss my hand, I will not wish it, and yet I will want you to." The plan proceeds, but Arlequin breaks the rules by pretending genuine grief at her refusal of her hand, whereupon she gives it to him. Even innocence can employ trickery. For the moment, naturalness is forced into the unnatural in order to protect its rights from a greater unnaturalness.

When Marivaux in later plays moves farther within the area of social comedy, his lovers retain their delicacy but cease to be quite so innocent; they breathe an atmosphere of nuances, latencies, arrière-pensées. But in *Arlequin*, if the serpent has communicated with Eve, she has not yet taken his message.

Marivaux frequently risks sentimentality but almost always evades it through his irony, wit, and humor. The sweetness of Arlequin and Silvia is kept within the bounds of comedy by a vigilant sense of the absurd. Marivaux is not loath to make fools of those he values most. And in her way, the Fairy protects the comic frontier. We are aware that innocence (which could destroy comedy) is threatened by the world the Fairy represents. The lovers' naturalness is threatened by what *she* thinks is natural. She is engaged to Merlin, but in the first scene she says to Trivelin, "Is there anything more natural than to love what is lovable? . . . The one [Arlequin] has made me forget the other; that too is very natural." In Arlequin naturalness is a lack of affectation; in the Fairy it is a pursuit of desire that can turn ruthless. As Trivelin says in reply to her self-defense, she is "taking nature a bit too literally." His criticisms of her are cool and light, but they hint at the corruption and decay of eighteenth-century France. Even in this early play, Marivaux's romantic comedy is stiffened by his unillusioned social sense.

Despite the gap between romantic and ironic comedy, the two are linked by the laughter of a consensus. This can range from gentle laughter at naiveté to harsh laughter at defeated selfishness or crass stupidity, for most audiences are capable of both laughters. But what if laughter turns to acute discomfort as the audience realizes it is being attacked? Shaw said that he cured his audience's folly as a dentist cures a toothache, by pulling the tooth, but he added, "I never do it without giving you plenty of laughing gas." Where the awareness of being attacked dominates—and the laughing gas runs out—we may have reformist drama or the "theatre of cruelty," as in Genet. But where there is a sense of a world in which folly or crime must always triumph, the state of things ceases to be the fault of the audience and we have irony, or what Frye calls low-norm satire.[6]

Romantic and ironic comedy are also linked by the overall movement of the plot. What I have called the divine average triumphs over the peculiar, even if it be the *status quo*. Traditionally, vigorous, normal youth triumphs over crotchety or obsessed age; *The Frogs*, where Aeschylus defeats Euripides, and *Major Barbara*, where Undershaft is the real winner, give the victory to the older contestant, but in each play, he is supernaturally vigorous.

Middleton's *A Trick to Catch the Old One* illustrates ironic comedy threatening to plunge into a fully ironic or satiric universe but stopping just short of the leap. Witgood, a young profligate, and his Courtesan outmaneuver two miserly old men, Hoard and Lucre, the latter being Witgood's uncle. Witgood gets free of his debts, including his obligations to his uncle, and wins the hand of a wealthy and attractive girl. He also tricks Hoard into a marriage with the Courtesan. In the last scene, Hoard discovers the identity of his wife, but instead of flinging offstage with an oath, he bows to his fate, exclaiming, "Cursed be all malice." Middleton wants his comic ending. Finally we get tongue-in-cheek repentances from the hero and his "whore"—who, it appears, has trespassed only with him. Both are kneeling. He announces that he is giving up

> Soul-wasting surfeits, sinful riots,
> Queans' evils, doctors' diets,
> Pothecaries' drugs, surgeons' glisters,
> Stabbing of arms for a common mistress,
> Riband favors, ribald speeches,
> Dear perfumed jackets, penniless breeches,
> Dutch flapdragons, healths in urine,
> Drabs that keep a man too sure in. . . .[7]

Considering his excellent prospects, why should he not?

Tht play is full of harshly sexual double-entendres which push it toward irony and satire; the conduct of the action is completely unsentimental and tough-minded, as we might expect from the author of *The Changeling*; and with the exception of the evanescent ingénue, Joyce Hoard, all the characters devote themselves to venal pursuits. There is Mistress Lucre, who puts her son on the track of the Courtesan posing as a widow; a pack of Witgood's creditors, who swing from obsequiousness to inexorable demands as the occasion warrants; Moneylove, who joins the crowd pursuing the widow; Hoard's brother, Onesiphorus (profit-bearing), whose name adequately describes him. Witgood differs from the others in youth, vigor, love of pleasure, and cheerful cynicism. When he observes Hoard rushing to marry the supposed widow, he says to her, "O for more scope. I could laugh eternally. Give you joy, Mistress Hoard. . . . Y'ave fell upon wealth enough, and there's young gentlemen enow can help you to the rest" (III,i,295–300). Here Middleton strikes the keynote of the entire play.

The zest of the profligate, Witgood, keeps the play within the circle of comedy. Granted that most men are committed mainly to their own interests, Middleton implies, the race can and should go to those best able to enjoy the fruits of victory; and as the audience hopes it is among those with talent for pleasure, it will enjoy not only Witgood's success but his joking manner at the end of the play. Where a greater work, the *Mandragola* of Machiavelli, emphasizes the disappearance of social decencies more than the pleasure in the hero's plotting, *A Trick to Catch the Old One* celebrates successful vitality. *Mandragola* is irony; *A Trick* is comedy.

Comedy is ironic and romantic; even in *A Trick* there is hasty obeisance to love, even *Arlequin* sets in motion some ironic reflections. Some balance between the two poles will guarantee the writer's grasp of experience. Yet comedy is neither irony nor romance. Could it be otherwise? Could there be a day in which audiences would receive high entertainment if not high comedy from mere wish-fulfillment or savagery? In the adult world the prospects for romance as comedy are not bright. One sign of a general unwillingness to equate the two is the tendency to reinterpret, more darkly, distinguished writers who may too often have been called charming. Marivaux is a good instance. It is harder to deny a comical future to plays presenting as material for laughter a postulated sado-masochistic structure of personality. Such plays will be rich in black or ochre humor: Arrabal's *Automobile Graveyard* may help to point the way. If the butt of the humor is always "the other," the result will be satiric or sadistic; if it is ourselves, the enjoyment will be masochistic. But only if the criticism of the audience is well veiled or if the playgoer's appetite for punishment enlarges greatly will it be possible to see Walpurgis Night as kômos.

NOTES

1. Cf. Arthur Schopenhauer, *The World as Will and Idea*, trans. R. B. Haldane and J. Kemp (London, 1891), III, 218–19; and Eric Bentley, *The Life of the Drama* (New York, 1964), pp. 297, 301.

2. "A Contribution to the Study of Wit," *Psychoanalytic Review*, XXXII (1945), 33–61.

3. Oscar Wilde, *The Importance of Being Earnest*, 6th ed. (London, 1912), pp. 31–32.

4. J. L. Styan, *The Dark Comedy* (New York, 1962), p. 281.

5. On romance, see Northrop Frye, *Anatomy of Criticism* (Princeton, 1957), pp. 186–206.

6. Frye, p. 226.

7. V, ii, 220–27, in *Elizabethan and Stuart Plays*, ed. Charles Read Baskervill et al. (New York, 1934).

CHAPTER THREE

Types of Comic Structure

In comedy one is usually aware of the contest between chance and plan. Even in a predictably unpredictable farce by Labiche the known appetites of the characters help to impel the action to its destination; even in a battle of masterful crooks one glimpses the Goddess Fortuna between the canvas clouds. But comedies in which chance dominates are clearly distinguishable from those in which intrigue—used here to mean the elaborated ruses of the characters—rises to prominence. These two kinds of structure, both emphasizing plot, are in turn quite different from the kind in which plot is subordinated to other elements in the design. Here too the struggle of chance and plan is at least visible.

Despite this dialectic, one probably leaves most comedies with the feeling that on the level of action—what goes on—chance has somehow been victorious. On the level of plot, which belongs to the author, one is varyingly aware that the playwright has been deliberately putting his creatures through their paces. Often the writer's design imposes a life of chance even though the comedy is bursting with intrigue. Many of Peter Sellers' films could provide illustrations; for example, *Your Past Is Showing*, in which two women drug and "murder" the wrong man, who returns only to be unintentionally drugged again. The ruses of the intriguer frequently happen to recoil upon himself, as in Jonson's *Volpone* or Congreve's *Double Dealer*, and even where he is successful, he plays a game in which he cannot know what card his opponent, human or otherwise, will play next.

Although comedies differ greatly in the emphasis laid on human ingenuity, they are alike in that the action, so lacking in the inner direction of tragedy, seems in retrospect a release of energy, reflexes, and ideas that "occur" to the characters, and not the issue of deep consideration and thoughtfully weighed alternatives. If tragedy is metaphysical, comedy is more nearly behavioristic. This quality in comedy can be briefly shown in Shaw's *Man of Destiny*.

A woman has stolen, or rather embezzled, a packet of letters meant for Napoleon. In an excellent scene typical of the play, Napoleon, who knows that the lady has hidden the letters beneath her fichu, attempts to get them from her. The passage is crowded with moments in which ingenuities and attitudes are suddenly exploded by a combination of planning by one character and automatic responses in the other. A character will rack his brains at one moment and cry out with rage the next. At first the scene emphasizes the clever dueling of the opponents, as the following schematic paraphrase indicates. Napoleon speaks first: You are brave; be sensible. —I am not brave. (*Display of feminine emotion. He reaches for the letters.*) I will get them from my room. —I shall accompany you. —I could not permit that. —I shall go alone. —They aren't there. —I know.

Up to this point we are in a comedy of intrigue. Shaw clearly admires the quick-wittedness of the Lady and the cool realism of the great man. The Lady now begins to present him to himself as the Man of Destiny. After he too denies that he is brave, we have this dialogue:

LADY. . . . You were not born a subject at all, I think.
NAPOLEON. (*Greatly pleased . . .*) Eh? Eh? You think not?
LADY. I am sure of it.
NAPOLEON. Well, well, perhaps not. (*The self-complacency of his assent catches his own ear. He stops short, reddening. Then, composing himself into a solemn attitude, modelled on the heroes of classical antiquity, he takes a high tone.*) But we must not live for ourselves alone, little one. . . . Self-sacrifice is the foundation of all true nobility of character.
LADY. (*Again relaxing her attitude with a sigh.*) Ah, it is easy to see that you have never tried it, General.
NAPOLEON. (*Indignantly, forgetting all about Brutus and Scipio.*) What do you mean by that speech, madam?[1]

Repeatedly, she drives him from realism to unconscious attitudinizing and back. When she thoughtlessly drops an incriminating phrase, he is jerked back to reality and consciousness. Soon he is chasing her around a table. When she decides to stop and poses as a martyr, he takes his time.

LADY. . . . Well: what are you going to do?
NAPOLEON. Spoil your attitude.
LADY. You brute!

[p. 162]

In a few moments she surrenders the letter.

The scene is not yet over, for the crucial letter turns out to be a revelation of Josephine's infidelity. The sharp reversals continue throughout the play, the characters alternately taking the roles of victor and
victim, planner and dupe. As usual in Shaw, the woman is the more
alert, but at the close Napoleon seems to have been driven out of his
heroic "humor." Yet the play interests us chiefly because the young
general repeatedly yields to the self-deceptions that are the fortune
of many a man of destiny.

Of the three main types of structure to be analyzed here, the first two,
the structure of chance and the structure of intrigue, are largely controlled by plot. *The Man of Destiny* falls somewhere between the
two. It is a "plotty" play. Shaw wrote the comedy in 1895, the year when
as play reviewer he attacked *The Importance of Being Earnest* for indulging in the "anachronism" of plot! But the exactly plotted play need
be no less expressive than the play developed largely through theme,
character, or language, or some combination of these. *An act can be as
symbolic as a word.* There are critics who prefer Molière's farces in
perpetual motion to his more serious plays in verse, and Molière may
have agreed. He spoke his last word not in *The Misanthrope* but in
The Imaginary Invalid.

His early farce, *Sganarelle, or The Imaginary Cuckold,* shows how
well a great writer can build on the structure of chance, in this instance a series of misunderstandings caused by the dropping of a portrait. The setting is outside the houses of Célie and Sganarelle. Célie
and Lélie are engaged, but while Lélie is away, the girl's father, Gorgibus, decides to marry her to another. Alone with her servant, Célie faints
from grief and drops a portrait of Lélie. Sganarelle appears, bends over
Célie's reclining form, tests the warmth of her flesh, passes his hand
over her bosom, and at the servant's request carries the girl into her
house. His wife appears at a window just in time to observe the panto-
mime. She assumes the worst. She picks up the portrait, and as she
voices ecstasy over the beauty of Lélie, Sganarelle reenters and observes. Each misinterpreting the behavior of the other, they quarrel
noisily. He snatches the portrait, she regains it, and he chases her from
the stage. At this point, enter Lélie and his servant, Gros-René, after a
long, hard ride. Sganarelle returns, studying the portrait. Accosted by
Lélie, he reveals that the picture had been in the hands of his wife.
Lélie assumes that he is referring to Célie. Alone, Lélie almost faints in
his turn, but seeing his distress, the Wife invites him to rest in her house.
After they go off, Sganarelle has a short scene with his father-in-law,
who warns him not to jump to conclusions. As the older man leaves,

Sganarelle thinks for a moment that he may have been too hasty, but he then sees his wife and Lélie coming from the house. As Lélie makes his exit he says to Sganarelle: "Oh, you are too happy in so beautiful a wife" (xv). Célie, at her window, has watched this moment. In an extremely clever scene, Célie concludes that Lélie is having an affair with Sganarelle's wife. She touches Sganarelle by her indignation, for he thinks she pities him. Heartbroken, she decides to bow to her father's choice of husband.

After additional complications, including Sganarelle's abortive attempt at revenge, Molière brings all four victims together as the Wife enters to reproach Célie for "certain very discourteous passions." Sganarelle replies: "You tremble with fear that your gallant will be taken away" (xxii). He is, of course, referring to Lélie; but the latter assumes that the gallant is Sganarelle. At this point, Célie's servant conducts a rational inquiry which succeeds in clearing up the imbroglio. When Célie's prospective father-in-law suddenly enters and releases her from the engagement her father had forced upon her, she is free to marry Lélie.

The errors multiply as the play proceeds. The first three misunderstandings occur at intervals, but the next four come close together. This spiraling effect suggests that the comedy should be played with increasing speed. The duller characters are deceived first and thus establish the atmosphere of misunderstanding or non-understanding. The stage is then set for the duping of the more refined if not more intelligent lovers. Certain details omitted from the summary help to "justify" the deceptions of the lovers. Célie's servant, for example, has said that the absence of Lélie appears suspicious. But complaints about the improbability of the plot are largely beside the point. If it be said the lovers would hardly believe that either one could be attracted to the crude bourgeois or his noisy wife, the answer is that in farcical comedy, there is no time, place, or available thought process for reflections of this kind. A character will be allowed to reason, as Sganarelle does in his long soliloquy, only if comic profit is to be obtained. At the close, the reasoning of the servant is a way of ending the work and departing from the world of farce. But we notice that after all has been clarified, the moral drawn by Sganarelle does not at all follow from the premises. "When you see everything," he concludes, "believe nothing." He has swung from one absurd extreme to the other.

When divided accordng to the French method of indicating a new scene for each entrance or exit, this one-act play has twenty-four scenes. No scene is longer than three pages in the Pléiade edition of

Molière; many scenes are very short. During most of the action, one,
two, or three persons hold the stage, but each of the last five scenes
brings on an additional character. This constant alteration of person-
nel emphasizes the shocks to which the four members of the quadrangle
are repeatedly subjected. One could imagine that Bergson's phrase,
"the lifeless encrusted upon the living," were devised for this play in
particular.

The stress on accident is strongly linked with the brilliant theatricality
of the work. The sudden appearances of characters at windows, door-
ways, or side entrances suggest a puppet show. The traffic is heavy
though the cast is small. In production, movement will naturally be
of great importance. After a long soliloquy in which he debates the
question of taking revenge on Lélie, Sganarelle comes in, carrying a
sword and muttering, "War, mortal war on the thief of honor" (xxi).
The lovers are reproaching each other. Sganarelle nears Lélie while his
back is turned. Célie points out the victim of Lélie's supposed misbe-
havior. Lélie turns and Sganarelle retreats. Then Lélie paces away and
Sganarelle follows threateningly. The stage director can elaborate at
will. Thematically, a move toward Lélie expresses Sganarelle's purpose, a retreat represents the inner chances, the surges of cowardice to
which he is subject.

Molière has devised dialogue to support and extend the domination
of chance. Often, if a fact had been exposed clearly or even a bit differently, the confusion would have disappeared. Sometimes one is aware
that it must have been difficult for the playwright to find the words exactly required for ambiguity. In the scene just analyzed, when Célie
points out Sganarelle to Lélie she says, "That object ought to discon-
cert you." She means that Lélie should be abashed at the sight of a
husband he has wronged, but the young man thinks she means that
since she is married to Sganarelle, Lélie ought to drop the tone of the
angry lover. When Lélie remarks vaguely on her "fine choice," we have
this exchange:

CÉLIE. Yes, I've made a choice one cannot reprehend.
LÉLIE. Go to, he's a man you do well to defend.

[xxi]

She refers to her despairing decision to accept her father's command;
Lélie supposes that Sganarelle is the "choice."

In a line quoted in the last paragraph, Célie refers to Sganarelle as
an "object," a good term to describe a plaything of circumstance. Appropriately, the text is sprinkled with words like *accident, sort, destinée,*

heureux, malheureux, disgrâce. Gros-René tells Lélie that their long journey has caused him an accident in a place he will not mention. Though this has nothing to do with the plot, it puts before us a notion of the way things happen in *Sganarelle.* René says of himself:

> . . . if I don't eat,
> The least bad luck throws me off my feet;
> But when I'm full up, my soul can stand firm. . . .
>
> [vii]

That is his solution to the problem of *la substance qui pense* in relation to *la substance qui est étendue.* But like most characters in farce, he is more an unthinking object than a thinking subject; he overestimates his independence.

If Gros-René is substantially comic, Lélie and Célie are light parodies of tragic lovers pursued by fate. Thinking that Célie is already married to the stupid Sganarelle, Lélie has an aside:

> Ah! mon âme s'émeut et cet objet m'inspire . . .
> Mais je dois condamner cet injuste transport
> Et n'imputer mes maux qu'aux rigueurs de mon sort.
>
> [xv]

> Ah, my soul is stirred, and that object arouses—
> But I ought to condemn so unjust a state
> Of mind, and impute my evils to fate.

In themselves the lines sound passably tragic; in context they are ludicrous, since a character led by chance is talking like a tragic hero in a struggle with fate. Célie too recalls high tragedy. When she concludes that Lélie is faithless, she says to her father:

> Oui, je veux bien subir une si juste loi,
> Mon père, disposez de mes voeux et de moi.
>
> [xviii]

> Yes, I wish to yield to paternal laws.
> Dispose both of me and my marriage vows.

She could hardly have come closer to the thought and cadence of Pauline, the heroine of Corneille's *Polyeucte.* But since this is a farce, chance will make unnecessary so grand an exhibition of will. Indeed it is comic that this charming puppet should adopt the tone of Corneille's famous tragic figure.

Naturally there is more to *Sganarelle* than a series of mindless errors accidentally prompted. Molière's genius for comic characterization is apparent from the first. In a few lines we have before us the crudely materialistic and sublimely confident Gorgibus, who says that if Valère, his choice for Célie, has twenty thousand ducats, "I guarantee he's a very honest man" (i). In a single speech Célie's servant reveals the earthiness of Dorine in *Tartuffe* or Juliet's Nurse. Sganarelle is, of course, the major creation; to him goes the honor of speaking a couplet that might serve as an epigraph for a study of comedy:

> Aller en l'autre monde est très grande sottise,
> Tant que dans celui-ci l'on peut être de mise.
>
> [iv]

> To go to the next world is sheer infatuation
> When you can stay right here in circulation.

The soliloquy (xvii) in which he is torn between revengefulness and cowardice—a farcical variant on the love-honor theme—is the high point of the play.

Sganarelle has just been overwhelmed by Célie's seeming desire to avenge his honor. Her rage (the tragic *courroux*) now inspires him with grandiose ambitions. At moments his handling of the admired alexandrine is elevated, but he keeps falling back to the humdrum level where he belongs. As he reflects on Lélie's impressive mien, he begins to take pride in his own pacific nature. What use will his honor have if he is stabbed in the paunch? Recalling Falstaff, he asks whether the news of his death will make this honor weightier (*plus gras*)—again we have a confusion of the two substances. It is better to be a cuckold than a corpse. Why should his back be loaded with blows because his forehead sprouts? Life is, anyhow, adequately subjected to evil mischances. "We must suppress our sighs and tears" (*Mettons sous nos pieds les soupirs et les larmes*): the imagery highlights the movement away from consciousness. Besides, he is by no means alone in his plight, and many solid citizens keep such misfortunes to themselves. (A serious reflection prefiguring Molière's first masterpiece, *The School for Wives*). Yet his bile is filling him with *courroux*. But how will he vent it? "I will go tell everyone he sleeps with my wife" (xvii).

During this speech Sganarelle is not so much the thinker as the victim of thoughts which strike like the blows he fears from Lélie. Instead of holding two or three alternatives in his mind for contemplation and comparison with a view to action, he sees one, seizes it, staggers under the impact of another only to be laid low by a third. It is in this sense that his "thinking" can be regarded as a series of chance occurrences. He becomes a split personality within which *I, we, you, he* and *my honor* struggle without regard for the total self. If "my honor" cries for revenge, "we" will tell "him" he can talk as much as he pleases. The soliloquy almost becomes a comedy in itself, with Molière, who played Sganarelle, acting half a dozen roles. Though the speech parodies tragedy, it completely negates or distorts the tragic emphasis on will issuing in decision. So far as Sganarelle thinks, he does so within the structure of chance.

Partially because it is too "literary," *Sganarelle* does not pass completely into the area of automated farce. Modern French farce often does. Labiche, Feydeau, and Courteline sometimes recall the farce of the Middle Ages, sometimes prefigure Ionesco. Critics have likened Feydeau's constructions to mathematics, chess, and physics. On the other hand, the stage property in Feydeau is said to operate like a Greek god intervening in tragedy.[2] In *Keep an Eye on Amélie!* (*Occupe-toi d'Amélie*), Feydeau leads his characters through a maze far more complicated than that devised for Molière's short play. Each setting, minutely described by the author, is completely functional. If three doors are specified, they are absolutely necessary as the lovers of Amélie tramp from sitting-room to bedroom to bath. If a bed has a footboard, a girl will be concealed behind it. The marriage chamber at City Hall is an obstacle course through which a small girl struggles laboriously to carry a collection plate while the Mayor attempts to read the Civil Code. As the clerk reads the marriage contract, the entire gathering excitedly discusses a bump on the Mayor's forehead. Contemplating the indignities to which the characters are subjected by seemingly adventitious objects, one may feel that farcical chance has become an appallingly attentive fate.

In the second main type of comic structure to be discussed here, the play of intrigue, volition has a much greater role than in the play of chance. The chief intriguer is either a clever rogue, like the Roman slave, or a lover, such as the witty gentlemen of Jonson and Restoration comedy. Sometimes the lover is a rogue: it is difficult to make a significant moral distinction between the hero and the villain in *The Way of the World*. If the hero is the villain in certain Elizabethan "tragedies," including *The Jew of Malta* and *Richard III*, this is also true in Wycherley's *The Country Wife* and Molière's *Don Juan*.

Beaumarchais' first great dramatic success, *The Barber of Seville*, is a handsome example of the comedy of intrigue. Coming a century after Molière and following many decades of critical debate on the relative importance of character, manners, and intrigue in comedy,[3] *The Barber* gave advocates of intrigue the play they had been anticipating. Much more elaborately engineered than the plays of Molière, the comedy brought the métier of playwriting to a high point of development. Yet to suggest that Beaumarchais prefigured the well-made play of the nineteenth century would be to diminish him.

A romantic lover removes an attractive girl from the grip of her jealous tutor and marries her—the proper conclusion for a comedy; but Beaumarchais took justifiable pride in the alertness with which the tutor, Bartholo, resists the lover's plot. When a critic in the *Journal Encyclopédique* complained that Bartholo had acted too stupidly, the author pointed out in his prefatory letter that the critic himself had been unable to follow the intrigue of the lover, Count Almaviva, and his *machiniste*, Figaro. During most of the action Bartholo penetrates a deception as soon as it is attempted. Rosine can complain that he doesn't miss a single detail. Figaro himself indirectly acknowledges the cunning of Bartholo, for when the old man attributes his defeat to lack of precautions (*faute de soins*), Figaro replies, "To lack of sense [*faute de sens*]. Let's tell the truth, Doctor. When youth and love unite in deceiving an old man, his every effort can rightly be called *The Useless Precaution.*"[4]

An account of Act Two will show how the play moves. Having drugged the servants, Figaro prepares Rosine to receive Almaviva kindly, and takes a note from her. As Bartholo approaches, Figaro hides. After a scene with his henchman, Bazile, Bartholo begins to cross-examine Rosine on her morning's activities. Knowing that she has had an interview with Figaro, he at first accuses her of taking a note from the barber, then concludes that she has given one. The dialogue that follows is typical of the whole play. Bartholo mentions the ink on her finger; she asserts that she put it in the inkwell because she had burned it. He points out that the notebook contains one less sheet of paper than earlier in the day; she replies that she has wrapped some candies for Mistress Figaro. Then why is the pen wet?

ROSINE (*aside*). This man has an instinct for jealousy! (*Aloud*) I used it to trace a faded flower on the jacket I was embroidering for you at the frame.

BARTHOLO. How edifying! If you want me to believe you, my child, you must not blush when lying. But you haven't learned that yet.

ROSINE. Who would not blush, sir, when you draw wicked conclusions
from things so innocently done?

[II,xi]

The dramatic movement of this dialogue depends on the sharp opposition of a clever girl and a clever old man. In spite of the rapidity of
the exchange, however, Beaumarchais is able to introduce an ironic
counterpoint through little suggestions in the language. When Rosine
says that Bartholo has an instinct for *jalousie*, we may recall that he
keeps his *jalousies* (blinds) locked. These blinds will be extensively
used in later acts. We notice, too, that Rosine is embroidering a faded
flower on the old man's jacket—a way of combining domestic loyalty
and sarcastic comment. Such moments help to guard against the danger
of exclusive concentration on intrigue.

Bartholo had locked the street door early in the act, then Figaro had
unlocked it. Bartholo now warns Rosine that he will soon have a double
lock—whereupon the Count enters in a military disguise, as if to under-
line the uselessness of Bartholo's attempts to lock out competition. This
sequence of locking and unlocking parallels the back-and-forth movement of the letters, the juggling of the keys and ladder in later acts, and
the alternating current of the dialogue. All help to keep the spectator in
a condition of suspense. As Beaumarchais wrote in one of his letters: "I
believe that what sustains interest in a play up to the last moment is the
accumulation of all the kinds of uneasiness the author can put into the
spectator's mind, and then an unexpected escape from them."[5]

The Count's masquerade as a drunken officer develops from a quarrel-
ing scene with Bartholo into another attempt to communicate with Rosine by word and letter despite the continuing presence of Bartholo.
When Rosine hints that she will catch the spirit of his words, the Count
fingers a note and replies, "No, take hold of the letter literally [*attachez-
vous à la lettre à la lettre*]" (II,xiv). Suspicious that this is not an official
document, Bartholo insists that the letter must go to him; the Count
must therefore substitute the false order for billeting. In a moment
we have the following skirmish:

1. The count drops the note to Rosine.
2. Bartholo reaches for it.
3. The Count picks it up, declaring that Rosine, not he, has dropped
   it.
4. She takes it.
5. The "officer" is ejected by Bartholo.

But Rosine still has to convince Bartholo that the paper has not come from the officer.

The skirmish presents in a small figure the structural pattern of the entire play. Neither of the chief opponents is successful for more than a few seconds at a time, since each thinks fast enough to subject the other to *facheux contretemps*. This quality in the action is both heard and seen. As the false officer makes his exit he ironically asks Bartholo to pray for his success in battle: "life has never been so dear to me"—since he has just passed a note to Rosine. Bartholo sourly replies: "If I had so much credit with death . . ." (II,xiv). As a parting shot the "officer" remarks that death is already in Doctor Bartholo's debt. The verbal triumph makes the pantomimic success the sweeter.

The play teems with reversals. These are so numerous that at times the play seems to be nothing but a series of blows and counter-blows, marches and counter-marches. Comparing Racine and Beaumarchais, Jacques Schérer points out that in the earlier writer, a reversal of situation endures long enough to produce "a considerable enrichment in the analysis of feeling. But in proliferating, the peripety was condemned to lose this psychological function. . . . In passing from the two peripeties of *Phèdre* to the thirty-odd reversals in *The Marriage of Figaro* we leave the domain of increasing profundity for that of accumulation."[6] But though very frequent reversals are harmful to tragedy—as in Jonson's *Sejanus*—they are proper to comedy, which endows its people and its universe not so much with spiritual depths as with quickness of mind and movement. If the comic world is one of uncertainty and suspense, to recur to Beaumarchais' letter, that world will accommodate both plays of chance and plays of intrigue.

At the close of *The Barber of Seville* we hardly know Figaro, Almaviva, and Bartholo more fully than we did at the end of the first act. Rosine, it is true, has an emotional role, and we are able to watch her feelings develop, though Beaumarchais does not have Mozart to help him here. She becomes increasingly outraged at her enslavement. In the third act we can see and hear the growth of her love. In the fourth, we observe her horror at the news of the Count's treachery and her overwhelming joy at the discovery that the news is false. In this act her emotional expression is more characteristic of the eighteenth-century *drame* than of tragedy. Seeing the supposedly false lover kneel before her, she cries, "Stop, wretched man! . . . You dare to profane. . . . You 'adore' me! . . . Go, I no longer find you dangerous. . ." (IV,vi). The stiffness of the speech is not far from that of Lessing's *Miss Sara Sampson*. On the other hand, when she learns the truth, her reflections on what might have been take the antithetical form of Beaumarchais' comic dialogue: "I would have spent my life detesting you. Ah, Lindor! the most frightful punishment is to hate when one feels one is made to love" (IV,vi). But time does not permit a more supple analysis of feeling, for Bartholo and the police are to arrive in a few minutes. Beaumarchais had already made his choice between a comedy of intrigue and a drama of emotional depths.

The critic in the *Journal Encyclopédique* could not see why Almaviva took so much trouble to transmit a letter, especially since Figaro had access to the house. Beaumarchais refuted this objection rather easily, but the critic had identified a weakness in the play. So much effort is expended on problems like transmitting letters or unlocking windows that the comedy loses stature; one feels the gap between ingenuity and what is achieved by it. The elements that enlarge the work—themes, characterization, imagery—do not always merge with its essence.

The social and political overtones are sometimes relevant; for example, the old man who represses youth also opposes new ideas. In a dialogue with Rosine, Bartholo attacks *La Précaution inutile*, which she is studying, as some newfangled *drame*. Since Beaumarchais had already advocated this new genre in an essay, his point here is not doubtful. The scene continues:

BARTHOLO. H'm, the journals and the authorities will prove me right! Barbarous century!
ROSINE. You're always attacking our poor century.
BARTHOLO. Pardon me! What has it produced that it should be praised? New kinds of nonsense: liberty of thought, gravity, electricity, toleration, inoculation, quinine, the Encyclopedia, and dramas [*les drames*].

[I,iii]

At this moment Rosine drops her music from the window. Here Beaumarchais' integration of dialogue and action expresses both the life of his time and a major theme of comedy in all times, the conflict of the generations. At other moments, however, the attempt to widen dramatic significance is forced, as in Bazile's famous speech on slander (II,viii). Though vividly written and suggestive of Beaumarchais' personal difficulties, it is not really justified. It varies the play only by diverting it from its course. Bazile tells his employer, Bartholo, that he will fight Almaviva by slandering him and then proceeds to a magnificent encomium of slander which, though speaking in prose, he presents poetically and musically as well as comically and satirically. But it does not appear that Bazile ever carries out his intention or that the plan could be useful, or even that Bazile is deliberately making a fool of Bartholo. The speech is an excellent *jeu d'esprit* but no more than that.

One other strand in Beaumarchais' dramatic pattern should be mentioned, his use of song. In Acts One and Three the playwright stops the headlong movement of the intrigue, first for a musical exchange of sentiments and later for a significant development of dramatic feeling. The second passage, Rosine's aria in Act Three, is especially important. Made possible by Almaviva's pretense that he has been asked by Bazile to give Rosine a singing lesson, the aria is a still point in the action, permitting Rosine to express musically her growing love for Almaviva, as Bartholo dozes in a chair. The words of the aria create an atmosphere of pastoral love while commenting on the situation of the intriguing lovers. The song concludes:

> Si quelque jaloux
> Trouble un bien si doux,
> Nos amants d'accord
> Ont un soin extrême . . .
> . . . De voiler leur transport;
> Mais quand on s'aime,
> La gêne ajoute encor
> Au plaisir même.[7]

[III,iv]

If some jealous rival troubles so sweet a pleasure, our lovers take great care to veil their passion. But when we love, danger adds to pleasure.

Near the end of the aria Almaviva covers Rosine's hand with kisses, and there is a retard. Overcome, she can hardly continue. All of this is important to the design of the play since it provides dramatic emotion, making it clear that the almost constant maneuvering does not exist merely for its own sake. Although the first-night audience disapproved his excursion into opera, Beaumarchais' instinct was right. To fall in love is a chance that should be extended even to a pert minx in a comedy of intrigue.

In the third main type of comic structure, the "commanding form" of the plot gives way to broader and more varied concepts of design. The playwright takes some combination of story, character, theme, and language as his chief organizing principle. One element or another may assume prominence. In *The Bourgeois Gentleman* and *The Imaginary Invalid*, it is character, though these plays are more than "comedies of character." In many plays of Shaw, it is theme, not necessarily thesis: *Getting Married* has an unmistakable theme, but the contrapuntal handling of story and the use of something like a double parabasis remind us of the Elizabethans on the one hand and Aristophanes on the other. In *Love's Labour's Lost*, the play is not only verbally clever but about verbal cleverness, to which it accords a story and administers a lesson. The comedies of Aristophanes, which are close to ritual without being ritual, combine traditional formulas derived from the kômos with story, character, theme, and language to produce a dramatic celebration of life together with a criticism of it as it is lived. *The Acharnians* and the *Peace* are good illustrations of this fusion, the *Peace* being the more clearly unified, *The Acharnians* the more complex.

For F. M. Cornford, when he wrote *The Origin of Attic Comedy* (1914), Aristophanes' plays were unified by an underlying fertility ritual signalizing the victory of the New Year over the Old or the destruction of the Old followed by his rebirth. The victory is followed by a sacrifice of the defeated agonist, a feast in which the "good" principle celebrates its victory, and a sacred marriage. Cornford's fascinating and highly influential book makes Aristophanes seem a grand type, even archetype, of comedy in all periods, since comedy in general is certainly concerned with love and sex, the struggle of the generations, and the life force itself. When we are told by Cornford, Murray, and others that the same ritual underlies both tragedy and comedy, the hypothesis becomes even more daring and therefore more attractive, for it appears to unify vast tracts of myth and literature.

Cornford pointed to many myths and rituals, ancient and modern, illustrating some part of his ceremonial pattern, and in reviewing the comedies of Aristophanes, he was able to show that a certain play presented a battle of youth with age, a sacrifice, a feast, or a marriage, sacred or otherwise—perhaps two or more of these. But he could not prove that the Greeks ever performed a ritual arranged in just his pattern, and in no play of Aristophanes, with the exception of *The Birds*, could he show a reproduction of the "canonical" Agôn, Sacrifice, Feast, and Marriage, in that order. Furthermore, it is often unclear who is supposed to represent the good principle—in *The Knights* is it Agoracritus or Demos?—or who stands for the bride of the victor: frequently there is none. In *The Clouds*, Strepsiades, an old simpleton, attempts to get new ideas from the radical Socrates, who rejects Zeus and the

old order, but Strepsiades proves too stupid to learn and is later beaten
for his pains by his newly educated son, Pheidippides. This might
seem to be a victory for the New Year, but Strepsiades takes his revenge by burning down the laboratory of Socrates. Are we to say that
the Old Year, harboring the good principle, has been rejuvenated and
has defeated what has seemed more vital but really was not? To say
the least, the argument would be forced.[8] Although the works of Aristophanes contain many reminiscences of the Attic kômos, a fertility ritual, the plays have a structure that is clearer than their substructure.

They regularly include a Prologue recalling Greek tragedy, a heavily
stressed choral entrance (Parodos), a struggle (Agôn) often reaching
a climax in the first half of the play, a long choral address to the audience (Parabasis), and a succession of scenes and choral passages concluded by a general departure from the stage (Exodos). The second
half of the play has been subject to frequent critical attack. A generation ago Gilbert Norwood remarked that after the Parabasis we find a
"jumble of little scenes."[9] The article on Aristophanes in *The Oxford
Classical Dictionary*, though less blunt, makes a similar point. Yet at
least one critic, Paul Mazon, had shown that the second half of an
Aristophanic play, far from being a jumble, is carefully guided by a
feeling for design, balance, and climax.[10]

Each comedy has a very simple plot constantly interrupted or pulled
up short by parodies, scenes of matched lines intended more to point
contrasts than to develop the action, and direct appeals or humorous
insults to the audience; but within this seemingly loose arrangement
there are immensely elaborate lyrics in which each syllable must have
its place. When there is a dominating character, he is vivid but un-
explored; he may remain the same or suddenly take on new characteristics. Things happen according to the will of the poet, not in ob-
servance of dramatic logic. One is always conscious of the poet's voice.
The focus of the events is the theatre as a public meeting ground. If
the spectator is tempted to identify himself with the hero or the Chorus,
the playwright is quick to shock him into a detached attitude. Literary sophistication and brilliant theatricalism contrive to reduce dramatic illusion to a minimum without destroying it altogether. The playwright is intent upon provocative, ironic entertainment involving both
criticism of Athens and endorsement of life as an ever-renewed
phenomenon.

The Acharnians (425 B.C.), Aristophanes' first surviving comedy, is
the kind of play just sketched. It is largely indifferent to the unities of
time and place, though preoccupied with Athens in the sixth year of

the Peloponnesian War. The stage, anticipating the simultaneous settings of the Middle Ages, indicates three separate areas: the Athenian Pnyx or public Assembly, the house of Euripides, and the home of Dicaeopolis (Just Citizen), in the fields beyond the city walls. The action begins about noon at the Pnyx, which was shaped like a theatre, and when the Assembly begins, the real audience will be looking at the backs of the actors playing citizens; that is, viewing itself engaged in political life—a touch of realism soon to be negated. Dicaeopolis has been waiting since dawn for the session to begin and will soon complain about Athenian inattention to high matters of state. But he begins by farcically bemoaning a life so miserable that he has known only four pleasures—the arithmetic evidently burlesquing the dry recitals in some of Euripides' prologues. Yet he has mentioned only two pleasures when his sorrows distract him. They have to do with bad Athenian musicians and bad Athenian politics. At the end of his long speech he announces his determination to shout down any public business except the all-important question of peace.

The rest of the Prologue shows the Assembly refusing to make peace with Sparta and Dicaeopolis arranging a private peace between Sparta and himself. But word of this accommodation reaches the Chorus of Acharnians, the ancient but warlike charcoal-burners from an Athenian deme.

On their entrance (Parodos), the Acharnians begin to attack the hero with coals. After threatening to sacrifice a basket of coals, held as a hostage, Dicaeopolis places his head on a chopping-block and prepares to speak in his own defense. Even comedy, he says, knows what is right. His oration, mingling serious and farcical arguments, wins over half the Chorus; the rest are converted, in the Agôn, when the hero points out that young draft-dodgers receive better treatment from the government than do patriotic veterans like the charcoal-burners.

In the Parabasis the Chorus praise the author and his fight for justice, or "the right," and speak proudly of their role at Marathon—sixty-five years ago.

In the second half of the play, a series of short scenes demonstrates the joys of peace and the sorrows of war. Various characters, including the military officer, Lamachus, beg Dicaeopolis for small allotments of the peace he holds in a wineskin, but to no avail. At the close, the wounded Lamachus is taken to a surgeon while the hero receives a prize for victory in a drinking contest.

The methodical madness of an Aristophanic play results from many antinomies. Three seem to stand out: (1) the tension between the artist's mastery of traditional form, as seen particularly in the epirrhematic construction of the extensive lyrical sections, and his practice of regularly scrapping this form; (2) his constant and deliberate oscillation between realism and fantasy, as well as between illusion and theatricalism; (3) his manipulation of dramatic movement, or temporal form, and stasis, or "spatial" form.

The first of these antinomies is mainly lost to the modern reader unless he is willing to study the playwright's elaborate metrics, often impossible to reproduce in English. Even a brief examination of Starkie's metrical analysis in his Introduction to his great edition of *The Acharnians*[11] reveals that the play was far more musical than translations indicate. This aspect of the comedy must have increased its artistic seriousness as opposed to its political seriousness, its fantasy as opposed to its realism, its stasis as opposed to its movement.

Aristophanes' use of fantasy has little in common with *Peter Pan*. A fantasy, however, is believable to those with a strong desire to believe it. At the same time, its removal from actuality serves as a protection against its possibly distasteful ideas. Presumably the aristocratic party in Athens found Aristophanes' ideas attractive and his fantasy not, therefore, completely fantastic, while the partisans of the demagogues were of another mind. But he was not writing for a party, he was a poet of the city; his own statements and his successes would indicate as much. His balancing of realism and fantasy cannot be regarded merely as a kind of literary politics, with fantasy for the aristocrats and realism for the commoners; it is an essentially creative act awakening extremely varied but related responses in the whole man. For this reason his highly original universe is provocative but not prescriptive. In *The Acharnians*, the treatment of the characters alone, shot through as they are with ironies, should warn us against tagging him too neatly. At the end of the play, the story is complete, but the issues are not settled.

The shuttling between realism and fantasy is paralleled by the zigzagging from dramatic illusion to theatricalism and direct speech. The former alternation continually transforms the world represented, the latter destroys it as the idea of representation is negated. The opening ten lines are "presentational"; they resemble a barker's spiel or a circus parade designed to lure customers inside the tent;[12] but as the long first speech continues, it turns inward and begins to arouse some feeling for an honest old citizen thwarted by stupid or corrupt politics. Then, as the Assembly begins, we have moments of almost serious state business broken by Dicaeopolis in the manner of a vaudevillian or "stand-up" comic. Throughout the play, Aristophanes clings to this technique for keeping the spectator off balance but alert.

Dramatic illusion depends on dramatic movement. Just as Aristophanes regularly scraps illusion, so he regularly stops his action. The swing from movement to stasis and back is inherent in choral drama, but a long stasimon in the *Agamemnon*, let us say, may be more active than a short ode in Aristophanes, since the Aeschylean Chorus of Elders, even when not obviously engaged in action, will be painfully struggling to understand the world and the gods: the *pathei mathos* involves inner activity. In Aristophanes, however, the Chorus does not seek to understand, it *knows* this or that. In the Parodos of *The Acharnians*, it knows that the war is right; later, half the Chorus, then all, know it is wrong. The playwright makes little or no attempt to show movement of mind. We see the Chorus and other characters at particular stages of thought but not clearly moving from one stage to the next. Even the Agôn, ordinarily the most dramatic part of the play, presents not so much a developing struggle as an unchanging opposition between the antagonists, Dicaeopolis and Lamachus. The later scenes between the two are similarly devoted to stasis—that is, to certain *stands* (one meaning of the Greek *stasis*). Naturally, movement does occur in Aristophanes, but his method puts a far greater emphasis on the stand than is true of the types of comedy previously discussed in this chapter.

This way of pulling up short helps to crystallize certain social and political positions as well as literary themes. It also serves to emphasize divergent aspects of character. Despite some long monologues and one lengthy soliloquy, the hero is not viewed from the inside but projected in various directions. Aristophanes treats his *eiron* ironically. Though nominally an old farmer suffering from bad government and a rampant enemy, he exists primarily as a funny man with ideas. A ruthless opponent of sham in high places, he becomes an exhibitionist. A rustic hating commerce, he becomes a master entrepreneur. A critic of pederasty, he chortles over Copaic eels and the *choiroi* of young girls. A "just" citizen, he becomes an exclusive beneficiary of the wine of peace. The Chorus envies him for his wisdom or good counsel (*euboulias*) but even more for his feasting (*euôchias*). He superintends his cooking scene with the cries of a tragic hero in pain.[13] Yet he does not seem fundamentally different in the second half of the play from what he was in the first. What unites the disparate moments is his boundless energy and his irreverence for everything including himself. When his life is threatened by the fierce Acharnians, he is unable to speak seriously. Daring to seek the aid of the famous Euripides, he is astonished at his own courage; yet this astonishment is one more joke at the expense of the tragic playwright. Dicaeopolis himself is a joke with something to say. About what? About war, peace, Athens, and a human nature which, rationally considered, might lead to despair but vitally considered is seen to achieve a recurring victory over fantastic odds, including those self-created.

The role of image patterns in the structure of a play has often been distorted. When a play is in motion, the language is part of the movement; indeed, a given word can hardly mean the same thing twice. A particular word or phrase, even if often repeated, does not necessarily have a meaning which can be arrested and detached from the flux—from the changing situation, the altering atmosphere, and the developing attitudes of the characters using the words. A metaphor may occur a number of times without being revelatory of the world (Denmark or Athens) purportedly described. The ineptness of the image can be the author's comment on the speaker. Nevertheless, since Aristophanes' writing teems with the stuff of life and since he so often stops his action to present sensuous contrasts, we should expect that the imagery of *The Acharnians* would be a significant part of the total structure. In his masterful study of Aristophanes, Cedric Whitman has already shown that this is so.

Since the play strongly contrasts the pleasures of peace and the pains of war, the imagery tends to fall into two large groupings. Associated with peace are the fertility of the land, the agricultural life, the production and enjoyment of food and drink, sensuous pleasure of all kinds, including the music at banquets, as well as Cypris, Eros, and the Graces. War is connected with the contentiousness of urban life, markets, shipbuilding, the coals and stones of the fiery men from Acharnae, monsters such as Geryon, and the warlike Acharnian muse. The sweet smell of peace is contrasted with the smell of the pitch used in building warships and with the armpits of scoundrels dangerous to the city. The terrible plumes of the warrior oppose the wings of thrushes being cooked for the feast. Even a casual reading of the play reveals an extraordinary number of references to birds (braggart peacocks, crows, and the "hail of birds" which the Boeotian offers the hero) and to their plumes, feathers, and wings. Pretending terror at the sight of Lamachus' arms, Dicaeopolis asks for a plume so that he may tickle his throat and vomit. The contrast between the warlike and the peaceful uses of birds reaches a climax as Lamachus, preparing for battle, asks for his plumes while the hero requests pigeons and thrushes (ll. 1103–4).

All this is part of the "spatial" structure of the play. But in the playwright's ironical scheme of things, the spaces can shift, symbols can change their valency. Wine, couches, and sex are "bad" when enjoyed by the wrong people, especially ambassadors living at public expense, but "good" when the hero enjoys them at the conclusion. Though mercantile conflict has been a cause of war, Dicaeopolis becomes a redoubtable merchant. One may question the Chorus' assurance that those who trade with him will not be cheated. The Acharnian muse can sound a call to arms or inspire the old men with harsh music in behalf of the peacemaker. In his cooking scene the hero can discard feathers in the grandiose style associated with the *alazôn*, Lamachus. Growing things can be symbols of fertility or of violence in self-defense. A reed (*skoinos*) can hold a few drops of peace or serve as an image of the Acharnians' desire to stab the enemy. As Whitman points out, Lamachus' ankle wound is caused by a vine-prop (*charaki*, l. 1178).[14] In general, despite his partisanship, Aristophanes can see that vice and violence are not confined to Cleon, Hyperbolus, and the host of shabby fellows he usually attacks.

The importance of a thematic word or image cannot be judged by the frequency with which it occurs. In *The Acharnians*, a word like "plume" or "vine" is significant when it contributes to the dramatic movement or when it is found in a cluster of supporting or ironically contrasted phrases or other scenic elements. In the stasimon following Dicaeopolis' scene with the Boeotian, images of fruitfulness and vigor, which have been strikingly in evidence, reach a concerted climax as the reformed Chorus invokes Peace. As so often at moments of lyric concentration in Aristophanes, the imagery looks two ways—toward the elevated and the ludicrous. Except for the first and last lines to be quoted, the passage is in regular paeonic tetrameter catalectic,[15] a meter impossible in English. Perhaps the best approximation would be a rendering in dactyls:

> Intimate friend of the fairest of goddesses, friend of
>   the Graces,
> Little we knew that your face was so beautiful.
> O that the God of Love, crowned with a wreath of flowers,
> Seizing us both, might bring us together now.
> Can you have thought of me gerontologically?
> Ah, but I see myself grasping and throwing you.
> First I will strike with a long row of vine-plants,
> Next to them placing the shoots of the fig.
> Last, cultivation octogenarian.

Round the estate a circle of olive trees
Good for anointing us both at the New Moon.

[ll. 989–99]

Some scholars think that Peace herself appears just before the invoca-
tion, but this is unnecessary, particularly since she has nothing to do.
The first lines are calm, reverent, as the Chorus sees her in its mind's
eye. The brief reference in the Greek to the painting of Eros, "crowned
with a wreath of flowers," increases the feeling of stasis. Soon comes
the humorous thought, slightly exaggerated in my translation, that the
men are too old for love, and then the astounding surge of aged vigor:
these men, as already mentioned, had fought at Marathon two generations ago. The remainder of the lyric keeps two lines of thought running simultaneously, one concerning the old farmer engaged in the
works of peace, the other presenting the old prodigy as a sexual partner. The healthy bawdiness of the second picture prevents the gentleness of the first from becoming too sweet.

The language opposes the aggressive and the peaceful, the masculine and the feminine. The row of vine-plants and the shoots of the fig
balance the wreath of flowers and the circle of olive trees. Both here
and elsewhere, the old men think of peacetime as an opportunity for
sexual attack. Although such ironies do not destroy Aristophanes' advocacy of peace, they suggest that in the Athens of his imagination the
cessation of hostilities will transpose without muting men's restless activity.

There is much in *The Acharnians* that marks it as Old Comedy. In
this respect it is not a permanent type of comic structure. But apart
from its purely local characteristics, it sets a standard for poetic comedy
in all times and places, though its pattern has never been followed
both closely and successfully in later times. Yet Shakespeare's greatest
comedies, like those of Aristophanes, are a poetic fusion of many elements, and their movement resembles that of the Greek in their passage
from a frustrating to a satisfying state of things. In Shakespeare the
happy ending is liberally distributed. In Aristophanes, on the other
hand, the critic in the playwright may withhold benediction from the
alazôn. Malvolio will get an apology, but Lamachus will not. In
Shakespeare the whole action spells out a comic meaning, in Aristophanes the victory of the positive feeling is most clearly visible in the spirit
of the poet himself. The structure of Aristophanes' mind is such that he
constantly moves from satiric attack to comic blessing.

The three types of comic structure I have described are dominated
by chance, intrigue, or the author's design emphasized as design. In

Aristophanic comedy, which exemplifies the third type, chance and intrigue are of course present, but the writer's design keeps them under so strict a control that we are likely to attend more to what the playwright is doing than to what his characters perform or suffer as fictive entities. The method permits a freedom of maneuver of which the comic poets of the future might make excellent use. Brecht, of course, has many points of contact with Aristophanes, and the very gifted John Arden, who began writing not many years ago, has already shown that in the twentieth century, comedy can be a theatrical poem of a high order.

It has been said that there is "something inherently absurd" about plot complications.[16] *Sganarelle* and *The Barber of Seville* support the idea. The "complications" in Aristophanes are the dazzling feats of the equilibrist himself as he leaps from the elevated to the low and back, from the real to the fantastic, from representation of life to purely theatrical activity, he himself the tricky servant who deceives his masters in the audience, he the buffoon who explodes the pretences of the boasters, hypocrites, and parasites, asserting by his felt presence the strength, breadth, and health of a vital humanity.

NOTES

1. *Man of Destiny,* in *The Complete Plays of Bernard Shaw* (London, 1934), p. 161. Citations from Shaw will be to this edition.

2. See the essays on Feydeau in *Cahiers de la Compagnie Madeleine Renaud —Jean-Louis Barrault,* XV (Jan., 1956); and cf. Marcel Achard's discussion in *"Let's Get a Divorce!" and Other Plays,* ed. Eric Bentley (New York, 1958).

3. See Edna C. Fredrick, *The Plot and Its Construction in Eighteenth-Century Criticism of French Comedy* (Bryn Mawr, Pa., 1934).

4. IV,viii, in *Le Barbier de Séville,* ed. E. J. Arnould (Oxford, 1963). Citations from *Le Barbier* and its prefatory letter will be to this edition.

5. Quoted by Jacques Schérer, *La Dramaturgie de Beaumarchais* (Paris, 1954), p. 143.

6. Schérer, p. 145.

7. The frequent rhymes (lost in translation) are clearly intended to mesh with the stage business to be invented by the director.

8. For a cogent criticism of Cornford's theory, see A. W. Pickard-Cambridge, *Dithyramb, Tragedy, and Comedy* (Oxford, 1927), pp. 329–49.

9. *Greek Comedy* (Boston, 1932), p. 299.

10. Paul Mazon, *Essai sur la composition des comédies d'Aristophane* (Paris, 1904).

11. *The Acharnians of Aristophanes,* ed. W. J. M. Starkie (London, 1909). My translations and citations are based on this edition.

12. Cf. Mazon, pp. 177–78.

13. See Starkie's note on line 1042.

14. Cedric H. Whitman, *Aristophanes and the Comic Hero* (Cambridge, Mass., 1964), p. 74.

15. Starkie, p. lxxxiv.

16. Northrop Frye, *Anatomy of Criticism* (Princeton, 1957), p. 170.

CHAPTER FOUR

Character

ALTHOUGH COMEDY includes characters who are not comic, all comic characters are fools or dwell in the ambience of folly. Their behavior ranges from fooling through foolishness to folly outright. In Aristophanes all the characters are in a wide sense buffoons, whether ironical men, boasters, or combinations of the two. In Shakespeare the professional and semi-professional fools speak a language very close to that of Benedick, Beatrice, and Rosalind, and when they ridicule the Malvolios and Shylocks, we see fooling ranged against folly. A character like Viola is not so much comic as romantic, but even she can indulge in fooling or fall into a laughable antagonism with Andrew Aguecheek. The sweet Hero can play with the emotions of Beatrice and make a fool of her. In Jonson, can it be said that the rogue is not a fool? In Molière there is usually a clear opposition between those who are foolish-comic and those who are not—Orgon and his mother against Elmire, Alceste against Philinte, Arnolphe against Chrysalde—but in the farces, fools are everywhere, as in *Monsieur de Pourceaugnac*, where the wonderfully lively fooling of Sbrigani and Nerine, the *homme* and *femme d'intrigue*, exercises itself upon the stupidity of the central character. Shaw takes pleasure in making fools of his wisest or cleverest men and has his cowards triumph over the brave or seemingly brave. In all periods the wit is one who makes a fool of language.

No one has matched the myriad-minded folly crowding Shakespearian comedy; it is a presence so ubiquitous that to reject it as contemptible would be like rejecting life itself. The fools are the stupid, the clever, the wise, the wisely foolish, the foolishly wise, the harmless, the vulnerable, and the dangerous. The clever gentlemen in *Love's Labour's Lost* surprise by their stupidity, the clownish Costard and Bottom surprise by their wisdom; Feste can make a phrase seem an adequate way of life, Lucio will throw away moral responsibility for a phrase; Trinculo would be dangerous if he were more intelligent, Angelo is intelligent enough to be dangerous. Though comedy attacks some kinds of folly, the panorama of fools in Shakespeare finally leaves one with the feeling that he who knows himself for a fool is on the way to salvation, and even he who does not may have a place in Limbo. One of the qualities preserving even Shakespeare's lightest comedies from triviality is the sense, both humbling and inspiriting, that the Benedicks and the Costards, however far apart in rank, belong to the universal brotherhood of fools.

Where Shakespeare and Aristophanes accept or revel in comic folly, Molière and Jonson regularly attack it. The first stance is festive, the second critical. Aristophanes chooses as comic victims a vast array of types and individuals, but the attackers are as ludicrous as the victims. The champion of reform in *The Knights* is as impossible as the demogogue he replaces, but no one is troubled by the fact. In *The Clouds* most of Just Logic's argument is on a rather high plane, but he ends by asserting that the Athenian advocates, tragic poets, and demogogues, and even the spectators at this comedy are "broad-arses" and that his cause is therefore lost. Perhaps the most serious character in Aristophanes is Lysistrata, but even she relaxes for a few phallic jests. What would be bitter in Juvenal or Jonson is turned toward joking or poetic fantasy. The mask of Aristophanes is ceaselessly genial. As Hegel wrote, "The characters he has imported into . . . his amazing artistic creations he runs into the mould of fool from the start with a sportive fancy that seems inexhaustible, so that the very idea of a rational result is impossible."[1] He is seriously unwilling to take his own most cherished ideas too seriously.

Jonson and Molière were in a sense more classical, more rational than Aristophanes. Jonson's plays and critical writings show him in agreement with Sir Philip Sidney's opinion that comedy represents human error as scornfully as possible. Holding this view of comedy, Jonson could hardly be friendly to folly. Characters in his plays with names like La Foole, Daw, Cokes (dolt), and Littlewit are certain to suffer for their stupidity. On the other hand Volpone, Mosca, and Subtle are well and truly fooled at the ends of their plays. Volpone is allowed a vivid judgment on his own folly:

> To make a snare for mine own neck; and run
> My head into it wilfully! with laughter!
> When I had newly scap'd, was free and clear!
> Out of mere wantonness![2]

This knave was a fool, and the chief fools in the play have been inferior knaves. Yet Volpone, Mosca, and their peers are admirable knaves, and even the contemptible fools in Jonson are seldom revolting. There is something delightful about Tribulation Wholesome, whose theology Jonson hated. Old Corbaccio's mad struggle to go on enjoying life is stunning. Epicure Mammon could almost convert a saint to debauchery. Even the loathsome Corvino, perhaps the worst man in comedy, has a boiling imagination that produces admiring laughter. Jonson shed his own prodigious energy over the grotesques he struck most viciously.

Jonson studied folly, lashed it, and created great imaginative projections of it. Molière saw it at closer range as somehow belonging to us. If he reveals unsparingly the obsessions of his jealous husbands and tyrannical fathers, he makes them such fertile sources of laughter that it is impossible not to regard them with a certain strange affection. Most of them are unconscious of their folly; they have a joyful devotion to their idiocies—their worthless medicines, their false religion, their pedantries; one can share, with a fine actor, Monsieur Jourdain's delight in the discovery that he is speaking prose. Although the nineteenth century may have overestimated the "humanity" in Molière's representation of folly, the suggestion that he viewed it with merely cold rationalism or anger is no more satisfying. Out of social ambition, the wealthy bourgeois, George Dandin, has sought and obtained the hand of an aristocratic girl, Angélique. He has courted not her but her parents, and there is no indication that he loves her. When the play begins, he already knows that she is ready to deceive him, and he curses his folly in marrying her. But despite his attempts to defend his marital rights, she and her parents fool him three times in a three-act play. In the last act he is forced to kneel to his wife for forgiveness. He is petty, ridiculous, cowardly, and we cannot pity him on the ground that he has given his love in vain. But the very fact that this little man is humiliated by shoddy aristocrats introduces sympathy into the laughter at his expense. Strictly speaking, he deserves what he gets, but the play does not encourage strict judgments.

In Book II of the *Nicomachean Ethics* (1108a20–29) Aristotle discusses truthfulness and pleasantness as moral qualities important in social intercourse. The truthful man is the mean between the mock-modest (*eirôn*) and the boaster (*alazôn*). The pleasant man is the mean between the boor (*agroikos*) and the buffoon (*bômolochos*). In a later passage (1128a23) he mentions the indecency or buffoonery characteristic of Old Comedy. Presumably at a later time, a short, anonymous work, the now famous *Tractatus Coislinianus*, divided comic characters into *bômolochoi, eirônes,* and *alazônes*; the *agroikos* is not mentioned. For F. M. Cornford the most striking opposition in Aristophanic comedy is between the buffoon combined with the ironic man, and the impostor. But as Cedric Whitman has recently pointed out, the ironic buffoon may himself become an impostor.[3] Indeed, all four types tend to merge in action. The buffoon turned impostor does not really wish to be taken seriously; he assumes boastfulness mainly for the amusement of the audience. Even the *agroikos* can merge with the buffoon. In *The Knights,* Demos, described as a boor, proves to be a clever rogue who is enjoying himself at the expense of others. In Jonson's *Epicoene,* Morose is the boor, but there is a scene in which he and the somewhat buffoonish Truewit, who certainly strays from the golden mean, trade superlatives in a style reminding us that they are both, after all, related to the ancient *bômolochos.*

The buffoon is the type of types, the comic character par excellence. Indecorous vitality existing for itself, he may or may not have a plot in mind. In Aristophanes he gets a brilliant idea which he carries through; in other writers he can be a "mere" entertainer. In all periods he is the man the populace wants to see, from the mimes of Epicharmus and the Atellane farces to the Turkish Karaghöz and the modern Greek Karaghiozes. Like the protagonist of Aristophanes, Karaghöz combines the ironic and the buffoonish. According to N. N. Martinovitch, "Karaghöz represents the common Turkish people stripped of exterior gloss; he seems to be very naive, simple and crude, but possesses in reality great natural wit and cunning. He laughs and jokes with everybody, including his own friend, Hadjeivat. He is often punished for this, but to no avail."[4] Martinovitch prints a short piece, *A Picnic to Ialova,* featuring Karaghöz. Insignificant in terms of plot or other development, burdened by apparently insoluble problems of translation, the play nevertheless communicates the indefeasible spirit of the buffoon. Karaghöz is a true clown, and as Susanne Langer writes, "the clown is Life, he is the Will, he is the Brain, and by the same token he is nature's fool."[5]

The apotheosis of the buffoon is Falstaff. He swallows down the braggart soldier, the Vice, the parasite, and the jester like so many cups of sack. He is Riot and Dishonor issuing a standing challenge to the world of responsibility, especially when it produces the instability of the history plays. He is a liar, but a liar who doesn't expect to be believed, even by himself during a soliloquy: does he really think, for example, that anyone will credit his pretense of killing Hotspur? His lies and shifts are most brilliant when he has been thoroughly exposed, his wit is most penetrating when he has most definitely been proved a fool.

He is a scapegoat who repeatedly escapes harmless, like the reviving
heroes in the St. George plays, only to be rejected at last, not really for
moral reasons but because one cannot be a buffoon forever. The plot
contains him like a girdle; if it did not, he would spread over the entire
play. As it is, he shares the stage at Shrewsbury with the great antagonists, Hotspur and the Prince. After Falstaff has fallen, supposedly
dead, under the sword of Douglas, and Hal has slain Hotspur, the Prince
says to his enemy:

> This earth that bears thee dead
> Bears not alive so stout a gentleman.
> [*Henry IV*, Part I, V, iv, 92–93]

Since he has not yet seen Falstaff on the ground, he cannot have intended a pun, but we must take it as such. The fallen buffoon is momentarily confused with the fallen Harry Percy, for both are "stout." Seeing
the point, we laugh, but then we may wonder about the entire system
of values suggested by the play.

Shakespeare frequently juxtaposes the buffoon and the serious man:
Falstaff and Hotspur, Toby Belch and Malvolio, the Fool and Lear.
One of the most daring of such confrontations brings together Cleopatra and an unnamed Clown. Depending on the buffoon, the juxtaposition can exalt or downgrade the serious character and his values.
When Henry V's call to the breach is followed by Bardolph's, the triviality of the clown makes the heroism of the King all the more salient.
But when the buffoon is Falstaff, buffoonery takes on compelling force
as a way of life. Both Falstaff and Toby Belch put forward the attractively subversive doctrine that virtue is not for all men, Falstaff with
his "Well, God be thanked for these rebels, they offend none but the
virtuous" (Part I, III,iii,213–14), Toby with his famous question about
cakes and ale. Merely by appearing in his characteristic stance, Falstaff can qualify the feeling of a scene that precedes or follows. At the
end of Act Two in *Henry IV*, Part II, Falstaff is ordered to return at
once to military duty but instead retires for the night with Doll Tearsheet. In the following scene, the King enters in his nightgown and has
the great soliloquy in which he envies the peaceful sleep of "the vile /
In loathsome beds," ending with the words "Uneasy lies the head that
wears a crown" (Part II, III,i,15–16, 31). Assuming there is no inter-
mission after Falstaff's scene, the memory of this scene will penetrate
the second, and the proximity of the two passages will raise a serious
question whether the usurping King has chosen a way superior to the
buffoon's. Who sleeps in the more loathsome bed?

Falstaff is as close to heroism as any buffoon has ever come, yet he is an anti-hero in the sense that his whole life is a criticism of what the heroes of his time stand for. As Enid Welsford writes, "Falstaff cracks a joke and the tavern becomes more reputable than the battle-field or the council chamber."[6] He turns his back not only on responsibility but on time. The past and the future concern him as little as possible. His life is pure spontaneity, a continuing triumph of improvisation over plan, as where he "forgives" the Hostess after she has been completely exonerated of the charge of robbing him. Considering the impediments in his way—his flesh, his deplorable reputation, his risk-taking—his successes are heroic. If he is a hero, he is heroism attained through prodigious expansiveness, for he is in sober terms worse than the average man, who can therefore laugh at him contentedly, but obviously superior to all other men in histrionic gift, slippery wit, and zest. In the first of his great Boar's Head scenes, when he takes off the King, he has no sooner spoken his first brief line, "Stand aside, nobility," than the Hostess cries, "O Jesu, this is excellent sport, i' faith" (Part I, II, iv, 430). Did ever an actor attain a more instantaneous success? As for his wit, literary and social history would seem to confirm the truth of his statement to his Page, "The brain of this foolish-compounded clay, man, is not able to invent anything that intends to laughter more than anything I invent or is invented on me" (Part II, I, ii, 8–11). He is, perhaps, Shakespeare's greatest artist, reminding us that the fool, the artist, and the outcast have sometimes been thought of as one.[7]

In *Aristophanes and the Comic Hero*, Cedric Whitman speaks of the beast-man-god structure in characters like Peithetaerus, Trygaeus, and Dicaeopolis, a structure representing the Greek feeling for the unity of the world and the range of man within that world.[8] But Falstaff is a more fully perceived embodiment of this trinity than any protagonist in the Greek plays. He is both real in the sense that he is constantly recognizable and beyond reality as we know it, a character if there ever was one and a symbol of what lies beyond individuality. His mythic quality has been increasingly observed. "What wonder," says H. C. Goddard, "that this contradictory being—as deminatured as a satyr or a mermaid—who is forever repeating within himself the original miracle of creation, has taken on the proportions of a mythological figure."[9] The beast in him is constantly insisted upon, but when he is likened to a Manningtree ox prepared for a festive table, when he speaks of himself as a wassail candle, when he falls in "death" and rises again, and when his long holiday is finally terminated, his role as the Spirit inspiring seasonal rites is unmistakable. It is indeed easy to see him as the Year Spirit in all its phases, so irrepressibly youthful is this "latter spring," this "all-hallown summer," despite his white hairs.

Attempts to reduce Shakespeare's Gargantua to a function of plot are unconvincing, but one must add that the change in Falstaff between the two parts of *Henry IV* is congruent with the tonal differences between the plays as wholes. If the first part is comical history, the second is tragical. The first bristles with vigor. Falstaff's spontaneity is supported by the fervor of Hotspur and the passionate self-belief of the brilliant Glendower. The death of Hotspur awakens regret that this vessel of youthful and essentially innocent energy had to be destroyed but raises no profound doubts concerning the governance of the world. Part II emphasizes age, sickness, and a sense of general decline. The evil Northumberland, who would "let one spirit of the first-born Cain / Reign in all bosoms" (Part II, I, i, 157–58), and Prince John, who destroys opposition by a low trick, are totally unlike the leading warriors of Part I. As for old Jack, the staff must fall. It is, indeed, hard to be a "pure" buffoon for ten acts. One sign of his declining purity is the subtle alteration in his soliloquies. In Part I, they are highly dramatic, partially because they occur in the heat of felony or battle. They tend to be constructed in rapid questions and answers, a method used not only in the famous catechism on honor but in the hasty inquiry into counterfeiting, which ends in the decision to wound the dead Hotspur: "Why may he not rise as well as I?" (Part I, V, iv, 127–28). One watches his mind responding to the thrust of immediate circumstance. His reality is inordinate; under each check it swells into preponderance. In Part II, spontaneity is turning into calculation, as in the soliloquies on Justice Shallow. In neither of these is Falstaff driven by immediate need—the situation which always brings out the comical sublime in him. One soliloquy shows him planning to "fetch" off the old countryman, for "I do see the bottom of Justice Shallow." And the speech ends with proof that the timeless Falstaff is stooping to the world of time: "Well, I'll be acquainted with him; and 't shall go hard but I will make him a philosopher's two stones to me. If the young dace be a bait for the old pike, I see no reason in the law of nature but I may snap at him. Let time shape, and there's an end" (Part II, III, iii, 352–57). The very reference to nature as a hierarchy suggests a way of reckoning new to Falstaff. The other soliloquy also presents him in his new role as cool strategist, for he will "devise matter enough out of this Shallow" to keep Hal laughing for a specified time (Part II, V, i, 86–87). The younger Falstaff had used the Hostess outrageously, but one cannot imagine him devoting a soliloquy to his plans for cheating her.

It is she who, in *Henry V*, restores Falstaff to the "green fields" where every "christom child" and pure buffoon has his rightful place. In comedy it is only the pure buffoon who can persuade us that gaiety, emancipated from time, fate, and responsibility, is the one thing needful, that gaiety is the key to unending freedom. But Shakespeare chose to show the world's greatest buffoon in ultimate collision with the facts of life, with history.

Where tragedy focuses attention on a single hero, comedy keeps its eye on the spectacle of human folly. For this reason the term "comic hero" must always seem paradoxical, indeed ludicrous. The common humanity of the hero keeps thwarting his claim to heroic status, or if he is a god, his divinity will be contradicted by, let us say, his hopeless love for a mortal woman. The comic hero is insecurely poised between his excellence and his absurdity. Possibly because of the chivalry of comic playwrights, "he" is more often a woman than a man, especially where the accent is on *hero* rather than *comic*. The hegemony of women over men in comedy can be seen in *Lysistrata, The Women of the Thesmophoria*, and *The Women of the Ecclesia*, in *As You Like It*, where poor Orlando offers no competition to Rosalind, in Restoration comedy, where the Millamants overshadow the Mirabells, and in Shaw, where the vital woman triumphs over the intellectual male. In Molière, the wife is usually saner than the husband, but she is hardly a heroine. There are, indeed, no comic heroes in Molière, except, perhaps, for the misanthrope in the play who breaks most rules, including Molière's.

The comic hero is not a mere parody of the tragic hero. Nor is he anyone who happens to play the title role. One might describe him in this way. First, since he is comic and not merely a part of a comedy, he is foolish. He is likely to be "hipped" on something, as is the Benedick who thinks himself the essence of bachelorhood or the John Tanner who purveys Shavianism so volubly as to make it laughable. At the point where he becomes a *malade* like Argan or Orgon, he ceases to be a hero, comic or otherwise. On the other hand, a "healthy" monomania, like that of some of Aristophanes' buffoons, does not appear to be incongruent with comic heroism. In Aristophanes the fantastic plans of a Dicaeopolis or a Lysistrata are sane enough when measured by the madness of the Peloponnesian War.

Secondly, the comic hero is vigorous and, whether young or old, full of youthful spirit. The astonishingly vigorous old man has at least the makings of an excellent comic hero. Since drama is action, the hero must have enough vitality to institute or resist opposition. A possible exception to this generalization might be a gentle, comic saint, like Shaw's Androcles. Here the innocence of the hero becomes a substitute for comic vigor and accomplishes tasks like taming lions through kindness. But a lazy fellow like Khlestakov, in *The Inspector General,* is either no hero or a hero in spite of himself, for the author has placed him within a circle of energetic townspeople who largely sustain the play. Though there is truth in Bergson's observation that the comic character approaches the puppet, the association of comedy with youth and fertility means that those propelling the action must be at least vigorous puppets, usually more than that. Bergson's theory is far more applicable to Molière than to Aristophanes, Shakespeare, or Shaw, and even in Molière it is Geronte (old man), not the dynamic servant, Scapin, who keeps repeating mechanically, "What the devil was he doing in that galley?" (*The Cheats of Scapin,* II, vii). Scapin is the real hero of the play.

The vigor of the comic hero is not directed by a highly developed consciousness but is characteristically unself-conscious. The audience will take him as an expression of its own lively, if bumbling, impulses. One sign of his lack of sharply personal quality is his habit, as Albert Cook has noticed,[10] of speaking asides instead of soliloquies. One might say that he cannot think quite alone but only in concert. He needs to share his ideas with someone, and the audience will do if no one else is present. Consequently, his soliloquies, when they occur, are extra-dramatic—passing beyond the frame of the action proper. This can be seen in speakers as different as Richard III, who begins his first soliloquy by making a pun for his listeners ("Now is the winter of our discontent / Made glorious summer by this sun of York"), and Viola, whose private reflections are conventional compared with those of Shakespeare's tragic heroes.

Early in the second act of *Twelfth Night* Viola soliloquizes on the evidence that Olivia loves her, not Orsino. The speech is that of a comic heroine:

> I am the man! If it be so, as 'tis,
> Poor lady, she were better love a dream.
> Disguise, I see thou art a wickedness
> Wherein the pregnant enemy does much.
> How easy is it for the proper-false
> In women's waxen hearts to set their forms!
> Alas, our frailty is the cause, not we!

> For such as we are made of, such we be.
> How will this fadge? My master loves her dearly;
> And I, poor monster, fond as much on him;
> And she, mistaken, seems to dote on me.
> What will become of this? As I am man,
> My state is desperate for my master's love;
> As I am woman,—now alas the day!—
> What thriftless sighs shall poor Olivia breathe!
> O time! thou must untangle this, not I.
> It is too hard a knot for t' untie!
>
> [II,ii,26–42]

The speech is comic in its appeal for help to time (and in its earlier appeal to Fortune), in its certainty that the situation controls the three lovers, who are seen as slightly absurd victims, in the speaker's way of referring to herself in the plural and as merely one member of a sex "made" according to unalterable specifications. She sees herself as lacking the will necessary to clear up the confusion. Women, she thinks, are not personally to blame for such contretemps; for everyone knows that women's frailty directs *them*. One might contrast Helena's belief in will-power as voiced in the relatively somber *All's Well That Ends Well*:

> Our remedies oft in ourselves do lie,
> Which we ascribe to heaven. The fated sky
> Gives us free scope, only doth backward pull
> Our slow designs when we ourselves are dull.
>
> [I, i, 231–34]

As Viola compares herself to other women, she should look directly at the audience, preferably at a party of women. Helena's lines are far more "inner-directed."

The quick-witted but unreflective vigor marking the comic hero is admirable yet laughable. Whether his cherished plans ultimately succeed is not important. We can laugh at his victims but also laugh at the superabundance, the prodigality of his invention, or enjoy seeing him caught in a trap of his own making. But he will be less attractive and less comic if he is the cold tactician selected as the protagonist in Restoration comedy than if he has at least a touch of romanticism. Alfred de Musset's unique blending of witty scepticism and romantic feeling made him especially well qualified to create comic heroes. During the larger part of his *Don't Swear to It* (*Il ne faut jurer de rien*), the hero,

Valentin, behaves like a Dorimant of 1660, but there is a difference. We first see him as the witty scapegrace tormenting his wealthy bourgeois uncle, Van Buck. His wit rises, however, out of a natural gaiety and poetic élan uncommon in the Restoration. He is as cheerful as Charles Surface in *The School for Scandal* but a good deal cleverer. When his uncle reproaches him for extravagance, he offers him pie and chocolate and assures him that he can easily afford to pay Valentin's bills. When Van Buck insists that he marry an attractive and wealthy girl, Cécile de Mantes, he replies with a pointed anecdote implying that he once seduced a young married woman and has no intention of sharing her husband's fate. In a long speech emphasizing phallic imagery an Elizabethan would have enjoyed, Valentin pictures the husband, preparing to leave the lovers together and putting on green gloves, ripped at the thumb, as a faint smile "sketched in shadow the two dimples" of his wife's cheeks.[11] For Valentin it was a joyful moment, but in memory the delight is mingled with the *triste* and *piteux* as the hero sees two large red hands struggling with gloves. And he concludes: "I have sworn that no woman in the world will glove me with such gloves." The speaker is a nineteenth-century Benedick. His imagery closely parallels Benedick's vaunt that he will never "hang [his] bugle in an invisible baldrick" (*Much Ado*, I,i,243–44). But the shadow in the wife's cheek is romantic. Indeed, it soon becomes clear that Valentin's cynicism about women is the other side of his belief that a young girl should be "a flower of the forest, not a plant in a vase" (I,i). The scene ends with the bewildered Van Buck agreeing that if Valentin can seduce Cécile within eight days, he need not marry her; if he fails, he will accept marriage.

The idea would have appealed to Wycherley. The plot is so arranged, however, as to frustrate the wager. Valentin visits Cécile's estate incognito, but she immediately recognizes him as the young man chosen as her fiancé. Failing to understand his wish to seduce her, she gladly accepts a rendezvous. Besides, as she says to him, the meeting will strengthen her mother's wavering approval of the match, and she innocently adds, "Voila ma ruse." This is the pre-eminently comic moment for Valentin. In an aside, he says, "Am I a fox caught in his own trap, or a lunatic [*fou*] regaining his reason?" (III,iv). He is both and therefore a comic hero. Inhabiting neither romance nor satire, he is poised between the two, acknowledging love but also seeing the absurdity of his confident planning, over which Cécile has triumphed through a combination of purity and sensible femininity.

Unfortunately for pure comedy, he does not retain this balance of emotion and humorous awareness of it. Shortly after the aside just quoted, he has another: "Either I am in the hands of the trickiest devil hell has ever let loose or an angel is speaking to me and opening the road to heaven." In a few moments he has plunged into a mélange of amorous and pantheistic emotion too extended and too deeply felt to be taken comically. As Cécile gazes at the stars, Valentin develops the passionate theory that the heavenly bodies are moved by love. All life is so moved, "from the ocean rising under the pale kisses of Diana to the beetle jealously sleeping in its cherished flower." Théophile Gautier found the passage ravishing. But in the speech ending the scene, the balance is righted. Cécile has just said, "What is the matter with you? You're shivering." On his knees he replies:

I shiver with fear and joy, because I'm going to open to you the depths of my heart. I'm the worst kind of madman, though what I'm about to confess isn't worth a shrug of your shoulders. I have done nothing but gamble, drink, and smoke since my wisdom teeth came in. You have told me that novels shock you; I have read many of them, and some of the worst. There is one called *Clarissa Harlowe*; I'll give it to you to read when you're my wife. The hero loves a beautiful girl like you and wants to marry her, but first he wishes to test her. He carries her off and brings her to London, after which, since she resists, Bedford arrives . . . that is to say, Tomlinson, a captain . . . I mean, Morden . . . no, I'm mistaken. . . . Anyway, to make a long story short . . . Lovelace is a fool, and so am I for wanting to follow his example. . . . God be praised, you haven't understood me. . . . I love you, I'm going to marry you: nothing in the world is true but the ravings of love. (*Enter Van Buck,* [*the Baroness,*] *the Abbé, and several servants lighting the way.*)

[III,iv]

In this speech Valentin moves from perfervid romanticism to an *état d'âme* oscillating between romantic absorption in love and objective inspection of his own behavior. Where he had taken himself with utmost seriousness, he cannot now speak of himself as a wicked fool without downgrading his Byronic stance by means of bathetic details. This elegant young man had complained to his uncle about Cécile's use of such homely words as "sprain" (*foulure*) and "bouillon"; now he talks about shoulder-shrugging and wisdom teeth. He clearly sees the absurdity of his summary of *Clarissa Harlowe* and knows that he is a *sot* as well as a *fou*. He retains an affection for his amorous confusion, but to see it is to get somewhat beyond it.

It is useful to realize that there is a peculiarly comic kind of hero, for the fact points to something important in the comic attitude. If the tragic hero indicates the ultimate achievements of the individual under conditions of gravest jeopardy, the comic hero embodies what common humanity can attain to, not in dreadful isolation, but in concert with others whom we can recognize for their tricks, disguises, contretemps, and happy chances. The tragic dramatist makes his hero accessible to the many. The comic dramatist, through his hero, enables us to find a justification for Walt Whitman's phrase, the divine average, for this hero is clearly one of us yet better or larger than most, and when he ascends the skies—like Peithetaerus or Trygaeus—we too are escalated.

The line between the comic hero and other comic characters is not always easy to draw. The comic hero shares with the others his folly, his tendency to sane madness (to paraphrase Bergson), and his lack of a highly developed consciousness. His abundant vigor is his own. The unheroic comic character might be described as a comic hero *manqué*. He is a less distinguished member of the same foolish family, whether he is a "blocking character" or one who forwards the action.

Can the comic character, heroic or otherwise, be specified more sharply? In his Preface to *Joseph Andrews*, Fielding attempts to delimit "the ridiculous," if not the comic:

The only source of the true ridiculous (as it appears to me) is affectation. . . . Now, affectation proceeds from one of these two causes: vanity or hypocrisy; for as vanity puts us on affecting false characters, in order to purchase applause, so hypocrisy sets us on an endeavor to avoid censure, by concealing our vices under an appearance of their opposite virtues.[12]

For Fielding, both hypocrisy and vanity are conscious, dishonest poses. These attitudes are not, of course, always found in comic characters. Even in *Joseph Andrews* the vanity of the saintly Parson Adams is certainly not deliberate or adopted to "purchase applause"; it is largely unconscious. And of course the novel includes many comic incidents having nothing to do with affectation; for example, the very funny episode in which Fanny fears an attack from an unidentified male whom the reader knows to be Adams himself. Fielding's view of the ridiculous, far from applying to all comedy, does not cover his own great work.

Bergson maintains that unsociability amounting to rigidity is the universal comic trait.[13] But as his volatile discussion continues, it turns out that unsociability is equivalent to automatism, absent-mindedness, somnambulism, obsession, obstinacy, and vanity. The last is said to be the ideal comic trait. These mental states are obviously not, however, the same. So far as character in comedy is concerned, vanity, conscious or unconscious, seems the best of these keys. Certainly the comic hero escapes mere automatism, and as we shall see, even the obsessed man dear to Molière sometimes does so.

Fielding and Bergson can agree on the central importance of vanity in the comic—or at least ridiculous—character. (Perhaps Fielding would agree that a comic hypocrite must be vain to think he can fool everyone.) But although comic characters are rarely without vanity, it is only in critical comedy that this trait is of the essence. Critical comedy was especially favored in the neoclassical age, which tended to equate the comic and the ridiculous in the sense of that which deserves ridicule.[14] The festive comedy of Aristophanes and Shakespeare focusses more strongly on the liberating aspects of character than on the constricting. The minor types—the cranks, the pedants, the gulls, and the fops—seldom carry the play. We are amused by the struggle between Philocleon and Bdelycleon in *The Wasps* or between Katharine and Petruchio in *The Taming of the Shrew*, but we are far from regarding the action as an object lesson in the perils of vanity.

One way of understanding comic characters is to divide them into the festive and the cautionary. Most writers on the subject emphasize the second group and tell us what the comic character lacks: he is deficient in powers of introspection, self-knowledge, the ability to change, inner life. But in the degree that he approaches heroism, the comic character cannot be described in exclusively negative, Bergsonian terms.

Freud read Bergson with great interest, but in his *Jokes and Their Relation to the Unconscious*, he shifted emphasis from the comic person to the one who laughs. In attempting to distinguish the comic from the witty or jocose, he suggests that a man is comic if he works too hard at what we take to be a simple physical task, like signing one's name, or fails to make the intellectual effort necessary to solve what we regard as a real problem. In each situation, Freud argues, we compare our own expenditure with that of the comic person. "The comic effect apparently depends . . . on the *difference* between the two cathectic expenditures— one's own and the other person's as estimated by 'empathy.' . . ." The odd fact that we may laugh at too much *or* too little effort is explained "when we bear in mind that a restriction of our muscular work and an increase of our intellectual work fit in with the course of our personal development toward a higher level of civilization."[15] It is clear that

Freud is thinking of the comic character as lacking that fullness of developed life to which we aspire and which the festive character can embody. Or in Freud's words, "what is comic is invariably on the infantile side."[16]

In the concluding section of his work, however, Freud finds a place for largeness of spirit, even grandeur, in the humorous as opposed to the merely comic character. Several anecdotes illustrate the point. In one, a criminal is being led to execution on a Monday morning and remarks, "Well, the day's beginning nicely." In Freud's terms, the speaker's insouciance enables us to economize on expenditure of pity. The discussion happily includes a brief but apt analysis of Falstaff. Freud shows that Sir John's wit, bulk, and age cause an economy of the indignation one might expect to feel at his unbuttoned career; but for us the most interesting point is the realization that Falstaff's humor arises from "the superiority of an ego which neither his physical nor his moral defects can rob of its cheerfulness and assurance."[17]

Whether we call the morally inappropriate but vitally fitting cheerfulness of Falstaff comic or humorous is of little importance. It is both. For us the conclusion must be that comic character cannot always be pasted with so restrictive a label as "vain," "absent-minded," "affected," or "infantile." Falstaff, who would be enough to upset any such rule, is not a cautionary character. In his presence, none of the critical tags I have mentioned seems of the essence.

Although the greatest comic characters cannot be reduced to functions of dramatic structure, the typical character in comedy does serve a variety of functions in relation to the work as a whole: he may be or become (1) an instrument of the dramatic movement or developing theme, (2) an element in an overall contrast or hierarchy, (3) a tone of voice commenting on action or character including his own (and therefore a signal for the actor to step slightly beyond his role), or (4) a surrogate for the dramatist himself. All of these uses of character can be seen in Molière.

(1) In *The Imaginary Invalid*, a hypochondriac, Argan, powerful in his own home and supported though deceived by an array of quacks, struggles with a group of reasonable characters including Toinette, Béralde, Angélique, and Cléante. Argan's second wife, Béline, and his doctors confirm his opinion that he should leave his money to her, force his daughter Angélique to marry, and continue his medical regimen. At the turning point of the play, Argan is convinced that Béline does not love him and that his daughter, Angélique, does. This crucial dis-

covery leads him to consent, first, that Angélique may marry Cléante, to whom Argan has been opposed, if the young man becomes a doctor, and, second, that his medical needs can be adequately served by his own entrance into the medical profession, a solution making the sacrifice of Cléante unnecessary. The play ends with a burlesque ceremony conferring a medical degree on the hypochondriac.

In Stanislavskian terms, the action of the play is "to make the 'truth' prevail." Argan's truth is found in the appearances provided by his wife and his doctors; the reasonable characters, headed by Béralde, know that truth is to be achieved by following nature. It is natural for the attractive young people to marry; it is natural for a sick man to get well if he avoids seventeenth-century medicine. For Béline, it is true that a young woman should make a fool of an old man idiotic enough to marry her. Diafoirus, like most doctors in Molière, evidently finds it true that medicine is for the benefit of the profession, but as Béralde points out, Purgon, another doctor, really believes in the efficacy of his prescriptions; the hilarious effect of his furious scene in Act Three depends in part on the sincerity of his outburst. In his devotion to truth, he, like the others, serves the thematic action.

Only one character in this play needs to develop in order that the play move. The action can in its progress present absurd types like Thomas Diafoirus or Fleurant mainly for their effect on Argan, who does change from scene to scene, depending on who his partner is, how hard he is pressed, and where he finds himself in the plot. At least three kinds of change in Argan can be distinguished: changes of mood amounting at times to changes of self, sudden departures from the basic mask, and the major change from anger to cheerful acceptance, accomplished in the bogus ceremony. All of these changes serve the total form.

A brilliantly theatrical example of the first kind of change is shown in the fifth and sixth scenes of Act One. Argan's dialogue with Toinette presents him as the ludicrous tyrant in opposition to the endlessly vivacious servant. Toinette brings out the best, the most laughably violent, in Argan. Molière emphasizes this aspect of the character not only because it is intensely funny and interesting in itself but because it is the element in Argan that must be exorcised if the happy ending is to be attained. Here he is insisting that he will put Angélique in a convent if she does not agree to marry Thomas. The following passage has Toinette speaking first: "You?—I. —Good!—What, good?—You shall not put her in a convent.—I shall not put her in a convent?—No.—No?—No.— Oh, what a joke. I will not put my daughter in a convent if I want to? —No, I tell you.—Who will prevent me?—Yourself" (I,v). Increasingly

excited, Argan is soon chasing Toinette about the room and threatening
to curse the silent Angélique if she does not stop the servant. When
Toinette runs off, Argan throws himself into a chair, exhausted.

Béline now enters, and we have the following:

ARGAN. Ah, my wife, come here.
BÉLINE. What's the matter, my poor husband?
ARGAN. Come here, and help me.
BÉLINE. What's the trouble, my little boy?
ARGAN. My sweetheart.
BÉLINE. My love.
ARGAN. I've just been put in a rage.

[I,vi]

The two scenes support each other. They also push the play forward
since each passage increases the intransigency of Argan toward Angélique. But in these scenes we see two opposing faces of Argan, the tyrannical and the sentimental. We get a sensation of suddenly re-routed or
discontinuous movement. It may be said that Argan does not really
change from scene to scene, that he merely reveals a new side of his
mask; but since there is no more to Argan than what he reveals, the
juxtaposition creates, in fact, a startling development. Character conceived as a unitary thing yields to process. First we see Pantaloon Enraged, then Pantaloon in Love. The antithesis in itself creates dramatic
vibrancy rather than dramatic movement toward a conclusion. But
thought of together, the two scenes produce horizontal movement or
movement toward the dramatic goal and also vertical movement or
movement of character.

The Toinette scene also illustrates departure from the basic persona,
what W. G. Moore has called the slipping of the mask. Just after the
lines already quoted from Scene Five, we have this dialogue, Argan
speaking first: "I?—Yes. You won't have the heart.—I will so.—You're joking.—I'm not joking.—Fatherly tenderness will prevent you.—It will not
prevent me.—One little tear or so, two arms around your neck, one 'my
dear little papa,' softly spoken, will be enough to move you.—All that
will mean nothing.—Yes, yes.—I tell you, I won't give up.—Rubbish.—
Don't say 'rubbish.'—Heavens, I know you, you're naturally good.—
(Enraged) I am not good. I'm bad when I want to be." Of such moments in Molière, W. G. Moore writes, "The point of interest for him,
and for us, is the point when the mask slips or falls, when the underlying man appears." Again: "The language of Molière's maniacs and fools
is no longer the vehicle of their intention, but conveys in its sweep and

force their condition also."[18] The machine has become a man. By implication, the change can be painful for him and for us. It should be said
that nothing in the remainder of the scene indicates that Argan has
experienced a fundamental change. Nevertheless, even a moment of appalling insight, later lost in the excitement, can do much to deepen the
comedy. Sensitive actors will be grateful for Moore's analysis of the
mask in Molière. For Moore is pointing to new and searching ways of
acting him. If this service appears inconsiderable to the critic concerned
only with words on the page, one may recall Molière's statement in his
preface to *Doctor Love*: "It is obvious that plays are written only to be
performed, and I would not advise anyone to read this one unless he
can visualize in the reading all the activity onstage."[19]

The mask can be removed by others, by the will of the masquer himself, or by inadvertence. The first of these is equivalent to the familiar
situation of the "enginer hoist with his own petard." The second occurs
in Act Five of *Tartuffe*, when the hypocrite suddenly drops his pious
manner and shows his ruthlessness. But the third is the most engrossing.
If the man who has been living falsely or superficially suddenly finds
himself behaving or thinking truly—if he suddenly finds himself out—
this may be profoundly comic, which means funny and moving at once.
Tartuffe's first interview with Elmire might be overwhelming in stage
production if he simultaneously revealed not only to her but to himself
the hidden power of his own sensuality. Similarly, in the scene with
Toinette, if Argan suddenly realized the *méchanceté* of his life, the play
would take on a previously unachieved dimension.

In his major change, Argan ceases to be a "blocking character" and
yields to the wishes of the reasonable party. The play brings this change
about partially through the discovery scene and partially through the
pretense that Argan will be inducted into the medical profession.

During most of the play, Argan is determined to choose Angélique's
husband—that is, he is determined when he thinks about the matter at
all. He is so largely the passive dupe of others that he has relatively
little time to play the tyrant. In various scenes Béline, Diafoirus,
Béralde, and Toinette-as-physician are imposing their "truths" on him,
so that the plot is subordinated to thematic action in which the *reac-
tions* of Argan play a glittering role. It is hardly worth arguing whether
action or character dominates this scene or that. Argan consists largely
of a series of responses; and the action consists of thrust and response.
He "is" the angry father, but he constantly swings from outcry to command and back again. Indeed his opening soliloquy is an extended answer to his large medical bills. He is a presence but not a fully developed

character in the sense of one who continuously attempts to work his will. One can properly speak of him—and of many another comic protagonist—as an instrument of dramatic action.

(2) A tragic character transcends his relations with others; the same cannot be said of comic character. Observing a comedy, we compare wise man with fool, fool with fool, and fool with rogue, who may also prove to be notably unwise. Comedy tends to develop a hierarchy of characters based not on social position or degrees of absolute merit but on common sense or, in subtler plays, on a developing dialectic. *The Misanthrope* is a subtle play, but the characters are rather definitely placed on a rising scale of sincerity. The most insincere are the fluttering marquises Acaste and Clitandre; Acaste, who has an egregious monologue of self-praise, is probably the ultimate of insincerity. Oronte, who wants a "sincere" opinion of his silly poem, is next on the scale. Though he may seem as absurd as the marquises, the Misanthrope admits he has some solid qualities. Arsinoé the prude is instinct with affectation, yet she reveals a disturbing undercurrent of malaise that awakens something like sympathy. Compared with Arsinoé, Célimène behaves honestly, but set against Philinte, Éliante, and Alceste, she emerges as a poseur. Speaking seriously though lightly, Philinte points out the coquettishness and scandal-mongering of Célimène; yet his whole attitude is a resigned acceptance of social duplicity. Éliante seems flawless. She offends no one and retains her own quiet dignity. She admires the rigorously sincere Alceste, who is at the opposite extreme from the ridiculous noblemen. Whatever judgment the audience finally passes on Alceste, it judges only after observing him within a world which is carefully divided into moral parcels. Whether he likes it or not, Alceste will be judged only in company with all the others.

(3) If comic character can advance thematic action and construct "spatial" contrasts on which judgments can be formed, it can also provide a base for choral commentary or "stand in" for the dramatist himself. Since comedy naturally tends toward parody, even young lovers can acquire tones in which they seem to be ridiculing themselves or others. In the opening scene of *The Miser*, for example, the lovers fall into a pseudo-pastoral manner that the author of *As You Like It* would have appreciated. In one of the most attractive scenes in *The Imaginary Invalid*, Angélique's languishing style permits Molière some good-natured laughter at the ingenuous girl. The actress would be quite justified in pointing up the slight absurdity of her lines; if she has no sense of humor and plays the scene "straight," it will lose vitality. Angélique is speaking of her admirer, Cléante:

ANGÉLIQUE. But just tell me, don't you find, as I do, something heavenly, something fated, in the marvelous way we became acquainted?

TOINETTE. Yes.

ANGÉLIQUE. Don't you think his action in coming to my defense without knowing me—wasn't that the behavior of a perfect gentleman?

TOINETTE. Yes.

ANGÉLIQUE. Could anything be nobler?

TOINETTE. Agreed.

ANGÉLIQUE. Didn't he do everything with the greatest charm?

TOINETTE. Oh, yes.

[I,iv]

After five additional exchanges, Toinette finally agrees to answer in more than two syllables. One might say that in this passage Toinette is more a character than is Angélique, for while both are in effect laughing at the ingénue, Toinette can do so from within her own role, but Angélique can not.

(4) Yet characters like Toinette and Dorine are more than characters; as Albert Thibaudet suggests, they symbolize comedy itself. Though not always essential to plot, they "embody the comic impulse."[20] They have only to enter the stage and the Angry Old Man begins to tremble. Though respectable in themselves, Toinette and Dorine bear a family resemblance to the disreputable intriguer who plays so vital a role in ancient and modern comedy. The *femmes* and *hommes d'intrigue*, represented in Molière by Frosine, Nerine, Sbrigani, and above all Scapin, can be traced to Roman comedy and beyond—the Alexandrian Herodas has a bawd with a lively comic spirit. But Molière, like Jonson, goes far beyond his sources. The intriguing Mosca towers over the parasite in Plautus; the Phormio of Terence can compete with Scapin in trickery but not in his sense of himself as a master of ceremony.

The lying valet Scapin is the triumph of brain over social rank, fortune, and morality. He is rich in that *ponêria* (comic villainy) attributed to the Aristophanic hero.[21] This demigod in uniform has had a slight brush with the law and has in consequence renounced all activity of any kind, for he, like Alceste in *The Misanthrope*, is "vexed with the ingratitude of the century" (I,ii). Like Mosca, he has a high opinion of his calling. For Mosca,

> your parasite
> Is a most precious thing, dropp'd from above,
> Not bred 'mongst clods and clot-poles, here on earth.

I muse, the mystery was not made a science,
It is so liberally profess'd!

[*Volpone*, III,i,7–11]

At his first entrance Scapin, Mosca's brother, "can say, without vanity, that the world has scarcely seen a more skilful manager of traps and intrigues, a man who has won more glory than I in this noble métier" (I,ii). Such genius as his cannot long remain idle, and when his young master begs for help in his romantic trouble, Scapin accedes with lordly calm. With good reason, he is supremely confident of success and soon takes on a second task for his master's cousin.

That his three acts are a series of victories is no surprise. What is most striking is his constant theatrical sense as he plays half a dozen roles in as many minutes and stages scenes in which everyone else performs clumsily. He is not only plot but, as Alfred Simon has said, producer and production. Simon's appreciation of him cannot be bettered: "Dethroning the Mascarille of the early plays, *fourbum imperator*, Scapin has received from Molière the sacrament of the comic. . . . He is the Hamlet of farce. Or like that other Shakespearian actor, Prospero, he surveys from the angle of the fly gallery the absurd couriers from that humanity hidden in the shadows. He looses on them his impostures, always ready to renounce his powers and receive these puppets with kindness if only they acquire a little sense. . . . As traitorous as Tartuffe, as demoniacal as Don Juan, as solitary as Alceste, he safeguards the power of laughter and of creating laughter. . . ."[22] Scapin is, then, far more important as a symbol than as a specific role. He is Molière's idea of comedy.

The comic role, more clearly than the tragic, is used, sometimes exploited, by the playwright for his dramatic action. Drama is character in action—character acting and acted upon by word, movement, and gesture. But one quality marking off comedy from other forms is the comic character's tendency to become indistinguishable from the action of which he is a part, the theme or idea he embodies.

To speak of comic characters is to speak of fools in their infinite gradations, including irrepressible fools, splendid fools, and hopeless fools—the John Falstaffs, the Epicure Mammons, and the Imaginary Invalids. It has been said that comedy teaches you to know a fool when you see one. This would be especially true of comedy in the Jonsonian or Molièresque pattern, where the poor fool is used, perhaps abused, by the playwright, then packaged and ticketed by the audience. But in Aristophanes, Shakespeare, and other festive comedy it is hard to keep a good fool down and in his place. For his nonsense may convert to wisdom, his clumsiness to grace. As he has liberated us, we will liberate him, feeling lucky at the chance to make him one of us.

NOTES

1. *The Philosophy of Fine Art*, IV; reprinted in *Hegel on Tragedy*, ed. Anne and Henry Paolucci (Garden City, N.Y., 1962), p. 78.

2. *Volpone*, V, xi, 1–4, *Elizabethan and Stuart Plays*, ed. Charles Read Baskervill et al. (New York, 1934). Citations from *Volpone* will be to this edition.

3. Cedric H. Whitman, *Aristophanes and the Comic Hero* (Cambridge, Mass., 1964), p. 26.

4. *The Turkish Theatre* (New York, 1933), p. 41.

5. *Feeling and Form* (New York, 1953), p. 344.

6. Enid Welsford, *The Fool: His Social and Literary History* (Garden City, N.Y., 1961), p. 52.

7. Welsford, p. 323.

8. Whitman, pp. 44–45.

9. *The Meaning of Shakespeare* (Chicago, 1951), p. 178.

10. *The Dark Voyage and the Golden Mean* (Cambridge, Mass., 1949), pp. 44, 51.

11. I, i, in Alfred de Musset, *Il ne faut jurer de rien*, ed. Jacques Nathan (Paris, 1941). Citations from *Il ne faut jurer* will be to this edition.

12. Henry Fielding, *Joseph Andrews* (New York, 1961), p. viii.

13. *Laughter*, in *Comedy*, ed. Wylie Sypher (Garden City, N.Y., 1956), p. 147.

14. Cf. the assertion of Addison: "The two great branches of ridicule in writing are comedy and the burlesque." *The Spectator*, No. 249, in *Eighteenth-Century Critical Essays*, ed. Scott Elledge (Ithaca, N.Y., 1961), I,32. See also W. G. Moore, "The French Notion of the Comic," *Yale French Studies*, No. 23 (Summer, 1959), 48–49.

15. Sigmund Freud, *Jokes and Their Relation to the Unconscious*, trans. James Strachey (New York, 1960), p. 195.

16. Freud, p. 225.

17. Freud, p. 232n.

18. *Molière: A New Criticism* (Garden City, 1962), pp. 33–34, 56.

19. *Oeuvres Complètes*, ed. Maurice Rat (Paris, 1956), II,ii.

20. "Le Rire de Molière," *Revue de Paris*, XXIX (Jan.–Feb., 1922), 331.

21. Whitman, pp. 29–36.

22. *Molière par lui-même* (Paris, n.d.), pp. 144–45.

CHAPTER FIVE

Speech

THE LANGUAGE OF COMEDY is in tension with the play as dramatic action and with the speaker. Though it is expected to and does serve action and express the speaker, it does more. A comedy in which all speeches merely said what was expected of them would read like a scenario narrated by no one in particular. The genius of comedy is such that the language is frequently on the point of surprising, of deserting, the theatrical and literary context. Or the speaker may desert the language which dramatic decorum has laid down as his proper idiom. If surprise takes a high place in the comic plot, it does so in the language as well. Although sustained verbal surprises may result in purple passages, preciosity, or confusion, they may also be among the greatest achievements of the comic poet.

In relation to the dramatic action, the language of comedy can be primarily functional, or prominent as a mode of acting, or even a substitute for action. In a particular play, style may be self-effacing at one moment and tyrannical at another, but each comic writer gravitates towards an individual norm: Molière's language is regularly more functional than Shaw's, but Shaw's is more so than Christopher Fry's, at least in Fry's early plays. In realistic prose comedy, much of the language will modestly defer to plot and character. Facts, states of mind, and dramatic purposes must be communicated, and often this should be accomplished as simply as possible. But simplicity does not preclude imagination. Most prose comedy suffers from please-sit-down scenes in which we are painfully conscious of the playwright's need to get on to something else, if only to a please-stand-up scene. Such writing can be fatal to the life of comedy. The language of Maugham, for example, which once appeared to sustain the English tradition of high comedy, has come to seem curiously flat. Although *The Circle* has a witty idea, sound structure, and creditable characterization, the play has already lost much of its appeal because of the low vitality of its language. The fate of this play suggests that only when language does more than is expected of it can a comedy retain its life. Ibsen's drama remains strong even in William Archer's obsolescent translations; Maugham's comedy has dated because its language has crumbled.

Molière's *The Doctor in Spite of Himself* presents language in close cooperation with action. Almost everyone who has discussed Molière's style mentions its verve. The acknowledgment easily becomes an excuse for passing quickly to his comic idea, his characterization, or his social bias. Molière's prose obviously has verve; what may not be so obvious is that this energy is regularly yoked to dramatic action. In *Le Médicin* one can distinguish three levels of speech, so far as its relationship to the dramatic movement is concerned. On the first level one is hardly aware of the language apart from what it reveals of the intentions of the speakers—what they are doing. After the opening scene, in which Sganarelle beats Martine for criticizing him, she has this soliloquy:

Va, quelque mine que je fasse, je n'oublierai pas mon ressentiment, et je brûle en moi-même de trouver les moyens de te punir des coups que tu me donnes. Je sais bien qu'une femme a toujours dans les mains de quoi se venger d'un mari; mais c'est une punition trop délicate pour mon pendard. Je veux une vengeance qui se fasse un peu mieux sentir, et ce n'est pas contentement pour l'injure que j'ai reçue.

[I,iii]

Believe me! Whatever face I put on it, I won't forget this. I'm just burning to find a way to punish these blows I've got. Of course I know a woman always has something handy to punish her husband with, but that's a punishment too delicate for my jailbird. I want a revenge he can feel a little better. *That's* no satisfaction for the blows I've had.

Following a violent scene, the speech will inevitably reverberate with rage. The first sentence will probably be accompanied by Martine's action of rubbing her bruised arms or shoulders. As one must frequently remark in Molière, the language is merely part of a physical statement. "Je brûle," for example, calls for tension in the head, neck, arms, and torso. Martine adds that she has "dans les mains" a kind of vengeance. The phrase is figurative, but clearly the movement of her hands must bring the image back to the activity she has in mind. Then we see her hastily rejecting the idea on "mais" and pausing for a sarcastic reflection on "délicate"—the word is beautifully apt but does not call attention to itself as language. Finally, the insistence on a punishment that can be "un peu sentir" redirects us to her body and the blows it has just received.

Realistic and totally theatrical from beginning to end, the entire speech is an inextricable part of the dramatic moment.

On the second level of speech we become gradually aware of the patterning as such, yet the precision still heightens dramatic tension. The opening scene of the play contains many matched speeches and a series of moments in which Sganarelle overturns Martine's thought with supersonic speed. Realistic language is heightened and sharpened by word-play and thought-play, but we are still not far from realism.

On the third level, illustrated by Act One, Scene Two, a neighbor tries to interrupt the beating but is put through an angry catechism, first by Martine, then by Sganarelle. Each passage ends with the same formula ("Et vous êtes un sot de venir de fourrer . . . ," "Et vous êtes un impertinent, de vous ingérer . . ." ["you're a fool to poke your nose . . . ," "you're a saucebox to meddle . . .]). In addition, each series of questions gets nearly monosyllabic replies from the flabbergasted neighbor, who is battered with metronomic regularity. In such passages, Molière creates so strict a dialogue that the form forces itself on our attention. The talk begins to assume a structure of its own. Instead of language in action we get language *as* action, but we have not arrived at language as a substitute for action. Molière was too theatrical a writer to push language so far.

A favorite pattern in Molière's prose dialogue is a series of short speeches placed in sharp opposition to one another and lifted above realism by repetition, antithesis, and other rhetorical devices. Even in a lengthy monologue, a speaker may conduct what is, in effect, an interior dialogue. Argan's opening speech in *The Imaginary Invalid* shifts back and forth between notes to himself and objections thrown at the absent Fleurant. But Molière's dialogue pattern is varied by true monologues often taking the form of burlesque orations. In these, the language ordinarily does not draw attention to itself as language. We observe the speaker developing his thought to the best of his frequently slight ability. On a somewhat different level are the monologues by the quacks who overwhelm their victims with floods of nonsensical verbiage. Here again, language, or non-language, becomes self-assertive, but it seldom conflicts with dramatic movement.

In English comedy the greatest masters of prose include not only Shakespeare and Jonson but G. B. Shaw. Style alone will be enough to save Shaw from oblivion. In his best writing, the sentence, the paragraph, the speech perfectly respond to his intellectual passion as his boiling energy scalds the victims of his attack. He could be garrulous, trifling, or merely facetious when making linguistic gestures long familiar to him, but when his feelings were deeply engaged, his prose was unmatchable, even in his old age. *Too True to Be Good* (1932) is one of his poorest plays, *On the Rocks* (1933) one of his best. In the earlier comedy, the talk has little structure or fundamental direction; Shaw will begin a speech without a real point of departure and continue through sheer momentum. In places we have a good deal of the old scarification of Victorian prejudices. Other passages show him reeling from the impact of twentieth-century nihilism, a mood he can neither express nor absorb. In *On the Rocks*, all is changed. Set in the Cabinet Room in Downing Street, the play is the perfect frame for the driving debates, and although the talk produces decisions and ultimately the hero's defeat, most of the speeches are so managed in themselves that they should get individual rounds of applause were it not that the succeeding speeches, always imminent, could not be heard. Between Acts One and Two Sir Arthur Chavender, the "Liberal" Prime Minister, makes a startling address in which he announces his intention to nationalize ground rents, banks, collieries, and transport, municipalize the building trades, prohibit private commerce in protected industries, introduce collective farming, and compel public service for all. In the second act the Cabinet, a great financier, a duke, and a labor deputation descend upon Downing Street. A debate develops, with a dozen speakers participating through orations of varying length spliced by shorter speeches. Though Shaw obviously favors the totalitarian argument, he allows every point of view exactly the same rhetorical force as every other. Even the reactionary Sir Dexter Hathaway, symbol of the Establishment, deploys with mastery his parallel clauses, stinging questions, illustrations, and climaxes. And since Shaw had been studying England's economic structure all his life, he had no trouble whatever with what the Renaissance called the "places of invention"—the logical and factual sources of argument.

There are scores of speeches supporting the generalizations just made. In one of the most brilliant outbursts, young Alderman Aloysia Brollikins (her last name means "little brat") attacks the English landowning class. So fiery is this speech that the Duke of Domesday, against whom it is directed, can plausibly say that Brollikins is the "greatest orator of my time." The fourth in a series, the speech rejects the Prime Minister's proposal to compensate landowners for the seizure of their property; but the words are thrown directly at the Duke:

It is from you that we shall exact compensation: aye, to the uttermost farthing. You are conspiring here with these capitalist blood-

suckers to rob us again of the value of what you have already stolen
—to make us give you gilt edged securities in exchange for the land
that no longer brings you in shooting rents; and you think we cannot
see through the plot. But in vain is the net spread in sight of the bird.
We shall expose you. We shall tell the story of the Domesday Clear-
ances until the country rings with it if you dare to lift your dishonored
head again in English politics. Your demand for compensation is dismissed, turned down: we spit it back in your face. The crofters whom
you drove from their country to perish in a foreign land would turn
in their graves at the chink of a single penny of public money in your
hungry pockets. [*She tears out a chair from under the table and flops
into it, panting with oratorical emotion*].

[p. 1205]

The speech builds on the opposition of "you" and "we," which become
rhetorical and dramatic opponents. After the first sentence, which replies to the idea that "you" want compensation, the speech (1) exposes
your plot, (2) details *our* triumphant counter-moves, and (3) appeals
for its climax to the moral history of the land. The transition from section one to section two is made by a slightly adapted sentence from the
Bible—"Surely in vain is the net spread for any bird" (Prov. i,17). Section two ends with a "dramatic" shift from the passive voice to the
active as *you* are repulsed and *we* "spit . . . in your face." The level of
discourse moves from the homely "aye" to the elegant Biblical inversion. Except for the metaphor from Proverbs, the imagery is not strikingly original. The exclusively literary critic might point his finger at
"bloodsuckers," "gilt edged," and "turn in their graves," but these familiar expressions suit both the Hyde Park oratory and the comic context so clearly indicated by the stage direction ending the speech. Such
writing might almost inspire a new fusion, as in the Renaissance, of
rhetorical and dramatic theory.

One might lightly assume that prose is more completely adapted to
action—the fundamental but changing urgencies of the characters—
than is verse. This would be true only of a realistic action. If we look
at two scenes in which Shakespeare moves between prose and verse,
we find that in the first, from *Two Gentlemen of Verona*, the verse is
more nearly functional than the prose, while in the second, from
Twelfth Night, the movement from prose to verse signalizes an increase
of dramatic feeling, a transition from a passage at arms to a deeper engagement.

The opening scene in *Two Gentlemen of Verona* consists of the parting of the friends, Valentine and Proteus, and a report from Speed,

Valentine's servant, to Proteus. The first section is in verse, the second in prose. In this early comedy of Shakespeare, the verse is musical and rhetorical but frequently inorganic; yet we notice that in the first scene it manages to convey a good deal beyond the sound of high spirits. The first two lines set the tone:

> Cease to persuade, my loving Proteus.
> Home-keeping youth have ever homely wits.

The first line states an action; the second indicates the drift toward word-play for its own sake. Soon Valentine lightly ridicules Proteus for being in love, and although the dialogue is quickly overweighted with puns, it sets up an opposition between the two men which will be ironically transposed later when Valentine himself falls in love and finds Proteus attempting to steal the affections of his mistress.

Speed, who has been on an errand for Proteus, enters in search of his master, Valentine, but he has left for the port. "And I have played the sheep in losing him" (I,i,73), says Speed, whereupon Shakespeare writes forty lines of wit-combat on the question: is Speed a sheep? The first few lines of this passage are in verse, a few more waver between verse and prose, and the dialogue then plunges into prose with this exercise in comic logic: "*Speed.* The shepherd seeks the sheep, and not the sheep the shepherd; but I seek my master, and my master seeks not me: therefore I am no sheep" (I,i,88–91). (This could easily be turned into verse, but the movement would be slowed.) Proteus makes an equivalent rejoinder. Within a few lines they are continuing the combat through puns on "mutton"—that favorite Elizabethan dish, "stick," and "pound," the last of which accumulates three meanings. This bravura passage has no implications for the rest of the play. It is action only in the sense that the two men, purely for fun, are seeking to outwit each other, and is less organic than the verse preceding it.

As readers have often seen, *Twelfth Night* reworks thematic material from *Two Gentlemen of Verona* but with greater subtlety and depth. Shakespeare has mastered the purely dramatic uses of prose and verse, but he constantly insinuates more than an audience could absorb on first hearing the play. The philosophic clown, Feste, plays tantalizingly with the nuances of "wisdom" and "folly"; actually he is nudging the other characters toward wisdom, and although they will not attain his kind of disengaged and mysterious understanding, they will have gone to school to him. He puts Malvolio through a harsh course (climaxed by a ventriloquist's act), obliquely lessons Olivia, teaches Viola something, and gains general respect. All this is done through his quicksilver prose. The verse is, perhaps, more lyrical than it has been in previous Shakespearian comedies, except for *A Midsummer Night's Dream*, yet at times one can hardly say whether it is ecstatic or smiling or alternating between the two. We can seldom announce with certainty: "This is comic poetry." Orsino's "If music be the food of love, play on" (I,i,1) is gorgeous but on the edge of the ludicrous; Viola's "She never told her love" develops a pathos to which she is not strictly entitled since it is clear that "concealment" will not long "feed on her damask cheek." If the prose is mercurial, the verse is opalescent, like the mind of Orsino.

The first meeting of Viola and Olivia opens with delicately sparring prose. At the beginning of the scene Olivia is veiled, and when Viola addresses her as "Most radiant, exquisite, and unmatchable beauty" (I,v, 181) the line immediately reveals the gulf between Orsino's passion and Viola's ironic attitude toward the supposed beauty. The jesting tone continues as Viola asks permission to deliver a speech in praise of Olivia, for "I took great pains to study it, and 'tis poetical" (I,v,206–7). After some amusing interruptions, still in prose, she asks to see Olivia's face, and when Olivia accedes, we reach a turning point in the style of the scene:

OLIVIA. . . . Is't not well done? [*Unveiling.*]
VIOLA. Excellently done, if God did all.
OLIVIA. 'Tis in grain, sir; 'twill endure wind and weather.
VIOLA. 'Tis beauty truly blent, whose red and white
    Nature's own sweet and cunning hand laid on.
    Lady, you are the cruell'st she alive
    If you will lead these graces to the grave
    And leave the world no copy.

[I,v,253–61]

In Viola's first speech she is still jesting, but what of the second? Is this the "poetical" speech she has studied? Even if it is, something has taken place within Viola: she has been moved by Olivia's beauty, until now a mere rumor, and reads her lines with feeling. One index of seriousness is the use made of the imagery of Shakespeare's early sonnets—particularly Sonnet 11, in which the poet urges the fair young man to leave a "copy" of himself in the world.

Olivia is not ready to desert prose. She says, "O, sir, I will not be so hard-hearted; I will give out divers schedules of my beauty" (I,v,262–63)—taking "copy" as a reference not to a child but to a legal document. But Viola's emotion helps to force the dialogue, just now called "skipping," to a level of sustained verse as she says:

I see you what you are, you are too proud;
But, if you were the devil, you are fair.
My lord and master loves you. O, such love
Could be but recompens'd, though you were crown'd
The nonpareil of beauty!

[I,v,269–73]

Viola declares that if she were Orsino, she would not understand
Olivia's denial:

OLIVIA.   Why, what would you?
VIOLA. Make me a willow cabin at your gate
        And call upon my soul within the house;
        Write loyal cantons of contemned love
        And sing them loud even in the dead of night;
        Halloo your name to the reverberate hills
        And make the babbling gossip of the air
        Cry out "Olivia!" O, you should not rest
        Between the elements of air and earth,
        But you should pity me!
OLIVIA.   You might do much.

[I,v,286–95]

So lyrical is this picture of the forlorn lover that we may fail to see
what the words are reflecting in the speaker and doing in the scene.
Since the lines recall the conventional swain, with his affinity for the
willow and despairing love songs, Harold Jenkins believes that Viola's
speech is to be taken as parody.[1] If so, the smiling comment comes from
Shakespeare, not the speaker. The urgent and hyperbolical narration
of what Viola would do if she were Orsino indirectly reveals how she
would proclaim her love for him, were that possible. It is Viola's love
that suffuses the "loyal cantons" pursuing the loved one far into the
night and as far as the elements reach; for as Orsino says of Viola later,
her "eye / Hath stayed upon some favor that it loves" (II,iv,24–25). The
speech is brilliant but not a purple passage.

Olivia's reply is the first major turning point in the play. Viola's love
for Orsino has made Olivia fall in love with Viola. The words "You
might do much" are the four most important syllables Olivia speaks.
Pregnant simplicity could go no further. Since Viola's speech is hyper-
bolic, we might think of Olivia's moving reply as meiosis, an understatement designed to increase the impression on the hearer. But it is
too early for Olivia to be setting verbal traps for Viola; this is the first

moment the Countess has been struck by the emotion of love. We must attribute the rhetorical strategy not to her but to Shakespeare alone.

Twelfth Night is free of scenes written primarily for verbal display. In this it differs from a good deal of Shakespeare's early work. If we turn to the twentieth century in a search for parallels to Shakespeare's youthful *jeux d'esprit,* we inevitably think first of two comedies which helped to make Christopher Fry's reputation, *A Phoenix Too Frequent* and *The Lady's Not for Burning.* Although most of the writing in these plays could probably be "justified" on purely dramatic grounds, it is often obvious that Fry was less interested in hewing to the line of action than in astonishing and delighting the listener with his daring fancies. In this preoccupation he succeeded. The conflicts in the plays are above all between the words, not the characters or their transacted intentions.

A Phoenix Too Frequent is a comic parable of death and regeneration, and the language keeps the theme prominent. The phoenix is too frequent because a widow intending to follow her husband into the grave resurrects him and herself within three days of his death, for she has fallen in love again and will use the corpse to save the life of the living man. The names of the characters are thematically significant. The wife is "Dynamene," the feminine form of the Greek adjective for "powerful." Her name suggests that she is too vital to devote herself for long to death. The dead husband is Virilius. The newly arrived lover is called Tegeus, from the Greek *tegos* (a roof or cover)—a name that Dynamene decides is too "thin" for this healthy, natural man, whom she renames Chromis, pronouncing it *krum-is* in order to combine the notions of color and solidity, for the new name suggests bread.

She is frequently associated with light, he with the physical world. When she embraces him after a brief separation, "Time runs again; the void is space again; / Space has life again; Dynamene has Chromis."[2] The spirit has rejoined the flesh.

The plot-action is extremely simple; the structure is fundamentally thematic and imagistic. Action, even inner action, is secondary. Apart from the thematic language, Fry's delight in words is such that they cut many a caper on their own. He is very fond of alliteration, consonance, and assonance, as in

> Let me unload something of my lips' longing
> On to yours receiving.
>
> > [p. 30]

The pleasure in such writing comes from an awareness of the laughable disparity between what the moment requires and what Fry crowds into it. He revels in puns, hyperbole, and references to his own style, descents from ecstasy into bathos, and anachronisms for comic effect. The action can accommodate most of these effects, or if not, can grace-fully retire while they provide an entertaining substitute for action; but sometimes they fall into cuteness, the laugh being at the cost of integrity. Early in the comedy, Dynamene is speaking her sorrow to her servant. The last section of a long and brilliant speech envisions the tumult of creation and ends with the widow's desolation as she contemplates the death of her husband:

> What a mad blacksmith creation is
> Who blows his furnaces until the stars fly upward
> And iron Time is hot and politicians glow
> And bulbs and roots sizzle into hyacinth
> And orchis, and the sand puts out the lion,
> Roaring yellow, and oceans bud with porpoises,
> Blenny, tunny, and the almost unexisting
> Blindfish; throats are cut, the masterpiece
> Looms out of labour; nations and rebellions
> Are spat out to hang on the wind—and all is gone
> In one Virilius, wearing his office tunic,
> Checking the pence column as he went.
> Where's animation now? What is there that stays
> To dance? The eye of the one-eyed world is out.

[p. 6]

The larger part of the passage shows Fry at his best. The lines are alive with the universal creativeness they celebrate. All is movement and ac-tivity as every form of life competes with every other in the sheer fury of its explosion into existence. But what of the cunningly devised anti-climax? Whereas Cleopatra's lament for Shakespeare's Antony ("Young boys and girls /Are level now with men; the odds is gone . . ." [IV, xv, 65–66]) risks the absurd with its quick foray into the colloquial, the end of Dynamene's speech courts absurdity too plainly. The lines place in a strong light the problem of comic poetry in the drama. How can the comic dramatist remain simultaneously true to his play, his poetic vision, his character, and his joke? Fry is of course implying that Dynamene's mourning is comic, that it is not true to her own vitality, but the heroic afflatus in "all is gone / In one Virilius" should not be so punctured by one who is speaking seriously unless she is extremely inept with words, as Dynamene is not. I began this chapter by saying that the language of comedy is in tension with the action and the speaker. The tension in the concluding lines of Dynamene's lament is too great. What Dynamene is doing—mourning an admired husband who has very recently died—and what she is saying are at this moment in flagrant opposition to each other.

A comic dramatist's love of words hardly offers grounds for complaint. And many readers, if not audiences, will prefer the structures that verbal patterns can create to the working out of a dramatic action. But the most mature comedy does not rest in "spatial" structure, to say nothing of self-indulgent word-play. The development of Shakespeare alone suggests that the greatest comic writing, however frequently it finds opportunity for thematic and other elaboration, is fundamentally committed to dramatic movement.

If one discusses the relation of language to the play as a dramatic action, it is obviously difficult to ignore the speaker as an influence on the words chosen, since dramatic effect depends on the illusion that characters are propelling the action, if not the plot. Those who place character in quotation marks or regard it as a mere dramatic device are as far from a sense of the whole as those who speak of metaphor as mere ornament. The principle of dramatic decorum according to the speaker, specified in Aristotle's *Poetics* and again in the Renaissance, has guided, but not manacled, both poetic and realistic comedy in all periods. Dynamene's words can hardly be separated from Dynamene, though most of these are recognizably the issue of Christopher Fry's highly original style.

In the following pages I shall consider the connection between speaker, or character, and language. As a first rough division one might think of the language of comedy as the languages of the clever and the dense or the witty, in a wide sense, and the witless. Normally the wit's mastery of language is a foretaste of his success in the play, and the verbal insensitivity of the witless indicates that he will be defeated. In *Twelfth Night*, Sir Toby assumes that because Aguecheek's written challenge to Cesario is stupidly phrased, Cesario will conclude that Sir Andrew is incapable of fighting well; Cesario will take the word for the deed. In Restoration comedy this kind of assumption is general. Usually there is a close correspondence between a man's verbal style and his standing in the play (not necessarily in the regard of the audience). Wits are courageous, energetic, skillful in alienating the affections of women; the witless are cowardly, clumsy, and destined to become cuckolds. In *The Man of Mode*, a Restoration lady values wit so highly that she says of a clever man, "I had rather be made infamous by him than owe my reputation to the dull discretion of those fops you talk of."[3] Wit, even by association, is better than good behavior. In Wilde it is better than truth, as when Algernon defends an epigram by saying that it is perfectly phrased and "quite as true as any observation in civilized life should be."[4] Although these two illustrations are extreme, they are evidence of a continuing tendency within the comic form.

Restoration comedy tirelessly contrasts the wit and the fool. To become a wit was to select a way of life, join a club, and adopt a mode of speech. The ideal is often far from what I have called the divine average. The Mirabells, Valentines, Dorimants, Harcourts, and Archers speak wittily, the Petulants, Sparkishes, Fondlewifes, and Sullens stupidly. But there are gradations. Witwoud, who supposedly speaks wittily only when he has memorized a *bon mot*, can perform well under the stress of a rapid-fire exchange. Of Sir Fopling Flutter in *The Man of Mode*, Dryden could say in the Epilogue:

> Most modern wits such monstrous fools have shown,
> They seemed not of Heaven's making, but their own.
> Those nauseous harlequins in farce may pass,
> But there goes more to a substantial ass;
> Something of man must be exposed to view,
> That, gallants, it may more resemble you.
> Sir Fopling is a fool so nicely writ,
> The ladies would mistake him for a wit. . . .
>
> [ll. 1–8]

And the characteristic rhetoric of the period can emerge from the mouths of a wide variety of speakers. The Restoration dramatists will allow clever servants like Foible or Jeremy some of their best lines. When a drunken shoemaker in *The Man of Mode* is chided by a gentleman for vices above his rank, he replies, "You would ingross the sins of the nation; poor folks can no sooner be wicked but they're railed at by their betters" (I, p. 13). In his variation on Restoration comedy, Wilde will convert this kind of satiric observation to his own use when he has Algernon declare that the lower classes should set "us" a good example.

Congreve's *Love for Love*, one of the best plays of its time, places its characters in the familiar categories—wit, fop, humorous character, and simpleton; but it cannot be said that each category has a constantly distinguishable language. The speech obviously intended to win approval as wit can be divided into three kinds: (1) rapid exchanges, (2) extended antitheses and paradoxes, (3) similitudes and metaphors, the latter sometimes developed into little allegories or parables. But there are some happy flights of fancy and grotesquerie that cannot be so grouped. The chief figures just listed are in oblique relationship to the characters. The members of the "club," Valentine, Scandal, and Angelica, use all three. Mrs. Frail has not played the Restoration game shrewdly enough, but her speech is shrewder than her behavior. Ben, though appropriately crude and habitually nautical in speech, is agile in repartee. At times his verbal technique is indistinguishable from that of the inner circle. Tattle, the "half-witted beau," is often on the edge of being witty. As he rattles on, finding as if by accident good things on his way, he has one speech in which he laments that if his tattling becomes generally known, his "visits will never be admitted beyond a drawing-room: I shall never see a bed-chamber again, never be locked in a closet, nor run behind a screen, or under a table. . . ."[5] This is the speech of one clever enough to capitalize on his silliness. Sir Sampson Legend, though typed as the heavy father, has some outbursts of legendary verbal energy in which he thoroughly enjoys himself. Even Foresight, "an illiterate old fellow," is permitted one or two ripostes proving that his study of astrology has not been entirely wasted.

The chief functions of the rapid exchanges in matched lines are to create dramatic tension and a vivacious tone. At one point, the three wittiest characters have the following duel:

ANGELICA. You can't accuse me of inconstancy; I never told you that I loved you.

VALENTINE. But I can accuse you of uncertainty, for not telling me whether you did or not.

ANGELICA. You mistake indifference for uncertainty; I never had concern enough to ask myself the question.

SCANDAL. Nor good-nature enough to answer him that did ask you; I'll say that for you, madam.

ANGELICA. What, are you setting up for good-nature?

SCANDAL. Only for the affectation of it, as the women do for ill-nature.

ANGELICA. Persuade your friend that it is all affectation.

SCANDAL. I shall receive no benefit from the opinion; for I know no effectual difference between continued affectation and reality.

[III,iii]

Scandal's first speech is aggressive and has the sweet smell of success, but Angelica immediately puts him on the defensive. In his second speech he is backing down politely though wittily. She has forced him into a dilemma at which he must either boast of his good-nature or chivalrously admit that he is less good-natured than Angelica and the rest of her sex. Angelica's reply means either "I already know it [your affectation of good nature] is false" or "Your friend *ought* to be persuaded of your ill nature; you don't deserve his friendship," or both. In the last speech quoted, Scandal subtly answers that even if he persuades Valentine that the good nature is affected, Valentine will realize that continued affectation becomes reality; Scandal is or will be a good-natured friend. The contest ends with Scandal eking out a narrow victory. This is in accord with his position in the play's hierarchy of intelligences.

A more showy and easily detachable dialogue, in Act One, opposes Valentine, the witty rake, and Mrs. Frail, the town flirt:

VALENTINE. Well, lady galloper, how does Angelica?

MRS. FRAIL. Angelica? manners!

VALENTINE. What, will you allow an absent lover—

MRS. FRAIL. No, I'll allow a lover present with his mistress to be particular;—but otherwise I think his passion ought to give place to his manners.

VALENTINE. But what if he has more passion than manners?

MRS. FRAIL. Then let him marry and reform.

[I,ii]

Here Congreve does not distribute the wit on the basis of the character's rank in the play. In action Valentine is the clever, successful hero, Mrs. Frail the light-headed schemer who is to be tricked in the final act. But in these lines she more than holds her own. Since both characters, however, are consistently sophisticated, one feels no definite violation of decorum here.

In the last scene, as Valentine is approaching his victory, Tattle and Mrs. Frail enter the stage. Valentine's junta has tricked them into a marriage which neither has wanted. We now get the following exchange involving Mrs. Frail, Tattle, and Angelica:

MRS. FRAIL. . . . Nay, for my part I always despised Mr. Tattle of all things; nothing but his being my husband could have made me like him less.

TATTLE. Look you there, I thought as much!—Pox on't, I wish we could keep it a secret! why, I don't believe any of this company would speak of it.

MRS. FRAIL. But, my dear, that's impossible; the parson and that rogue Jeremy will publish it.

TATTLE. Ay, my dear, so they will, as you say.

ANGELICA. O you'll agree very well in a little time; custom will make it
   easy to you.
TATTLE. Easy! pox on't! I don't believe I shall sleep to-night.

[V,ii]

Once again there is a blend of the characteristic and the independently
witty. Though befooled and subject to ridicule, Mrs. Frail is still poised
and pretends to dislike her fate more because that attitude is modish
than because she actually suffers. She has attained a husband of her
own rank. Tattle, as usual, teeters between silliness and an awareness
of the effect he is making. The two "my dears" are double-edged, giving an amusing suggestion of overhasty subjection to marriage but also
implying that the partners retain an ironic sense. And the line quoted
last may be an indication of sexual inadequacy *or* a sly hint that Tattle
expects the marriage to be pleasurable after all. There is tension between speech and speaker, but no definite break.

The wit sees both sharp distinctions and surprising similarities. In
Love for Love, Congreve assigns his little essays in antithesis and paradox mainly to Angelica and Scandal. Long speeches built exclusively on
this method are likely to be arid, as are the opening speeches in *The
Way of the World*. In *Love for Love*, when Scandal tells Angelica that
she loves Valentine, she replies:

Acknowledgment of love! I find you have mistaken my compassion,
and think me guilty of a weakness I'm a stranger to. But I have too much
sincerity to deceive you, and too much charity to suffer him to be de-
luded with vain hopes. Good-nature and humanity oblige me to be
concerned for him; but to love is neither in my power nor inclination;
and if he can't be cured without I suck the poison from his wounds, I'm
afraid he won't recover his senses till I lose mine.

[IV,i]

There are more glittering displays of antithesis in the play. The present
speech is more dramatic and less sententious than others. Angelica's
pride and pique repel Scandal's suggestion with a cool show of "judgment"—one synonym for wit during the Restoration.[6] Read for its style
alone, the speech is a bit verbose, but we can see the heroine working to
disguise her feelings, already intimated in an aside, as she accumulates
over a half dozen antitheses or distinctions. The rather strained quality
of the speech is qualified, however, by the metaphor, which could suddenly occur to the actress and lend an air of improvisation to the last
sentence.

In a letter written in the same year as the play, Congreve makes an important statement on the relation of language to character:

The saying of humourous [in the modern sense] things does not distinguish characters, for every person in a comedy may be allowed to speak them. From a witty man they are expected, and even a fool may be permitted to stumble on 'em by chance. Tho' I make a difference betwixt Wit and Humour, yet I do not think that humourous [in the old sense] characters exclude Wit. No, but the manner of Wit should be adapted to the Humour. As for instance, a character of splenetic and peevish Humour should have a satirical Wit. A jolly and sanguine Humour should have a facetious Wit. The former should speak positively; the latter, carelessly. . . .[7]

In *Love for Love*, Congreve at least approaches this ideal. Tattle stumbles across some lively similitudes, including this: "I have more vizor-masks to inquire for me than ever went to see the Hermaphrodite, or the Naked Prince" (III, iii). The comparisons are unquestionably vivid, but Tattle is stripping himself, indicating both his vanity and his dubious masculinity. Scandal illustrates the "splenetic and peevish Humour" and its satiric wit; Valentine is the more "jolly and sanguine." The first shows more judgment, the second more fancy.

Congreve, like Etherege, is devoted to the similitude. In *Love for Love*, almost every character who has more than a few lines uses this figure. Prue and Foresight are exceptions, since she is extremely simple and direct, and he is so rapt in his fancies that he cannot distinguish what I. A. Richards calls the tenor from the vehicle.[8] As the chief raisonneurs, Angelica and Scandal use the similitude to generalize. Scandal, for example, believes "some women are virtuous . . . ; but 'tis as I believe some men are valiant, through fear" (III, iv). When characterizing women, Valentine prefers metaphor: "You are the reflection of Heaven in a pond, and he that leaps at you is sunk" (IV, iii). Scandal's similitude is abstract and flat; Valentine's metaphor reminds us of the great age preceding him. One of the strongest similitudes comes, in fact, from a man of an older generation, Sir Sampson: "Odd, I love to see a young spendthrift forced to cling to an old woman for support, like ivy round a dead oak: faith, I do; I love to see 'em hug and cotton together, like down upon a thistle" (III, iii). The hand is the hand of Congreve, but the voice is the voice of Sampson. Though the similitude becomes a mannerism, it can take on life—both halves of Sampson's last clause benefit from the time he has spent in the country—and Congreve knows how to vary the figure from speaker to speaker.

In shifting emphasis from the rapidly moving figures of the early seventeenth century to the leisurely similitude, the neoclassical age gained clarity but sacrificed power. And though Congreve is more realistic than the Jacobeans, his similitudes are no more realistic than metaphor. At any rate, the language of *Love for Love* is most vigorous when it returns to metaphor and related tropes. With the rather tame similitudes in which the play abounds, compare the following:

Did you come a volunteer into the world? or did I, with the lawful authority of a parent, press you to the service?

[Sampson,II,i]

You know my aunt is a little retrograde (as you call it) in her nature. Uncle, I'm afraid you are not lord of the ascendant, ha! ha! ha!

[Angelica,II,i]

No, no, to marry is to be a child again, and play with the same rattle always. . . .

[Tattle,V,ii]

Partially because he is the most frequently given to metaphor, Ben threatens to run off with the play. Though the content of his imagery becomes monotonous, his mode of speech might well be envied by the more polished characters. When he sticks to metaphor, he is admirable, but when he brings in locutions beginning with "as" or "more than," he reveals the debilitating influence of the in-group.

The recent critical reaction against Restoration comedy, led by L. C. Knights,[9] is mainly a dissatisfaction with its language. Exclusive attention to Congreve's conscious wit may lead to boredom. One may also recall that much of a greater dramatist's wit seems to have been on the borders of his consciousness.[10] But in attacking what he considered the thinness of Congreve's wit, Knights ignored the language of Congreve's fools. This is often more poetic and reflective of keener observation than the language of the wits. Some of the foolish Sampson's speeches in *Love for Love* are extremely vital, and in *The Way of the World*, Lady Wishfort's "boudoir Billingsgate," as Meredith called it, has the very force and concrete detail that Knights missed in the speeches of Mirabell, Fainall, and their peers. Her tirade at the beginning of Act Five develops a truly Jonsonian power as it pictures Foible "washing of old gauze and weaving of dead hair, with a bleak blue nose over a chafing-dish of starved embers." Congreve's language sometimes hints at an inner, underground rebellion against the wit-fool dichotomy. This was good for the plays.

Jonson is a greater dramatist than Congreve largely because of the greater strength, density and mass of his language. His dramatic dialogue gives more than lip-service to the rule of decorum according to the speaker. In his *Timber; or, Discoveries* he advises the writer that words "are to be chose according to the persons we make speak or the things we speak of. Some are of the camp, some of the council-board, some of the shop, some of the sheepcot, some of the pulpit, some of the bar, etc."[11] If we examine the language of *The Alchemist*, we find that, up to a point, he had already followed this advice. Face and Subtle begin by using the low and vital invective appropriate to the rogues they are; Dol Common shifts from low to elevated language when it suits her purpose; Ananias speaks in Puritan jargon; Mammon is the sensualist *par excellence*; Dapper and Drugger are fittingly simple-minded in speech as well as action. But what finally stamps *The Alchemist* with greatness is Jonson's ability to move beyond the merely appropriate to a range of discourse far exceeding the capacities of the speakers if they are conceived in realistic terms. Where a lesser man might have unwittingly made his dramatic persons speak out of character, Jonson has them transcend it. This he accomplishes by the sheer weight and aptness of his detail, the piling up of hyperbole, and the significant use of metaphor, simile, and related figures of speech. No quacks, no pimps, no Puritans were ever so exceedingly themselves as are Jonson's men.

A large share of the dialogue goes to Face, Subtle, and Mammon. In their longer speeches, all three tend to combine the chief figures of Jonson's rhetoric. In discussing *Love for Love*, we found that certain devices—antithesis, for example—are associated with certain types. There is less specialization here, for Mammon, the chief gull, uses the same modes of speech as the rogues. Yet hyperbole and *accumulatio*, the "heaping figure" of the Renaissance, create very different effects on the lips of Subtle and Mammon.

In the great opening scene, Subtle and Face attack each other with monumental, baroque force and relish, a zest so thoroughly shared by Jonson, the audience, and the reader that one should avoid the hasty assumption that Jonson's attitude toward these men is one of mere disapproval or outrage. The Prologue states that the manners or humors of bawd and impostor (here Face and Subtle) have always been the subject of the comic writer's "rage or spleen," yet Jonson adds that he has aimed not to "grieve, but to better men." If the reader could be permitted to rewrite the Prologue, he might want to play down the "better" and play up the comic rage, a phenomenon combining positive and negative feelings toward the humors represented.

Each opponent exalts himself fantastically and degrades the other to dung. Face claims that he met his opposite

> at Pie Corner,
> Taking your meal of steam in, from cooks' stalls,
> Where, like the father of hunger, you did walk
> Piteously costive, with your pinch'd-horn-nose,
> And your complexion of the Roman wash,
> Stuck full of black and melancholic worms,
> Like powder-corns shot at th' Artillery Yard.
> . . . .
> When you went pinn'd up in the several rags
> Yo' had rak'd and pick'd from dunghills,
> before day. . . .[12]

I have quoted only a third of a twenty-five line outburst climaxed by a tremendous period. Since Jonson leans so heavily on hyperbole and the heaping figure, short extracts do not do him justice, though it is wrong to say that he does not appear favorably in single lines. The "meal of steam" alone is a hint of what he can do with a phrase.

Though the speech creates a generally naturalistic impression, it is rich in imagery. The picture of Subtle as the archetype of the hungry, constipated man is based on Catullus, but Jonson's poetic energy is not satisfied with the details taken from the Roman poet. Subtle's face must not only bear the marks of his unhealthy life, but the "worms" must look like grains of gunpowder. He must not only rake his clothing from dunghills but reach into the filth with his hands. As the passage continues, this restless activity increases in speed until Subtle breaks in upon the tirade.

Though Face is a bawd working with a whore and a quack, it is impossible not to admire him and his cronies in this scene. If they do not improve our morals, they "better men" by creating an indefeasible joy in the power of words to triumph over mean circumstance. Although Subtle and Face overvalue themselves ludicrously,[13] the words in which they do so confer on them something of the value they claim.

Subtle replies in kind. If Face sees Subtle as above all a dog, for Subtle, his partner is an insect, a scarab who has been scarcely worthy to "converse with cobwebs." (In this play "converse" regularly implies sexual conversation.) His most masterful denunciation takes an interrogative form:

Thou vermin, have I ta'en thee, out of dung,
So poor, so wretched, when no living thing
Would keep thee company, but a spider or worse?
Rais'd thee from brooms, and dust, and wat'ring pots,
Sublim'd thee, and exalted thee, and fix'd thee
In the third region, call'd our state of grace?
Wrought thee to spirit, to quintessence. . . .

[I,i,64–70]

Subtle has taken about a dozen technical terms from alchemy—most of
them are to be used later in the play—and applied them to his elevation
of Face. Just as the alchemist starts with worthless matter and in eight
stages, to be listed in Act Two, Scene Five, raises it to gold or the
philosopher's stone, so Subtle has taken Face from the dung and gradually refined him: the fourth stage, sublimation, and the last, fixation,
are specifically mentioned. But as Subtle goes on to say in lines I have not
quoted, improving Face has been twice as difficult as creating the stone,
for the original material was so vile. Now Face has been handsomely
clothed, given speech, spiritualized. He who was hardly equal to a
spider is ready for "more than ordinary fellowships": perhaps Subtle
means that Face is now so learned, he could become a university fellow.
For he has been taught not only the "great art" but many other learned
subjects like the art of cheating at cards and "whatever gallant tincture
else": Face now has certain tinctures of gallantry just as the alembics
hold tinctures of mercury and sulphur. The play of mind in all this is
dazzling, but Subtle seems unaware of any sardonic conflict between
the realm of spirit to which he has introduced Face and the cheating
arts he has been taught. In Subtle's defense one could remark that the
speech boils onward at such a pace that he hardly has time to notice
the harsh irony.

Subtle plays some half dozen roles, each of which has its own language. With Mammon, he is the artisan but also the sacred priest of
alchemy. His talk is all of bolt, athanor, and pelican—containers for
chemicals, of the toad, the crow, and the panther—colors of liquids, of
inceration, ascension, and projection—stages in the work; or else of
watching and patience, love and zeal—the moral qualities essential to
achieving the stone. With Kastrill he becomes Master Doctor, the philosopher learned in

. . . your divisions, moods, degrees, and differences,

Your praedicaments, substance, and accident,
Series extern and intern, with their causes,
Efficient, material, formal, final. . . .

[IV,ii,24–27]

For Dapper he becomes a priest of Faerie speaking rhymed incantation,
with Tribulation Wholesome, a crushing Jonsonian critic of Puritanism.
In most of these roles, he is above all a cheat, but during his attack on
the Puritans, we hear a scoundrel taking pleasure in tormenting Tribulation with sarcasms that Jonson evidently thought justified. Somewhat
surprisingly, Jonson speaks through the mouth of one already revealed
as morally worthless. With Face, as in the opening scene, the relation
of Subtle's character to his speech is complex. Although he hyperboli-
cally praises himself and degrades Face, there is a passionate sincerity
in his words. For the moment, at least, he has convinced himself that he
is a great master foully mistreated by a ruffian.

These shifting alignments of character to speech bring Subtle close
to the modern drama and novel, in which the individual ego may suffer
transformations, disappearances, and recurrences. One may think of such
a play as Pirandello's *Henry IV*, the hero of which is sometimes mad,
sometimes sane, and sometimes playing a game so strangely that though
he thinks he is sane, the audience is left in doubt. Subtle is more the
master of himself than is Henry, but at times his role-playing overwhelms
him.

Like Subtle, Face plays various roles. In his scenes with Mammon, he
is Lungs, the alchemist's assistant. Encountering Surly at St. Paul's, he
is a suburb-captain or bawd, though Dapper and Drugger take him to
be a real officer. At the end of the play, he returns to his post as Love-
wit's butler. In and through his language, he rises superior to his rascality
in a way that differs from Subtle's. His many asides place him in inti-
mate relationship with the audience, preventing absolute condemnation and communicating a sense of godlike ease. Even his regular dialogue may support his privileged position. There is a scene (I,ii) in which
he attacks Subtle in order to deceive Dapper, but actually Face gets
the double pleasure of taking in the simpleton and insulting the alchemist without risk of retaliation. There is double pleasure for the audience
as well, who in gratitude may bestow a kind of impunity on Face.

When making an argument or reporting an incident, Face takes positive joy in amassing illustrations of his point. In Act Three, Scene Three
he tells Subtle he has found a new gull in a Spanish nobleman,

A noble count, a don of Spain, my dear
Delicious compeer, and my party-bawd,

[III,iii,10–11]

who comes equipped with slops, trunks (trunk-hose), pistolets, and pieces
of eight, and who will

make his batt'ry
Upon our Dol, our castle, our cinque-port,
Our Dover pier, our what thou wilt.

[III,iii,17–19]

Here and elsewhere, the alliteration is merely a pleasurable fillip added
to his heap of literal and figurative details. The military image, which
will be picked up shortly as Dol enters, builds the picture of Face's
cheerful and tireless war against society. In his preface to the quarto
edition, Jonson condemned those "that (to gain opinion of copy) utter
all they can, however unfitly," but he himself was a master of copy
(copiousness), and Face is second to none in this mark of style. One who
enjoys language so immensely and so astutely is very hard to dislike.
Language so used becomes a secret agent undermining or at least quali-
fying the stated moral purpose of the writer.

When Dol asks, "How fares our camp?" Face replies:

As with the few that had entrench'd themselves
Safe, by their discipline, against a world, Dol,
And laugh'd within those trenches. . . .

[III,iii,34–36]

A shocking misuse of the ideal of discipline! Face's discipline issues in
his and the audience's laughter on this festival day, as he calls it a few
lines further on. An air of festivity flows around the speech and laughter
of Face. He has the temperament if not the morals we expect the successful to have, and this is probably Jonson's meaning when he gives victory
to Face in his civil war with Subtle.

Just as he speaks more asides than anyone else, so he has the largest
number of double-entendres, usually obscene. Like the low, festive
jokes in Aristophanes, they are a sign of vitality and that *ponêria* Whitman finds in the Aristophanic hero.[14] When the gullible Mammon in-
quires about Dol, Face replies: "So pleasant! She'll mount you up, like
quicksilver, / Over the helm; and circulate, like oil" (II,iii,254–55).
Critics are likely to view this sort of image as a stern moral reflection on
the link between sexual immorality and immoral moneymaking schemes,

as if the protean wickedness in Jonson were not at all delightful. In another scene the two cheats will draw lots for Dame Pliant, and the loser "shall have / The more in goods, the other has in tail" (II,vi,87–88)—the indecent reference swamping the legal idea of entailment. Examples could be multiplied.

The obsolete word "firk," usually glossed as "stir" or "rouse," occurs three times, always with a suggestive meaning. This is the way Face instructs Dol how to behave with the Spanish don, who supposedly knows no English:

> And—do you hear? good action!
> Firk like a flounder; kiss like a scallop, close;
> And tickle him with thy mother tongue.
>
> [III,iii,69–71]

The image has a Shakespearian density. No short passage could better express Face's energy and bawdy enjoyment in anticipation of success. Language and character are perfectly matched. Subtle's improprieties are comparatively heavy, as in his lines directed at the Spaniard: "Donzel, methinks you look melancholic, / After your *coitum*, and scurvy!" (IV,vi,20–21) Face has the address to put his sexual references in metaphors, similes, or imaginative quibbles.

Jonson is content to have his dullest characters, Drugger, Dapper, and Dame Pliant, reveal their stupidity mainly in action; flat rather than notably stupid, their speech does not boast the infelicities of a Dogberry or a Prue Foresight. With Mammon, the case is altered. As already mentioned, this magnificent fool uses the locutions and turns of speech favored by Subtle and Face. Like them, he is dissatisfied with one epithet when four will serve. At his first glimpse of Face, he calls him Subtle's "fire-drake,"

> His Lungs, his Zephyrus, he that puffs his coals,
> Till he firk nature up, in her own centre,
>
> [II,i,27–28]

lines displaying Mammon's verbal bounce, his happy sensuality, his fatuous belief that Subtle will rape nature especially for him. What separates his language most clearly from that of the cheats is that their imagery is always in touch with reality, while his builds ever higher a monstrous confusion of fact and fancy. As he prepares to receive Dol, whom he thinks a noblewoman, he says:

> She shall feel gold, taste gold, hear gold, sleep gold;

> Nay, we will *concumbere* gold. I will be puissant,
> And mighty in my talk to her!
>
> [IV,i,29–31]

For him, Jove's famous shower becomes not a symbol of the sex act but a substitute for it. The vehicle has become the tenor, and the tenor has disappeared. Yet, despite the comic rage in Jonson's portrait of Mammon, the feelings he arouses are not wholly negative. Besotted as he is, he can almost intoxicate with his vainglorious visions, moving us alternately to wonder and laughter. Since his sensual ambitions are so obviously unreal, one can more easily surrender, at moments, to an as-if attitude counterweighting detachment with a readiness to imagine that is untinged by guilt-feelings. He is a very great fool.

His most astonishing scenes occur early in Act Two. As he enters with Pertinax Surly, he begins dreaming aloud of what he can achieve with the stone. His promise to "purchase Devonshire and Cornwall, / And make them perfect Indies" (II,i,35–36) is merely one of his teeming fantasies, each more towering than the last, each marking him as the Jonsonian character most completely given over to illusion. For him the myth of Jason is merely one of a dozen "abstract riddles" signifying alchemy. When Face assures him that Subtle's chemical solution has arrived at "ruby"—the final stage of the great work of transmutation—Mammon's imagination flies to a height of comic poetry unsurpassed in Jonson and perhaps in English literature.

Immediately he envisions a seraglio filled with wives and concubines, and himself as a miracle of potency, thanks to the elixir. Then he sees himself in his dream world:

> I will have all my beds blown up, not stuff'd;
> Down is too hard. And then, mine oval room
> Filled with such pictures as Tiberius took
> From Elephantis, and dull Aretine
> But coldly imitated. Then, my glasses
> Cut in more subtle angles, to disperse
> And multiply the figures, as I walk
> Naked between my succubae. My mists
> I'll have of perfume, vapor'd 'bout the room,
> To lose ourselves in; and my baths, like pits
> To fall into; from whence we will come forth
> And roll us dry in gossamer and roses.—
> Is it arrived at ruby?—Where I spy
> A wealthy citizen or rich lawyer

Have a sublim'd pure wife, unto that fellow
I'll send a thousand pound to be my cuckold.

[II,ii,41–56]

As the uproariously funny first line and a half announces, the great speech
is fully comic poetry, an unusual phenomenon: great comic poetry is as
seldom seen as the phoenix. The inflating of Mammon's beds perfectly
images the swelling, the comic afflatus of his ego. The entire passage
propagates an attractively outlandish daydream of vice. Each vaunt enlarges the dream and helps along the bursts of laughter. Just as *all* the
beds are to be inflated, so the room will be *filled* with lewd pictures
suggested by the erotic author, Elephantis—an excellent name for one
furnishing monstrous models of lubricity far surpassing those of the in-
adequately evil Aretino. With his "glasses," Mammon will turn his already long list of concubines into a population explosion. Presumably
Mammon will walk naked, not between two succubae—female demons
who have intercourse with men in their sleep—but between two regi-
ments of them. The vaporous confusion is compounded in mists of per-
fume until Mammon and a platoon or two fall into watery pits that
drown them in delicious sin instead of washing it away. No one cleansed
of vice would dry himself in gossamer and roses.

His question "Is it arrived at ruby?" is not for information since he
knows it has, but for the joy of having Face confirm his happiness. Seeing Face nod or bow with assurance Mammon trembles with delight.
The question looks back to "roses" and forward to "sublim'd," for the
ruby will permit both the roses and the prostitution of the wealthy man's
wife. In any other mouth, Mammon's plan to convert the sublime to the
degraded—to reverse the supposed moral direction of alchemy—could
awaken horror, but since Mammon's hopes are so utterly unattainable,
his wicked image is pure comedy.

Throughout the speech, comedy and poetry are in sensitive relation
to each other and to Mammon, who is fully present at every moment.
We can see his vainglorious strut as he walks between his succubae. For
a moment his posture fades as he loses himself in mists, but then he returns with redoubled clarity as he splashes into the water. Like Aristophanes, Jonson will construct a vision that can briefly be taken seriously, whereupon he will break it into fragments. He encourages the
listener to "lose" himself in this Bower of Bliss and then tears down the
latticework. This method never attained a greater triumph than in his
presentation of Mammon, who bids fair to make a fool of his audience.

Wit unleavened by folly is unable to sustain the greatest comedy. We can occasionally sense in Congreve an enlarging sympathy with folly, but one measure of Jonson's superiority to Congreve is the greater splendor surrounding the older dramatist's fools—prodigies like Mammon, Ursula, and that rogue-fool, Volpone. This splendor is, of course, the creation of Jonson's comic poetry.

NOTES

1. "Shakespeare's *Twelfth Night*," *Rice Institute Pamphlets*, XLV (1959); reprinted in *Shakespeare: The Comedies*, ed. Kenneth Muir (Englewood Cliffs, N.J., 1965), p. 77.

2. *A Phoenix Too Frequent* (London, 1953), p. 38.

3. II,ii, in Sir George Etherege, *The Man of Mode*, ed. Bernard F. Dukore (San Francisco, 1962).

4. *The Importance of Being Earnest*, 6th ed. (London, 1912), p. 51.

5. *Love for Love*, I,ii, in *William Congreve (Complete Plays)*, ed. Alexander C. Ewald (New York, 1956). Citations from Congreve will be to this edition.

6. For a good analysis of wit in this period, see Thomas Fujimara, *The Restoration Comedy of Wit* (Princeton, 1952), Chapter II.

7. "Concerning Humour in Comedy," in *Dramatic Essays of the Neoclassic Age*, ed. H. H. Adams and Baxter Hathaway (New York, 1950), pp. 172–73.

8. *The Philosophy of Rhetoric* (New York, 1936), pp. 89–138. The tenor is what the figure of speech is "about"; the vehicle is that part of the figure communicating the speaker's attitude toward the thing in question.

9. "Restoration Comedy: The Reality and the Myth," in *Explorations* (New York, 1947), pp. 149–68.

10. See M. M. Mahood's penetrating study, *Shakespeare's Wordplay* (London, 1957).

11. *Timber; or, Discoveries Made on Men and Matter*, ed. F. E. Schelling (Boston, 1892), p. 60.

12. *The Alchemist*, I,i, 25–34, in *Elizabethan and Jacobean Comedy*, ed. Robert Ornstein and Hazelton Spencer (Boston, 1964). Citations from *The Alchemist* are to this edition.

13. Cf. E. B. Partridge, *The Broken Compass: A Study of the Major Comedies of Ben Jonson* (London, 1958), pp. 114–20.

14. See above, p. 94.

PART TWO

VARIATIONS

CHAPTER SIX

The Ambiguities of
The Birds

OF THE GREAT COMIC DRAMATISTS, Aristophanes is the most difficult to
hold in a firm grasp. A creature of earth, he constantly transforms himself into air, fire, and water, as if he were successively an embodiment of
each of the mutually contradictory pre-Socratic philosophies. Ultimately he is energy, not matter, for any shape he takes will soon be
disavowed if it becomes exclusive or restricting. In the course of his restless metamorphoses he strikes out right and left, but seldom with settled malice. One who can laugh at both parties to a dispute, whether
literary, philosophic, or political, presumably finds something valuable
in both and responds favorably to the world containing them. Aristophanes' catholic and uninhibited laughter is a unifying force in
comic poems of frequently dazzling complexity. His untiring verbal
and histrionic energy might seem to refute the idea, referred to earlier,
that his plays are often filled with great bitterness. Bitterness is tiring,
but Aristophanes never tires.

The fable Plato makes him tell in *The Symposium* is an interpretation
of his life's work, just as the Myth of Er at the end of *The Republic* is a
critical comment on Greek tragedy. According to the fable, men,
women, and androgynes were once round, having two faces each and
two sets of hands and legs; but angering Zeus, they were cut into halves
amounting to transverse sections. (And unless our behavior improves,
there is danger that we will suffer a second, longitudinal division.) At
any rate, each half-human being feels lost and isolated and constantly
seeks to mate with another. This is love or, in the famous phrase, "the
desire and pursuit of the whole." Since *The Symposium* was written after the fall of Athens, it is easy to give the fable a political interpretation;
if Greece is ever to prosper, it must unite. One thinks of Dicaeopolis,
driven to make a private peace with Sparta, or of Lysistrata joining the
Spartan women to make war on war. But the fable and its application

to Aristophanes should not be so limited. For the wholeness achieved by this poet is more than political; it is an implicit warning against all kinds of divisiveness or fragmentation of consciousness.

During the last hundred years and more, readings of Aristophanes have variously placed him as "the rallying point of political criticism"[1] in Athens and as a pure artist or pure jester "making fun" of the public figures and issues of his day, with a third school attempting to strike a balance between these extremes. Most critical thinking about Aristophanes analyzes his politics. Though this preoccupation has been excessive, it is in part justified by the vast number of contemporary allusions in the poet and by such assertions as the one in *The Acharnians* that "even comedy knows what is right" (1.500). For Werner Jaeger "comedy was the censorship of Athens. That is what makes Aristophanes' wit so deadly serious despite its mask of outrageous laughter."[2] Maurice Croiset's once very influential book, entitled *Aristophanes and the Political Parties at Athens*, studies the plays for the light they throw on the dramatist's politics. Both Jaeger and Croiset, however, recognize that Aristophanes cannot be neatly tagged with a political label.

Decisively rejecting the weight of opinion, A. W. Gomme insisted that Aristophanes must be read as a dramatic poet, not as a political pamphleteer. "For a dramatist," said Gomme, "you ask the question: 'Are his characters and his incidents probable, as Aristotle defined *probable* in the *Poetics*? Is his picture of Philocleon a probable one?'—an artistic problem; not, 'did he approve or condemn Cleon?'—a historical or biographical problem."[3] Gomme's vigorous polemic was needed. Yet in the face of Aristophanes' lifelong attention to educational, literary, moral, and political questions important to the life of the city, one is left somewhat dissatisfied with the attempt to exclude such issues from a study of the artist. The problem of the critic is not, of course, to discover the private opinions of the playwright, which are largely unrecoverable, but to determine how his assertions and half-assertions are used in the work of art as a whole. In his greatest works one would expect to find that the allusions are swept into the controlling movement, where they will reflect on the community not as literal statements but as signals looking two ways, toward the work itself and toward the city.

Most of Aristophanes' plays were up to the minute, both in plot and in the relevance of the dialogue to contemporary affairs. Among the earlier comedies, *The Knights* is at least partly stimulated by Cleon's rising political power, recently strengthened by his important victory at Pylos. The *Peace*, in which Trygaeus succeeds in bringing Eirênê to the

Greek people, was presented during the days when the Peace of Nicias (421 B.C.) was generally expected. But the plot of *The Birds*, presented in the spring of 414 B.C., has no obvious connection with current events. Two tired old men, sick of Athenian turbulence, search for Tereus in the country of the birds, hoping that he can direct them to a land where a "soft" life is possible. The adjective in Greek is *eueron* (fleecy, 1.121) and is far from suggesting an idealistic motivation. But one of the old men suddenly decides that the birds can become the rulers of the world. The rest of the play works out this idea. Men and gods yield all power to the birds, and the hero becomes the new Zeus. Not surprisingly, the comedy has often been treated as a comedy of escape.[4]

In the summer of 415 B.C., Athens and her allies launched an expedition against Syracuse, the chief Dorian stronghold in Sicily. The armada carried about 30,000 men, roughly the population of Athens at this time. Most Athenians, according to Thucydides, were "ignorant of its [Sicily's] size and of the number of its inhabitants, Hellenic and barbarian, and of the fact that they were undertaking a war not much inferior to that against the Peloponnesians."[5] The expedition was led by Alcibiades, Lamachus, and Nicias, but Alcibiades was soon recalled to answer grave charges of sacrilege. The galley sent for him, the Salaminian, is twice mentioned in *The Birds*, produced after Alcibiades' recall but before the campaign had reached a decisive stage. When Tereus suggests that the old men of the play might retire to a seaport on the Red Sea, Euelpides fears that if they should do so, the Salaminian might one day arrest them. Such allusions to recent history encourage the idea that Alcibiades' career hovers beneath the surface of the fantasy. Can the Sicilian expedition be the "true" subject of the play?

Or is the play, as F. M. Cornford thought, fundamentally a developed version of an Attic fertility ritual in which the New Year triumphs over the Old and celebrates his victory? *The Birds* is the one Aristophanic comedy in which Cornford was able to find all the parts of his ritual pattern and in the proper order. The hero, to be sure, is an old man, but he is rejuvenated by his great idea, overcomes the hostility of the birds, conducts a sacrifice involving a cooking scene, and at the close marries Basileia, the symbol of universal power. But there are serious objections to this view of the play. It leaves out a good deal of what is important in the plot; it selects as the antagonist the Chorus of birds, who can hardly be seen as the Old Year; and it emphasizes incidents which may have been fundamental in the ritual but are not critical in the play. Nevertheless, the spirit of the play has the mystery and exhilaration of a great and vital myth.[6]

The Birds is the most ambiguous of Aristophanes' comedies. It is at once Utopian and intensely topical; over a score of contemporary Greeks are mentioned by name, as well as many places significant in recent history, nor are these allusions introduced merely to give the play a spruce look. The *polos* (celestial sphere or sky) suddenly becomes a Greek *polis* (city). The two men looking for a quiet place (*topos apragmôn*) turn bird-land into the prodigiously busy Cloudcuckooland, an imperial realm. The birds express the innocence of an idyllic nature at one moment and a knowing irony the next. Nature itself, as so often in the late fifth century, is an ambiguous concept. Aristophanes, the scourge of the sophists, creates a "heroic" sophist *in excelsis*. The hero's name is Peithetaerus (Winfriend) and/or Pisthetaerus (possibly Trusty Friend), not to mention other possibilities. He begins as a tired searcher for peace and quiet but soon outdoes the restless activity of Alcibiades and ends his career as ruler of the world. The comedy is full of wordplay permitting radically different interpretations of the action: the *flight* of birds, for example, can be associated with innocence, escapism, flightiness, or warlike spirit. Incongruity is a guiding principle of the comic dialogue. The speech in which Prometheus identifies Basileia for Peithetaerus is entirely characteristic of the play: Prometheus explains (ll.1139–41) that she controls the thunderbolts of Zeus, wise counsel, law and order (the conservative ideal of *eunomia*), the *sôphrosynê* hymned by the tragic poets, but also dockyards, invective, financial officers, and the three-obol wage of the Athenian juror—reminders of the vices of popular government, vices Aristophanes had often satirized. Of such is the kingdom of heaven.

Aided by the ancient scholiasts, modern scholars have at least tentatively identified a large number of the individuals named by Aristophanes. They make up a comprehensive sampling of the community which the two men are fleeing but inevitably take with them. There are poets, sophists, a musician, a city-planner, politicians, generals, soothsayers, foreigners seeking Athenian citizenship, informers, sybarites, and degenerates, as well as a horse-dealer, a bird-seller, and a trainer of quails. No sooner is Athens-in-the-air established than a Colonial Supervisor arrives, asking for the consul who should be greeting him. Many men, and not the best, are acquiring bird names, and ten thousand human beings are applying for feathers. The point is not only that the worst are trying to take advantage of a good thing but that many, in resembling birds, are subhuman instead of superhuman. A young advocate of the newfangled "natural" freedom as against "law" ascends to Nephelococcygia because he has heard that cocks fight their parents; indeed, the birds have already said as much in the Parabasis. All of this creates an elaborate set of relationships between the real and the ideal. The birds are both better and worse than men. They are totally different from us but much the same. Consequently, the allusions to reality, which so often seem irrelevant or limiting in Aristophanes, actually reenter the work and increase its aesthetic complexity. When the one-eyed informer Opuntius is called a crow, when a noisy orator is called a magpie, we are forcibly reminded that man's ideals are not necessarily purer than his reality. "Birds" can be swans or nightingales; they can also be vultures or trivial noisemakers.

The coming of Peithetaerus and Euelpides converts the Chorus of birds to a way of life in which all their aggressiveness is put to new uses, yet the traditional association of birds with poetry and religion remains strong. The universal implications in the word *polos* reappear in the new *polis*. Deep religious feeling survives the decision to make war on the gods. This is apparent in the song of Tereus, the Hoopoe, to his mate and very striking in the great Parabasis at the center of the play.

Tereus' song immediately follows the opening scene, in which Peithetaerus persuades the Hoopoe that the birds can win hegemony by subjecting the gods to a Melian famine. This allusion to Athens' brutal destruction of Melos in 415 B.C., an action condemned by Thucydides and apparently by Euripides in *The Trojan Women*, definitely taints the hero's scheme, yet Tereus is delighted by the plan and wants to tell his wife and his people about it. Retiring to the copse where Procne is sleeping, he sings:

> Come, my companion, arise from sleep
> And release from your heavenly throat sacred hymns
> Lamenting your Itys and mine. Tawny-throat,
> Godlike is your song, ever new. It will echo
> And mount through the twining locks of the woodbine
> To the throne of Zeus. And there, golden-haired,
> Apollo will hear the elegy, stirring
> The strings of his lyre, inlaid with ivory.
> He places the gods in chorus. Deathless,
> Their voices rise in divine lamentation.[7]

Throughout this poem, which is accompanied by the aulos, the recently irreligious Tereus voices the spirit of natural religion. The songs of both Procne and the gods are called divine (*theios*). The poet refers to the throat or voice (*stoma*) of the bird and of the Olympians. In heaven Procne will stir answering music. But in his most brilliant image, often ignored in translation, Aristophanes sees the music rising through the twining foliage or locks (*phyllokomos*) of the woodbine to Apollo of the golden hair. The harmony between bird and god is complete. The lines are among the most moving in the play.

Next the Chorus of birds enters the stage. Horrified by Tereus' new friendship, they are about to make war on the two men, but Peithetaerus persuades them that with his help they can regain their ancient dominion over the gods. Once the hero has explained his strategy, the Chorus swears a firm league with the men. As Peithetaerus and Euelpides enter the Hoopoe's nest, the birds are left onstage for the Parabasis. Observing the standard arrangement in Old Comedy, the Parabasis consists mainly of a long section in anapaests followed by odes and epirrhemes (after-speeches) in alternation. It magnificently illustrates Aristophanes' double-edged poetry, now evocative, now abrasive, the satire often breaking but also enhancing the grave mood by contrast and isolation. The anapaests oscillate between the grave and the gay, the odes are exalted, and the epirrhemes sharply ironic.

The anapaests include many metrical variations, but the rhythm is well marked. What follows is an attempt to approximate the effect of the first sentence, spoken by the Leader:

Come, you men whose life is in darkness, you generation of leaves,
Whose strength is as nothing, clay-figures, a feeble, shadowy race,
You wingless, ephemeral, dark-fated mortals, creatures of dream,
To us the immortal, to us the undying, O lift up your thoughts,
To the spirits of air, to the ageless, whose counsels will never decay,
Then hearing all things from us rightly concerning far truths in the skies—
The nature of birds, the birth of the gods, of the rivers, Erebus,
Chaos—by me you can say to Prodicus: "Go, and be hanged!"

[ll.685–92]

Sheerly through his style, Aristophanes suddenly creates in his mortal audience a nostalgia for the infinite. The first three lines reawaken our dormant sense of our own fragility. Then, as the Chorus speak of themselves, they cease to be the amusing fowl of the choral entrance or the quarrel with Peithetaerus and become symbols of the flawless and immortal. There is no question of theatrical illusion here, as if the Chorus were enacting the infinite. It is rather that the long hypnotic lines create ideally and sonally what man knows he is not, yet longs to be. As the Chorus promises to inform mankind of *tôn meterôn* (things in the air or lofty speculations), a trace of characteristically Aristophanic satire may be creeping into the text. One recalls Socrates in *The Clouds*, sus-

pended in air the better to speculate and saying that if he had remained
on the ground, he would never have discovered anything about "things
that are above" (*Clouds*,1.238). Next, the mood is definitely broken as
the speaker points out that bird knowledge is so far superior to that of
the respected sophist Prodicus, he might as well close up shop. This is
Aristophanes' way of saying that the spell he has been creating is a form
of sophistry.

Benjamin Rogers has said that after Aristophanes creates a lofty or
ecstatic mood, he then feels the need to apologize for it. But since oscillating attitudes are fundamental in this playwright, it is better to assume
that from moment to moment he knows what he is doing. At any rate,
the poet's protean comic poetry simultaneously or in rapid alternation
stimulates a reaching out for the kind of certainties Socrates and Plato
insisted upon as well as an awareness that such values may be illusory.
James K. Feibleman has argued that comedy criticizes the failure of
reality to attain the ideal.[8] Aristophanes both encourages and laughs
at man's quest for the absolute.

The anapaests, so named in the text, go on to explain the development of the cosmos. At first there was only Chaos, Night, Erebus, and Tar-
tarus. Black-winged Night then hatched an unfertilized egg in the bosom
of Erebus, and from this egg Eros was born. Naturally, he too had
wings. "And when he had mingled with Chaos by night . . . , he brought
forth our race and led it up to the light of day" (ll.698–99). By this time
we know that three of the cosmic principles were air-borne. Only after
the syntheses of Love did heaven, ocean, earth, and the blessed gods
come into being.

Following this flight of fancy, the tone drops into sardonic farce:

And so we
Are by far the eldest of all the blest, and the facts make it plain
That we're children of Love; for we fly and we're always with lovers.
And masculine suitors through our strength alone have opened the thighs
Of many a beautiful, difficult boy, before youth is gone,
By the gift of a quail, a porphyrion, goose, or a Persian bird.

[ll.703–07]

From this point, the anapaests are mainly jocular, but as the poet places
the birds once again within the cycle of nature or has them say, "We
are your Ammon, Delphi, Dodona"—the spondaic feet underlining the
revered names—he demonstrates once more his astonishing ability to
escape from the patterns his own writing would seem to impose upon
him. He continually refuses to be taken in, even by his own formulations.

The strophe immediately following the anapaests and sung by the Chorus is written in logaoedic verse consisting of various meters in different lines and variations within the line.

> Poet encloistered,
>   tio tio tio tiotinx,
> Cunning singer, I with you
> In the valleys and in high places,
>   tio tio tio tiotinx,
> Taking my stand in the curling leaves of the ash,
>   tio tio tio tiotinx,
> As I draw from my tawny throat a melody,—
> For Pan I bring forth sacred hymns,
> For Cybele solemn pavanes,
> totototototototototinx,
> Where on high, like the bee,
> Phrynichus carried away
> Fruits of ambrosial melody,
> Singing his sweet song forever,
> tio tio tio tiotinx.
>
> [ll.737–52]

Addressed to the *Mousa lochmaia*, "Muse of the coppice," the poem treats the nightingale as more symbolic than actual, as the voice of man's highest aspiration toward the divine. For the moment, the contrasts between man, god, and bird have disappeared. The dramatic action is in a sense contradicted and replaced by a moving stillness. Peithetaerus, the Hoopoe, Procne, Athens, even the Chorus itself, dissolve in the hymn to creation. Not that the lines are without sensuous detail, in part reminiscent of the Hoopoe's song; but the particular is placed under the universal. Even the allusion to the pre-Aeschylean poet, Phrynichus, comes without the comic jolt usual in Aristophanes. Phrynichus lends his voice to the choir sounding in mountain and valley.

But as soon as the strophe concludes, the jolt comes in the epirrheme spoken by the Leader. He invites the spectators to join the birds if they wish to pass the rest of their lives "sweetly," for whatever is shameful (*aischra*) among men and condemned by law (*tô nomô*) is approved by the birds. Item, beating your father. In Greek tragedy the shameful is what is most to be avoided; in Aristophanes it is viewed ironically, as in the Leader's words here. The use of *nomos* also contributes to the tonal reversal. In the strophe it was the lofty song of the choristers; now it is a law to be broken with impunity among the birds. Aristophanes is of course satirizing the new advocates of *physis* as against *nomos*, but meanwhile he is using the birds as a multivalent symbol, for they can stand for what is lofty, innocent, orderly, or shameful in the life of man.[9]

Attempting to specify exactly what the birds "mean" in this play is dangerous, yet they are certainly put to significant uses. I believe it is wrong to suggest that their freedom from moral law justifies or even half-justifies the new advocates of *physis*. Aristophanes had already spoken very clearly of law and nature in *The Clouds*. Moreover, the birds are sometimes brought under law. Their songs are *nomoi*, which means that their melodies at least are in accord with musical law and tributary to the stream of nature conceived, at any rate in the odes, as a great and awe-inspiring harmony. As it invokes first Pan and Cybele, the Great Mother, and then Apollo, the Muses, and the Graces, the bird-choir is very far from a disorderly *physis*. The sardonic epirrhemes, on the other hand, tell us that many a scoundrel has used nature for his own shabby ends. In these parts of the Parabasis, the birds are in no sense the actual creatures of the natural world but are what the unscrupulous would impose upon it.

After the Parabasis, the Chorus declines in importance. They never again reassert the religious sense of a harmonious, all-embracing nature. When they speak of themselves as all-seeing and all-powerful (ll.1058–59), they immediately add that these gifts permit them to kill the insects devouring the foliage. In this stasimon, Aristophanes writes a romantic poem of the seasons, the birds dwelling by summer "in the leafy bosoms of the flowered meadows" (ll.1093–94) and by winter "in the hollow caves with the tree-nymphs" (ll.1097–98), but the poet no longer merges the natural and the divine. During the remainder of the play, the birds are either admiring assistants of Peithetaerus or cool, ironic observers of human absurdity, whether trivial or dangerous.

Clearly, the Chorus is not a character in anything like the Aeschylean or Sophoclean conception of choral character. It is rather an extremely versatile, imaginative device or point of reference. It works chiefly in these ways. (1) In the fight scene it is the angry antagonist. (2) When the Leader speaks, it is mainly a sardonic commentator on man, but as we have seen, Aristophanes can shift the Leader's stance with dazzling speed. (3) In the odes of the Parabasis, it is now the elevated voice of a creation bent on mysterious but benevolent goals and now the focus of the poet's romantic yet nontheological response to nature. (4) In the short scenes after the Parabasis, it is an assistant performing great feats at Peithetaerus' request while praising the happy ease (*hêsuchia*) of bird life. (5) During the later chorika it is an ironic poet, less direct in its commentary than the Leader had been.

At the triumphal close, the birds are completely happy. But have they been cheated? Though Peithetaerus had promised to make them the rulers of the universe in accordance with their august history, he has become an absolute master wielding the thunderbolt of Zeus. Since they do not complain, the query may be beside the point, but considering the character of Peithetaerus, it appears that they have been managed as many a nation has been by leaders like Alcibiades.

There is no more reason to suspect that Peithetaerus came to Tereus with dynastic plans than to suppose that Iago originally intended to destroy Othello. Ease had been the first wish of Peithetaerus. His ambition dates from his decision to found an ornithocracy. And if one feels the need to defend him against charges of excessive trickery and tyrannic plots, one can recall that it is Prometheus, enemy of the gods and friend of man, who first puts in his head the idea that he who would rule the world must acquire the lovely Basileia.

Like so many other elements in the play, the character of Peithetaerus is ambiguous. In what way is he superior to the fakers—the Soothsayer, the Colonial Supervisor, the Statute Seller, and the Sycophant (Informer)—he drives from the stage with ridicule and blows? Obviously in cleverness; perhaps in morality, at least by comparison with that lowest form of Athenian life, the Informer, to whom the Chorus devotes some telling lines. One way of solving the ethical ambiguity would be to say that Aristophanes distinguishes between the merry rogue and the outright scoundrel, but this is to rely on what he as a good Athenian must have felt, not on what he does in the comedy. Actually, the Informer's scene, as farcical as any other, does not carry a heavy weight of moral disapproval.

Cedric Whitman argues that the central characteristic of the Aristophanic hero is *ponêria*. The term is a development from the ancient Greek *ponêros* (worthless or villainous), but this insulting epithet sometimes has humorous overtones. At the opening of the play, for example, Euelpides cries out to his jay, "*O ponêr',*" because the bird has led him down the garden path, not to Tereus. "*Poneria* in modern Greek," says Whitman, "indicates not wickedness, but the ability to get the advantage of somebody or some situation by virtue of an unscrupulous but thoroughly enjoyable exercise of craft. Its aim is simple—to come out on top; its methods are devious, and the more intricate, the more delightful." It is a "kind of heroism . . . likely to arise during any struggle for

survival against heavy odds. . . ." Whitman finds this trait in various
Aristophanic characters, above all in Peithetaerus. He is "simply the
man of heroic *poneria* par excellence; more properly, he becomes that
in much the same way Dicaeopolis did."[10]

If Dicaeopolis is heroic, he is a heroic image, not a psychologically developed character.[11] Peithetaerus is more of a piece. Except for his
shift from the lazy to the dynamic in the opening scene, he is one of the
more consistent characters in Aristophanes. He is clever in the fight
scene, in exercising persuasion on Tereus and the Chorus, in disposing
of the intruders, and in handling the divine commission consisting of
Poseidon, Herakles, and the Triballian god. He is always ready with
word and action. When the Soothsayer reads aloud an oracle proclaim-
ing that he should receive gifts, Peithetaerus reads another saying the
fellow should be beaten. Annoyed by a wordy poet, he thrashes him with
a pair of wings, and when the poet reacts, taunts him, "So you don't like
to be winged?" (1.1402)—*pterodonêtos* meaning both "stirred by wings"
and "high-flown." As Iris enters Cloudcuckooland on her way to earth,
Peithetaerus intervenes and threatens to rape her, and when, in massive
Aeschylean language, she warns him of Zeus' mattock and thunderbolt, he ridicules her with her own splendid words. But his masterpiece is his success in persuading the Chorus to take up its divine mission.

His argument is a burlesque oration regularly interrupted by farcical
jokes from Euelpides and troubled questions from the Chorus. Peithetaerus proves that the birds were the first gods, then laments their sad decline to the dinner table, where they are served with sauces and grated
cheese, and finally shows in detail how birds can subdue gods and men.
If the lark, as Aesop says, had at first nowhere to bury her father, then,
forsooth, the lark must be older than the earth. If the cock is the Persian
bird, that is because he was once the king of Persia. In fact, even today
we all jump out of bed when we hear him crow. The eagle, not merely
the symbol of Zeus' royalty, was in fact that royalty itself. The hawk was
the power of Apollo, the owl was the wisdom of Athena.

The hero's assurance that men will yield to the birds is supported by
two excellent sophisms. When the Chorus fears that men will never accept birds ("we who have wings") as gods, Peithetaerus replies that
Hermes, Victory, Eros, and Iris have wings. The answer is formally correct but bypasses the real meaning of the question. Later, as the hero explains the benefits which the birds can legitimately offer men if they accept the new rule, the Chorus wonders if it can promise health, the gift
of the gods. He replies, "If things go well with men, isn't that good

health? Just remember that if things go badly, no man is truly healthy."
(ll.604–5). The denial of health to the unlucky neatly covers up the
failure to prove that the lucky are well.

In 414 B.C. Gorgias was one of the leading sophists in the Greek
world. A dozen years earlier he had sailed from Leontini in Sicily, urging
Athenian assistance to his city against Syracuse. Near the close of *The
Birds*, a choral ode charges him with making money by tricky use of his
tongue and even links him with the Athenian sycophants. But it looks
as if "Peithetaerus knows his Gorgias,"[12] or at least the kind of argu-
mentation associated with him.

A version of his philosophic work, *Not-Being and Nature*, has sur-
vived. In this treatise he maintains that nothing exists, that even granted
existence, it cannot be known, and that if known, it cannot be communicated. Since he made his living as a teacher of rhetoric, he seems to be
talking himself out of a job. This is a part of his argument:

> Moreover, Being does not exist either. For if Being does exist, it either
> has come into being, or always was, or both has come into being and al-
> ways was. But it neither has come into being, nor always was, nor both
> has come into being and always was, as we shall show. Being, then, does
> not exist. For if Being always was . . . it does not have any beginning, for
> everything which comes into existence has a beginning, but that which
> always was, not not having come into existence, does not have any be-
> ginning, and not having any beginning it is infinite. If, moreover, it is
> infinite, it is nowhere.[13]

If Gorgias was really arguing this way during the late fifth century, how
could a comic playwright react if not with Gargantuan laughter? There
is plenty of evidence that Aristophanes found the sophists vastly amusing, if also "unjust." As is appropriate to Nephelococcygia, the hero's
reasoning carries unreal verbal gymnastics to even greater heights than
any sophist is likely to have reached. We are in a realm where sober
logic and morality fall out of focus. The point of an argument is to miss
the point. Such is the atmosphere during Peithetaerus' triumph of persuasion.

Whitman's chapter on *The Birds* is entitled "The Anatomy of Noth-
ingness," as if to suggest the influence of Gorgias. But we should not
identify the comic logic in the play with the radical scepticism advanced
by the sophist. The thematic structure of the play is too fluid, disengaged, and ironic to suggest a positive commitment, even to scepticism.
Through his dramatic sleight-of-hand, Aristophanes can have his hero
push sophistic reasoning to extremes so absurd and so entertaining

that they cease to be immoral and even become sympathetic, while at the same time they imply a criticism of fraud in the real world. This criticism is made explicit in the choral ode satirizing Gorgias.[14]

At the end of the play Peithetaerus has overcome the opposition of the birds, the intruders, and the gods themselves, shown in person as a committee of three. Herakles and the Triballian god are burlesque figures. Poseidon is conceived differently. He is serious, intelligent, dignified, as a god should be. What do these two approaches to divinity signify? One should not assume that the scene is impious, for Greek religion tolerated liberties not permitted by Hebrew or Christian doctrine. But beyond mere playfulness, Aristophanes is probably suggesting that men conceive their gods in their own image. Triballos is the deity not only of barbarians but of barbarous men. Herakles is the god of those a step higher toward civilization. When Poseidon, outvoted by his stupid colleagues, exclaims at the sins committed in the name of democracy, Aristophanes may be implying that the Athenian view of the Olympians could be greatly improved. Certainly Peithetaerus ought to make a better ruler than an average constructed from the three commissioners.

Action, character, and language create for *The Birds* an iridescent plumage defying attempts to name the precise color of the comedy. Fantastic, ecstatic, buffoonish, grave, and satiric by turns as the light of the poet's mind strikes it from various directions, its total effect is one of flashing irony. Glancing at Gorgias, Prodicus, Alcibiades, Nikias, and indeed at the whole Greek community, it makes no prescriptions for Athens. But by its very form and quality, its brilliant shifts and conversions, it exemplifies that elasticity of mind a city always needs and seldom finds, except in its comic poets.

NOTES

1. A. Meder, as quoted by Victor Ehrenberg, *The People of Aristophanes*, 2d ed. (Cambridge, Mass., 1951), p. 9n.

2. *Paideia: The Ideals of Greek Culture*, trans. G. Highet (Oxford, 1939), I, 362.

3. "Aristophanes and Politics," *CR*, LII (1938), 97.

4. See, for example, Gilbert Murray, *Aristophanes* (New York, 1933), pp. 135–63; and E. M. Blaiklock, "Walking Away from the News," *Greece and Rome*, 2d series, I (1954), 98–111.

5. Thucydides, VI,i, *The Peloponnesian War*, trans. R. Crawley (New York, 1934), p. 338.

6. See Webster's discussion of Cornford's theory in A. W. Pickard-Cambridge,

Dithyramb, Tragedy, and Comedy, 2d ed., rev. by T. B. L. Webster (Oxford, 1962), pp. 192–94.

7.   *The Birds*, ll. 209–22. The lines are in free anapaestic measure. For the Greek text I have used *The Birds of Aristophanes*, ed. B. B. Rogers (London, 1906). Much of my information comes from Rogers' full and excellent notes.

8.   "The Meaning of Comedy," in *In Praise of Comedy* (New York, 1962). Cf. Walter Kerr: "Comedy will speak of nothing but limitation" (*Tragedy and Comedy* [New York, 1967], p. 146).

9.   There is an excellent analysis of *nomos* and other ambiguous words in the play in Cedric Whitman, *Aristophanes and the Comic Hero* (Cambridge, 1964), Chapter V. Whitman's book is much the best literary study of Aristophanes known to me.

10.   Whitman, pp. 30, 34, 170.

11.   See above, p. 69.

12.   Whitman, p. 174.

13.   From Sextus Empiricus, *Adversus Mathematicos*, trans. C. P. Osborne, in *Philosophers Speak for Themselves*, ed. T. V. Smith (Chicago, 1934), p. 66.

14.   The ode begins: "In Phanae [sycophant-land] there is a shifty race of Englottogastors who reap and sow and pluck and gather figs with their tongues." Gorgias is one of them. The tone flickers between the harshly satiric and the joking. The word for "pluck" (*trugôsi*, l. 1698) is related to *trugôdia*, a word for comedy. If there is a pun here, it helps to keep the satire from becoming too harsh. The grotesque compound "Englottogastors" also helps to preserve the balance.

CHAPTER SEVEN

The Role of Wit in Much Ado About Nothing

Much Ado About Nothing ranks high with audiences but somewhat less so with critics. Although they concede it to be a very witty drama, critics find it lacking in that profounder quibbling that characterizes Shakespeare's later work. In her book entitled *Shakespeare's Word-play*, M. M. Mahood gives a chapter to *The Winter's Tale* but not to *Much Ado About Nothing*. One may feel too that the play is less serious than Shakespeare's witty sonnets—for example, in its exploration of love. So far as the verse is concerned, it does not lead one to think of the play as a poem. It has a good deal of rather elementary rhetoric, as in Leonato's lamentations, and although there are passages of charm and delicacy, perhaps no one would maintain that as poetry the writing ever equals the opening of *Twelfth Night* or Viola's "Make me a willow cabin." In fact, one of the most successful verse passages in the play—Hero's satire on the "lapwing" Beatrice—has the salience of wit rather than the ambience of poetry. The main plot of the play is certainly not the chief interest, and the central characters in this plot would never stimulate an A. C. Bradley. Moreover, the three main strands of action do not at first seem very well joined. The sudden appearance of Dogberry and his men in Act Three, for example, comes as quite a jolt on the path of the action. The role of Margaret is mysterious, to say the least; only by straining can we think of her various activities as congruent.

William Empson once remarked that the greatness of English drama did not survive the double plot. Partially under Empson's influence, recent Shakespearian criticism is in general looking for Shakespeare's unities not in plot or character, or even characteristic action, but in theme. Actually the theme of a play, if dramatically significant, is worked out in action, and conversely a particular action can be translated into

139

theme. If one says, as does John Russell Brown,[1] that the theme of *Much Ado* is love's truth, the governing action (the activity guiding the characters) could be formulated as the search in love for the truth about love—though where this would leave Dogberry is a bit hard to say. In a keen study of the comedy, James Smith found pride, or comic hubris, the binding agent in an action presenting a shallow society whose superficiality is finally transcended by Benedick and Beatrice.[2] The analysis is illuminating, but I believe it pushes the comedy too far in the direction of satire and understates the role of wit, which in both its main senses drives the play.

During a performance of a Shakespearian comedy one sometimes notices that his neighbors are laughing at a line before the point has been made, or in ignorance of the exact meaning of the sentence, unless they have been studying footnotes. (This assumes that witticisms and jokes have exact meanings—not always a safe assumption.) One may feel a slightly superior sympathy for such an audience—they are so eager to enjoy what their piety has brought them to witness.

Yet this solicitude may be misplaced. For a witticism may be delightful and funny even if understood in a sense slightly different from that advanced by Professor Kittredge or Dover Wilson. When Beatrice says that Benedick "wears his faith but as the fashion of his hat; it ever changes with the next block,"[3] the audience laughs though it may not know whether "block" is a hat block, a fashionable hat shape, a blockhead, or some combination of these. Secondly, if the actor has been advised to "throw away" the line as highly obscure and to create instead a visual and musical impression of wit, the audience can hardly be expected to laugh for the "right" reason. And finally, if Susanne Langer is right, the point of the line is not primary anyway; for Mrs. Langer advances the interesting idea that when an audience laughs, it does so not at a particular joke or witticism but at the play. In *Much Ado*, at any rate, wit is organic.

The wit of Shakespeare's play informs the words spoken by the characters, places the characters themselves as truly witty and intelligent, inappropriately facetious, or ingeniously witless, suggests the lines of action these characters will take, and as intelligence, plays a fundamental role in the thematic action: the triumphing of true wit (or wise folly) in alliance with harmless folly over false or pretentious wisdom. I will further suggest that the comedy itself is a kind of witticism in the tripartite form often taken by the jests.

As language, the wit has a variety of functions. From the first it creates the tone of "merry war" which will resound through so much of the comedy, though the timbre will change as the scenes or speakers change. The merry war is primarily between Benedick and Beatrice, but in the opening scenes Leonato, Don Pedro, Claudio, and even Hero participate in the skirmishing. Even before Don Pedro arrives with his party, we find Leonato experimenting with word-play. Hearing that Claudio's uncle has wept at the news of the young man's martial exploits, Leonato remarks: "a kind overflow of kindness. . . . How much better is it to weep at joy than to joy at weeping" (I,i,27–28). It is as if he knew that some witty friends were coming to visit and he had better try out a pun and an antimetabole—a rhetorical figure popular in the earlier nineties. Since there has been no question of taking pleasure in tears, one tends to downgrade the speaker for this verbal flourish. But he may be more shrewd than this when, a bit later, he chides Beatrice for ridiculing Benedick: "Faith, niece, you tax Signior Benedick too much; but he'll be meet with you, I doubt it not" (I,i,44–45). Since "meet" and "mate" were pronounced alike, Leonato is not only referring to Benedick's powers of retaliation, but predicting the happy and voluble ending.

After establishing his fundamentally witty tone in the first three acts, Shakespeare almost destroys it in the church scene. But notice the language in which Claudio rejects Hero and Leonato responds to the scandal. There is the outburst of Claudio—

> O, what men dare do! What men may do!
> What men daily do, not knowing what they do!
>
> [IV,i,18–19]

—a rhetorical display so hollow as to bring on this burlesque from Benedick: "How now? Interjections? Why then, some be of laughing, as, ah, ha, he!" As the scene progresses, Claudio's speeches rely more and more on the verbal tricks recorded in the rhetorical texts of the time. His half-ridiculous, half-pathetic pun "O Hero! What a Hero hadst thou been" is a parody of the wit crowding the early scenes. When he says:

> . . . fare thee well, most foul, most fair, farewell;
> Thou pure impiety and impious purity . . .
>
> [IV,i,102–3]

the idiom is of the kind that Shakespeare will overtly ridicule at the turn of the century. Leonato's response to the rejection is equally conventional:

> But mine, and mine I loved, and mine I praised,
> And mine that I was proud on, mine so much
> That I myself was to myself not mine. . . .
>
> [IV,i,135–37]

The tone is precariously balanced between seriousness and levity. I believe that the scene has to be played for what it is worth and should not
be deliberately distanced; otherwise the grief and anger of Beatrice will
be unfounded; but if the dialogue is recognized as a distortion of wit,
the scene becomes a grim sequel to the opening scenes and not an absolute break with them.

It is often difficult to separate style for tonal effect from style for characterization. But to put it in Renaissance terms, the decorum of the
genre will sometimes take precedence over the decorum of the speaker.
Critics like Stoll and Bradbrook have shown that the Elizabethans were
frequently ready to drop consistency of characterization for tonal or
other reasons. Margaret seems to illustrate the point. She is a witty lady-
in-waiting, on excellent terms with both Hero and Beatrice, but the plot
demands that she play her foolish part in the famous window scene that
almost destroys Hero. After the rejection of her mistress, we see Margaret enjoying herself in a bawdy dialogue with Benedick, for all the
world as if we were still in Act One. It is true that Hero has just been exonerated, but presumably Margaret does not yet know this. At the end
of the preceding scene (V,i), Borachio has assured Leonato of Margaret's innocence of treachery to her mistress, but Leonato wants to
know more. The men leave the stage, whereupon Benedick and Margaret enter for a set of wit. It is well played. But if we are trying to make
sense of Margaret, we are puzzled. As she must be aware, her foolishness has been a main cause of all the distress, and she supposedly does
not know of the happy solution brought about by Dogberry's men; if
she does know, she also realizes that her role at the window is now revealed. Is she so indifferent to what has happened? Apparently we are
not supposed to raise this question. Margaret asks Benedick if he will
write a sonnet to her beauty.

BENEDICK. In so high a style, Margaret, that no man living shall come
    over it; for in most comely truth thou deservest it.
MARGARET. To have no man come over me! Why, shall I always keep be-
    lowstairs?

[V,ii,6–10]

In view of her involvement with the tool villain Borachio, one is tempted
to say, "That is where she belongs." But the moral reaction is uncalled
for. Margaret is here a representative of wit from the lady-in-waiting,
and her quibble is related to her earlier wit but not to her earlier sub-
stantive behavior. Her wit at this moment is a bit crude. When Beatrice
comes in a minute later, she will reveal a continuing concern for Hero

along with a continuing mental agility. We can say that the two women represent two varieties of wit, though Beatrice is also clear as a character.

One has to distinguish between the seemingly ill-timed roguishness of Margaret and the really insensitive banter of the Prince and Claudio in Act Five. Margaret makes no reference whatever to Hero, Leonato, or the painful episode of Act Four. But in Act Five, Scene One, after Leonato and his brother Antonio have quarreled with Claudio and Don Pedro over Hero and left the stage, Benedick enters, whereupon Claudio remarks, "We had liked to have had our two noses snapped off with two old men without teeth" (ll.115–16). This is bad enough. Then, in view of Hero's supposed death, his cheery "What though care killed a cat" is one of his worst gaffes. When Benedick challenges his friend and tells him he has killed Hero, Claudio promises that in the duel he will "carve a capon." As the scene continues he and the Prince struggle to revive the tone of Act One. As word-play, their language is much the same as ever, but neither Benedick nor the reader is in the mood for jocose references to "the old man's daughter," as if Hero were still happy. Stage directors and audiences seem ready to go along with the struggling wits at this point, but the reader's judgment is the right one: the scene makes a sardonic comment on the Prince and his young friend and gives supporting evidence of the ineptitude previously illustrated. The wit *in this context* downgrades the two lords.

Apart from placing the characters, the play of wit indicates in advance the way the action will go. Where the repartee is not clearly out of place, the wittier speakers will prefigure in language the wit or intelligence of their acts. Benedick and Beatrice are the shrewdest in speech and with the Friar are the first to reject the rejection of Hero. What of Claudio's jests? At first they seem technically equal to Benedick's, but on closer inspection, we notice that Claudio tends to repeat in somewhat different words the jests of the Prince. If Don Pedro heckles the amorous Benedick with "Nay, 'a rubs himself with civet. Can you smell him out by that?" Claudio will add, "That's as much as to say, the sweet youth's in love" (III,ii,48–51). There may be a groundswell of laughter in the second line, but its point hardly differs from the other. If Don Pedro says that Beatrice has been ridiculing Benedick and then sighing for him, Claudio will chime in: "For the which she wept heartily and said she cared not" (V,i,172–73). This echolalia illustrates the lack of independence which will cause him to swallow the slander of Don John and mirror the response made by the Prince. "O day untowardly turned!" says Don Pedro; and Claudio: "O mischief strangely thwarting!" (III,ii,127–28). Language is here the perfect expression of action, or rather of action descending toward comic automatism.

When Shakespeare was writing *Much Ado*, "wit" as mental agility or liveliness of fancy had rather recently come to supplement "wit" as intelligence. (A passage from Lyly is the first listing in *N.E.D.* of the newer use.[4]) Both senses occur frequently in the play, and there are examples of overlapping. It seems clear, for example, that in the following dialogue, Dogberry is preening himself not only on his intelligence but on a handling of language so ingenious that it will drive the accused out of their minds:

DOGBERRY. . . . We are now to examination these men.
VERGES. And we must do it wisely.
DOGBERRY. We will spare for no wit, I warrant you; here's that shall drive some of them to a non-come.

[III,v,57–60]

Benedick and Beatrice are witty and are described as witty and wise by their peers, and again both ideas get into the word "witty."

The word "wit" (or "witty") occurs over twenty times, and one-third of these examples cluster in Act Five, Scene One, the scene in which Don Pedro and Claudio are flogging the dialogue. According to Benedick the wit does no more than amble in spite of the whip. As the scene progresses, one becomes weary of the verbal effort. After Benedick leaves, the Prince comments on his uncooperativeness: "What a pretty thing is man when he goes in his doublet and hose and leaves off his wit" (V,i,198–99). Here the word suggests that for the idle nobility wit is a fashionable accessory you put on for lack of something else to do. In no other scene does this sub-sense (or Mood of "wit," in Empson's terminology[5]) make itself felt.

In the drama, a particular witticism has three dimensions: the character's motivation for the speech, the technique, and the effect in context. A full criticism of a particular mot would have to consider all three. As Freud points out in his study of wit, a joke may be far more powerful than an examination of its technique would reveal: it may be poor in technique but strong in motive or "tendency." In a play, if a character's motive is strong, it may justify, in dramatic terms, what would be merely crude. Or if we share his animus, we will give way to hard laughter. In Act One Beatrice sometimes attacks Benedick in terms so unsubtle as to amaze—unless we realize that the insults express a half-conscious anger over his past treatment of her. At such moments we see the "wild" spirit of the "haggard of the rock" (III,i,35–36), in Hero's phrase for her. The *effect* of a joke emerges in part from motive and technique but may extend far beyond these. After Beatrice has given a satiric picture of marriage, we have this:

LEONATO. Cousin, you apprehend passing shrewdly.
BEATRICE. I have a good eye, uncle; I can see a church by daylight.
[II,i,81–82]

Leonato's speech is a mild rebuke but also an appreciation. The power of her unforgettable reply is remarkable, considering the simplicity of the technique, ironic understatement; but apart from the doubt whether she is speaking modestly or proudly, the line looks back to her own hardly masked fears of spinsterhood and forward to marriage in general and Hero's ill-omened ceremony in particular, when Beatrice will not only see the church but see better than most what is really happening there.

The technique of wit in *Much Ado* might be classified under four main heads: (1) verbal identifications and contrasts including puns, quibbles, and sharp antitheses; (2) conceptual wit including allusive understatement and sophistical logic; (3) amusing flights of fancy; (4) short parodies, burlesques, etc. The first heading begins with the pun, as where it is said that Beatrice wrote to Benedick and found them both "between the sheets." Claudio calls this a "pretty jest," but Shakespeare uses the pun rather sparingly in this play. Much more frequent are the quibbles wherein a speaker deliberately mis-takes a word for his own purposes. Typically, a word used metaphorically is suddenly given a literal sense: the Messenger says that Benedick is not in Beatrice's "books," and she replies, "No. And he were, I would burn my study" (I,i,76). One is reminded of Bergson's principle that it is comic to introduce the physical where the spiritual is at issue. At the opposite extreme from the pun is the sharp antithesis, as in Don John's assertion, "Though I cannot be said to be a flattering honest man, it must not be denied but I am a plain-dealing villain" (I,iii,28–30). Here, of course, the wit includes paradox.

I would suggest that, in comedy at least, the pun is a sign of harmony, the quibble or mis-taking is a ripple on the surface of social life, and the antithesis an index of separation or selfishness. The pun is obviously social and in comedy is seldom bitterly satiric. Even Claudio's silly "what a Hero hadst thou been" is a sigh after vanished good relations. Or one could cite Margaret's use of the pun as coquetry in her scene with Benedick. The quibble may be petty, but it is heavily dependent on what has just been said and may tacitly accept it. When Don Pedro declares that he will get Beatrice a husband, she replies that she would prefer one of his father's getting. The new meaning does not reject the old but merely improves it. The antithesis of Don John, on the other hand, flatly rejects the concept of "honest man," for like Goethe's Mephistopheles, John is the spirit that always denies. Since *Much Ado* is neither a jolly farce nor a morality play, it fittingly emphasizes mistakings as opposed to puns and antitheses.

Freud's category of conceptual jokes or wit includes the play of ideas and playfully false logic.[6] The joke in Gogol, "Your cheating is excessive for an official of your rank," is conceptual, but it would become more abstract if transposed into the key of La Rochefoucauld as follows: "If a man appears honest, it is merely because his dishonesties are fitted to his position in life." Obviously the latter form is too abstract for *Much Ado* though not for the tragedies. But in the mercurial world of *Much Ado*, Shakespeare infiltrates ideas less directly:

DON PEDRO. . . . . I think this is your daughter.
LEONATO. Her mother hath many times told me so.
BENEDICK. Were you in doubt, sir, that you asked her?
LEONATO. Signior Benedick, no; for then you were a child.

[I,i,100–104]

Leonato's first pleasantry is standard social chit-chat, and no more critical than Prospero's "Thy mother was a piece of virtue, and / She said thou wast my daughter" (*Tempest*, I,ii,56–57). But Benedick's rude interruption, a quasi-quibble, pricks the complacencies of a cliché-ridden society. If his question is liberal, Leonato's reply is conservative: except for a few men like you, life in Messina is eminently respectable.

A good example of false logic in the service of true wit appears in Benedick's great soliloquy, which he speaks after hearing that Beatrice loves him. Faced with his own absolute opposition to marriage, he is capable of this: "Shall quips and sentences and these paper bullets of the brain awe a man from the career of his humor? No, the world must be peopled. When I said I would die a bachelor, I did not think I should live till I were married" (II,iii,236–40). Previously he had boasted that he would never decide to marry. Deserting that premise, he now pretends that the anticipated decision to marry can be taken as a mere occurrence happening to a thing innocent of choice. Involved in the complexity of the thought, however, is the speaker's awareness that to fall in love is to become a thing—an accident to which he gracefully acknowledges himself liable. The soliloquy promotes Benedick from social critic to self-critic. He is now ready to appreciate the *maxime* of La

Rochefoucauld: "It is a great folly to wish to be wise all alone."[7] It is a crucial moment in the play.

At moments, Beatrice or Benedick will launch into an extended flight of fancy that moves distinctly away from its environment, particularly because the play is dominated by prose. Benedick will describe a series of fantastic expeditions to escape Beatrice, or Beatrice will picture herself on a private harrowing of hell. Beatrice's comparison of wooing, wedding, and repentance to a Scotch jig, a measure, and a cinquepace is halfway between the conceptual wit just described and Shakespeare's more densely "tropical" style. Each of the dance steps is characterized as if it were a dramatic person, and all three encourage the actress to demonstrate. Like poor Yorick, Beatrice is a creature of "gambols," "of infinite jest, of most excellent fancy."

Outright burlesque or parody is used infrequently but significantly. When Beatrice asks Benedick if he will come to hear the news of Hero, he replies: "I will live in thy heart, die in thy lap, and be buried in thy eyes; and moreover, I will go with thee to thy uncle's" (V,ii,100–103). This good-natured burlesque of the Petrarchan tradition affirms what we already knew, that Benedick will never make a conventional lover. Beatrice parodies Petrarchanism with deeper ironic effect:

DON PEDRO. Come, lady, come; you have lost the heart of Signior Benedick.
BEATRICE. Indeed, my lord, he lent it me awhile, and I gave him use for it, a double heart for his single one. . . . Marry, once before he won it of me with false dice; therefore your Grace may well say I have lost it.

[II,i,273–79]

In this moment she moves close to the atmosphere of the more somber sonnets. The exploitation of the "usury" of love and of the dialectic of hearts recalls some of the opening sonnets as well as the more intense poems to the Dark Lady.

Although the technique of wit in Beatrice's speech is good, it seems unimportant except as a revelation of motive or "tendency," in Freud's language. Nowhere else does Beatrice reveal so much of the reason underlying her war with Benedick, merry on the surface but now clearly shown to be serious underneath. If the seriousness were not there, she could scarcely keep her place as the wittiest of Shakespeare's characters. Beatrice had given her heart to Benedick as interest for his, but at the same time he received his own back again. But clearly there was another occasion when Beatrice felt she had been deceived into uncover-

ing too much affection for him. In the nineteenth century such a motivation would bring on a suicide; in Shakespeare's play, it deepens the wit.

Seen as character, wit in *Much Ado* is awareness and the ability to act
discerningly. As is already obvious, the awareness is largely the property
of the talkative lovers. Such wit proves to be an Erasmian sensitivity to
one's own folly. I have already referred to Benedick's increasing knowledge of his own limitations. Beatrice understands herself earlier. In the
first scene she says to the Messenger: "[Benedick] set up his bills here
in Messina and challenged Cupid at the flight; and my uncle's fool, reading the challenge, subscribed for Cupid and challenged him at the bur-
bolt" (I,i,37–40). Dover Wilson thought she might be referring to a
jester appearing in an earlier version of the play, but David Stevenson
makes the excellent suggestion that the fool is Beatrice herself.[8] Other
details strengthen the idea. Beatrice recalls the loss of her heart to Benedick. At another moment she names this heart a "poor fool." She fears
that if she yields to Benedick, she will prove the "mother of fools." On
which side of the family does she discern the folly? After entertaining the
Prince with her merriment, she apologizes by saying: "I was born to
speak all mirth and no matter." If she were a professional fool, she would
not need to apologize.

At the masked ball, she calls Benedick the Prince's jester. The barb
stings, for Benedick does not yet know who he is. But since there is no
Feste or Touchstone in the cast, Shakespeare evidently decided to let
Benedick and Beatrice serve as surrogates for the "allowed" fool. Like
the court jesters, they stand somewhat apart from their society. Beatrice
is uncontrolled by an immediate family, and like Touchstone both lovers
shoot their wit from behind the stalking horse of a merry madness. While
he is heart-whole, Benedick thinks love a "shallow folly"—almost the
phrase Borachio applies to the Watch—but after being tricked by his
friends, he thinks Beatrice's love for him "no addition to her wit, nor no
great argument of her folly; for I will be horribly in love with her"— as
if the folly of his love would prevent folly in her. He would now rather
be a witty fool than a foolish wit.

Beatrice's soliloquy following Hero's fictional account of Benedick's
love has its place in a prettily lyrical scene in verse (III,i), and perhaps
for this reason Shakespeare does not permit her the prose to which she is
"native and indued." Instead, she speaks part of a sonnet—two quatrains
and a couplet in regular verse and simple sentiments. How should they
be spoken? They lack the conscious humor of Benedick's parallel soliloquy, and as ecstasy they are a bit subdued. Some performers attempt to
make this moment as romantic as possible, but I have seen an actress

give the whole speech as if Beatrice felt very foolish in this new situation, a girl suddenly not at all confident of her own wit and attractiveness, something of a hoyden who has just realized that her special superiority may be close to sham. This seems to me the right interpretation, though it may do some violence to the formality of the writing. The verse form itself embarrasses her, and she has only a few more lines of verse in the whole play; these occur in the first half of the church scene, when prose would be indecorous. When next we see her after the gulling scene, she has a cold, is taciturn, and has to be prodded into wit by Margaret. This scene confirms the anti-romantic interpretation of Beatrice's soliloquy; in both passages she is ill at ease.

Once Benedick and Beatrice have understood themselves, they are ready to act appropriately in the affair of Claudio and Hero. In the marriage scene Benedick immediately senses something deranged in Claudio's heroics, and when Hero faints under slanderous attack, Beatrice immediately reveals her judgment: "Why, how now, cousin? Wherefore sink you down?" (IV,i,109). Whereas Leonato is completely convinced by the evidence, Beatrice is certain that Hero has been "belied."

Only after Beatrice has spoken out does the Friar join the defense of Hero. He has accurately read her character in her face.

> Call me a fool;
> Trust not my reading nor my observations,
> Which with experimental seal doth warrant
> The tenor of my book; trust not my age,
> My reverence, calling, nor divinity,
> If this sweet lady lie not guiltless here
> Under some biting error.
>
> [IV,i,163–69]

At this moment he alone shares the wit of Benedick and Beatrice. Significantly, this man, who combines observation, insight, learning, and the favor of God, is ready to be called a fool.

If wit marks the style and characterizes the dramatic persons in varying degrees, it is also the key to the "action"—taking this word in the Stanislavskian sense as that focused drive which unites all the larger and smaller activities of the play. From this point of view, the action of *Much Ado* is the struggle of true wit (or wise folly) in alliance with harmless folly against false wisdom. Don John, Borachio, Don Pedro, Claudio, and even Leonato represent in very different ways the false wisdom which deceives others or itself; Benedick, Beatrice, and the Friar embody the true wit which knows or learns humility. If we group the characters in this way, the conclusion of the play becomes more than the discovery of the truth about Hero followed by the double marriage but includes the triumph of true wit over false wisdom. The dominant tone of the play, however, finally softens the dichotomy I have suggested. The stupidities of the fine gentlemen are half-forgotten in the festive spirit of the close.

This interpretation of the basic action throws light on moments which might otherwise seem weakly articulated. One of these is the apparently rambling recital of Borachio to Conrade, as the Watch listen. These men, of course, stand for harmless folly as Borachio represents false wisdom. It was he who devised the entire plan to destroy Hero and who said, "My cunning shall not shame me" (II,ii,55). His long digression under the penthouse emphasizes that although fashion—here equated with appearance—"is nothing to a man" (III,iii,119), young hotbloods will be deceived by it as Claudio had been deceived by Margaret's disguise. Borachio is shrewd enough to see the shallowness of the Claudios whom he can deceive but not wise enough to avoid boasting of his success.

Various references to fashion constitute a minor theme related to the theme of wisdom true and false. Preoccupation with fashion is a sign of immaturity or lack of wit. The unconverted Benedick is laughed at for being over-conscious of fashion, but in the climactic scene Beatrice flays the Claudios of society for their superficial and chic manners; "Manhood," she says, "is melted into cursies, valor into compliment, and men are only turned into tongue, and trim ones too" (IV,i,317–19). In his quarrel with Claudio, Antonio makes the same point. Antonio, who is often seen as a farcical dotard, strongly attacks "scambling, outfacing, fashionmonging boys" (V,i,94). Properly read, the speech puts this old man on the side of wit as opposed to shallowness and takes its place in the not always obvious hierarchy of wisdom and folly.

A good play, like a good witticism, has a beginning, a middle, and an end. *Much Ado* is not only like wit; it can be seen as a witticism in tripartite form—the joke, of course, is on Claudio. In Freud's study of wit, there is a classification called "representation through the opposite." Like many other kinds of wit, this kind has three parts. It makes an assertion, seems to reaffirm it, but then denies it. A good example occurs in the following exchange from *Henry IV*, Part I:

GLENDOWER. I can call spirits from the vasty deep.
HOTSPUR. Why, so can I, or so can any man;
But will they come when you do call for them?

[III,i,53–55]

Other witty exchanges can be reduced to the form: no, maybe, no—as here:

LEONATO. You will never run mad, niece.
BEATRICE. No, not till a hot January.

[I,i,89–90]

Beatrice agrees, seems to have doubts, then agrees doubly. Many other examples of this tripartite form could be cited. I shall merely refer again to the comparison of wooing, wedding, and repentance to three dance steps. Here the witty sketch is a three-act play in little.

In the examples just given, the final proposition is not, of course, a simple denial or affirmation of the first. If the wit is to succeed, the climax must gain power through an obliquity which deceives expectation. The same method appears in some of the more ingenious sonnets. Sonnet 139, "O call not me to justify the wrong," has the following structure. (1) The lover asks the Dark Lady to refrain from wounding him by her straying glances. (2) He argues that she is kind in looking aside since "her pretty looks have been mine enemies." (3) He replies that since her eyes have almost slain him already, they might as well kill him "outright" by looking straight at him. The conclusion returns to the opening, but with a crucial variation.

The beginning, middle, and end of *Much Ado* are not hard to name. The beginning is the successful wooing of the pure Hero. The middle is Claudio's conviction that she is impure: "Out on thee, seeming! I will write against it" (IV,i,55). The end is the exoneration of Hero; but notice the words of Claudio:

> Sweet Hero, now thy image doth appear
> In the rare semblance that I loved it first.

[V,i,252–53]

By this time the audience is convinced that the fashionmonging boy will never penetrate the reality lying beyond semblance. This is the joke on Claudio. He and his bride do not see the point, but the audience can hardly miss it.

As the play draws to its festive close, one might ask whether the friendship between Benedick and Claudio has essentially altered. The last scene would hardly be the place or time to say so. But in a final exchange, Benedick says: "For thy part, Claudio, I did think to have beaten thee; but in that thou art like to be my kinsman, live unbruised, and love my cousin." He must know that it will take some wit to do so.

NOTES

1. *Shakespeare and His Comedies*, 2d ed. (London, 1962), pp. 109–23.

2. "*Much Ado About Nothing*," *Scrutiny*, XIII (1946), 242–57.

3. I,i, 71–73, in *Much Ado About Nothing*, ed. David L. Stevenson, in The Signet Classic Shakespeare (New York, 1964). Citations from *Much Ado* will be to this edition.

4. But William G. Crane shows that this sense goes back another forty years or more. See his *Wit and Rhetoric in the Renaissance* (New York, 1937), pp. 19–20.

5. *The Structure of Complex Words* (London, 1951), pp. 17, 85.

6. *Jokes and Their Relation to the Unconscious*, trans. James Strachey (New York, 1960), pp. 74ff.

7. *Maximes*, III,231, in La Rochefoucauld, *Maximes suivies d'extraits des moralistes du XVIIe siècle*, ed. J.-Roger Charbonnel (Paris, n.d.), p. 24.

8. Introduction, *Much Ado About Nothing*, p. xxviii.

CHAPTER EIGHT

On the Edge of Comedy: Jonson's Bartholomew Fair

In *Bartholomew Fair*, Jonson presents a staggering society in which all men have lost their rightful places, each man preys on every other, and the ruthless scoundrels devour the kindly but unlamented fools. On a fairground where the familiar Jonsonian pimps, thieves, fools, and brutal gentlemen circulate in the dust and stench, an ironic comedy unfolds, less savage and far less moral than *Volpone* but even more authoritative in its representation of a deranged world.

As is well known, Jonson found many parallels between Jacobean England and imperial Rome—the Rome of Petronius, Martial, and Juvenal. The life of *Bartholomew Fair* is in part what Jonson's penetrating eye had observed in his city but it also owes a great deal to his reading. C. H. Herford has spoken of the "amplitude of squalid and unsavoury erudition"[1] in the play. It is not long before this erudition, savoured or not, makes itself felt, harmonizing as it does with the quality of Jonson's observation. In the opening scene, the fine gentleman, Winwife, has come to Littlewit's home, to court the rich widow, Dame Purecraft. Winwife's friend, Quarlous, soon appears and in a prodigiously long speech satirizes Winwife's suit. The speech can hardly have been given in full when the play was produced in 1614, for Jonson's Induction sets the running time of the play at two and a half hours whereas the text as we have it would surely run more than four. Moreover, the speech is full of that "license" of which Jonson, in his Epilogue addressed to King James, had said:

> *You* [James] *can tell*
> *if we haue us'd that* leaue *you gaue us, well*:
> *Or whether wee to* rage, *or* license *breake.* . . .

Jonson must have greatly expanded Quarlous's speech after the year of production, or restored the cut portions, in order to present more fully a life he found both fascinating and repellent.

153

The most vivid speeches in *Bartholomew Fair* are often the most pornographic, and this is one of the most vivid. As Jonsonian scholars have
pointed out, the climax of the speech adapts some particularly brutal
lines from Martial and Juvenal. To quote only the sentences inspired by
Jonson's classical reading:

I'll be sworne, some of them, (that thou art, or hast beene a Suitor to) are
so old, as no chast or marryed pleasure can euer become 'hem: the honest
Instrument of procreation, has (forty yeeres since) left to belong to 'hem,
thou must visit 'hem, as thou wouldst doe a *Tombe*, with a Torch or
three hand-fulls of Lincke, flaming hot, and so thou maist hap to make
'hem feele thee, and after, come to inherit according to thy inches. A
sweet course for a man to waste the brand of life for, to be still raking
himselfe a fortune in an old womans embers. . . .

[I,iii,70–79]

Quarlous—a gentleman—delivers this speech in the presence of Dame
Purecraft's daughter, Win-the-Fight. The speech is only a bit less sadistic than the comparable lines in Martial. (For example, where Jonson
speaks of the three handfuls of link, Martial writes: "intrare in istum
sola fax potest cunnum."[2]) In the cities of Martial and Jonson, the sym-
bolism of the funeral link or torch and that of the marriage torch have
become interchangeable. And as Juvenal puts it, the body of an old
woman has become the high road to success.[3] Since Quarlous himself
later chooses this road to wealth, we may feel that he cannot be Jonson's
accredited *porte-parole* at this point; but this would be confusing the intellectual and moral sides of Quarlous. Though a bad man, he is making
a conclusive, if vicious, criticism of venal marriages. In Molière, we have
to "like" the raisonneur fairly well in order to accept his argument, but
in Jonson the penetrating social critic may be as loathsome as those he
attacks. Instead of the clarity and serenity of classic comedy, Jonson offers a comic blade that cuts to the hilt.

The play is a massive and intricate structure of social confusion. It is
as far as it could be from Meredith's comic world, a society "founded in
common sense." For although Jonson masterfully presents differing social groups one after another: Puritans, gentlemen, countrymen, "Bartholomew-birds," and officers of the law, he just as masterfully eradi-
cates the distinctions between them; the play ending with the betrothal
of the disguised Quarlous to the old Puritan he despises, the conversion
of Rabbi Busy to puppet shows because the puppets are without sexual
organs, the exposure of a "wise" judge's imbecility, and the reduction of
his lady to the status of a drunken tart—a tart soundly beaten, moreover,
by Punque Alice. In his last speech, Justice Overdo affirms the repeal

of social distinctions by inviting his "good friends all" to supper: "I will haue none feare to go along, for my intents are *Ad correctionem, non ad destructionem; Ad aedificandum, non ad diruendum*" (V,vi,111–13). It is a genial but fatuous acceptance of the mad status quo which has just been created. The play as a whole is much less genial than the Justice's peroration.

In such a play it is proper that the extensive use of disguise should emphasize the theme. Overdo, in a "guarded coat," pretends to be half-way between a fool and a madman. Actually, he is more than half a fool and by Act Four is in the stocks under suspicion of theft, while the Watch go in search of the judge—Overdo himself—who should examine the suspect. The careful "governour" of Cokes succumbs to drunken-ness, a sort of disguise, and is arrested for disturbing the peace. Overdo escapes from the stocks and reappears in a second disguise, since the first is no longer safe. Quarlous disguises himself as a madman in order to determine whether he has won Grace Welborne but while in disguise awakens the love of Dame Purecraft, who finds him "mad in truth," like St. Paul after his conversion. (This phrase, which occurs a half dozen times, aptly describes the mad world of the play.) He decides that for the sake of a fortune, madness is not too high a price; in fact, he would be mad to stay sane. Dame Purecraft herself reveals her "true" character to the supposedly mad Quarlous; a "sincere" Purecraft is, of course, a woman in disguise. Two "good" women, Win-the-Fight and Dame Over-do, appear masked at the puppet show, the companions of a bawd and a pickpocket; for the simple-minded Win has been convinced that she may "lye by twenty" gallants yet remain an honest woman. "Tish com-mon, shweet heart," says Whit, "tou may'st doe it, by my hand. . ." (IV, v,45). And Knockem agrees that this is the "vapour of fashion."

Just as the hierarchy of the classes is breaking down, rendering suc-cess problematic, the identity of the man who succeeds is itself in doubt. If in Pirandello man uses his split personality as an excuse for his failures, here his instability raises the question: who has succeeded? As the play comes to an end, the successful characters are Quarlous, whose disguise brings him victories he has not planned; Edgworth, the civil cutpurse; and Winwife, whom Grace accepts as the result of an unconscious choice made by the madman, Troubleall. A fitting conclusion for a play taking place in a theatre as "durty as *Smithfield*, and as stinking euery whit" (The Induction, ll.159–60).

Attempts have been made to parallel Jonson with Justice Overdo[4] or with Overdo, Waspe, and Busy,[5] the reformers who are worsted at the close of the play. *Bartholomew Fair* would then stand to *Volpone* as *An*

Enemy of the People stands to *Ghosts*. The old compaigner sees at last the absurdity and hopelessness of his reforming zeal. But since Overdo, Waspe, and Busy are fools—the last a dangerous fool—the parallel is not very flattering to the author. The only character in *Bartholomew Fair* whose intellect approaches Jonson's is the clever and educated Quarlous, but he is a scoundrel. If one were determined to extract a lesson from the play, one could reflect that his is the outstanding triumph: he wins the hand of the wealthy widow, a payment compensating his loss of a rich girl, and to conclude, a free meal from the doddering Justice, who is still certain of the dignity of his mission. Though Jonson has given up the moral assertiveness of *Volpone*, he is not repudiating his earlier acerbity.

Technically, the play is remarkable for Jonson's method of placing each character in connection with as many other characters as possible. Whereas Sir Politick Would Be, in *Volpone*, leads a dramatic life which seldom touches the lives of the main characters, Bartholomew Cokes, by contrast, has short or long scenes with almost all the major characters in his play. In addition to his dialogues with his own party of friends, he is victimized by the Bartholomew-birds, suspects Overdo of complicity in theft, seizes him and turns him over to the Watch, tries to steal pears from a Costard-Monger, is himself robbed once more, and in desperation turns to the madman, Troubleall, for help. In the fifth act he becomes the chief spectator and constant interlocutor at the puppet show. Quarlous, though an observer during much of the play, manages to get involved with as many characters as does Cokes. Quarlous salutes Win-the-Fight as often as possible, pursues Grace, gets Purecraft, blackmails Edgworth, drives Ursula into a rage, fights the roarers, and draws his sword against his friend, Winwife. Even the naive Littlewit plots with Captain Dan Jordan Knockem the arrest of Rabbi Busy, in addition to serving Cokes, pacifying Waspe, and working with Leatherhead. The Watch collaborate with the bawd, Captain Whit, arrest three major characters, and are completely confused by Troubleall. In *Every Man out of His Humour*, Jonson had praised himself, through Cordatus, for the multiple connections of his characters (II,iii,195–200), but where the links were mechanical in the earlier play, they are fundamental here to form and meaning.

The temporal as well as the "spatial" structure of the play contributes to the picture of social derangement. In Acts Two and Three, for example, there is the following sequence: Edgworth steals from Cokes, Waspe suspects Overdo and beats him, Edgworth steals again, Cokes seizes Overdo and turns him over to the Watch, and finally, Quarlous

and Winwife, having observed the thefts, force Edgworth to commit another theft for them. The hunter becomes the prey, the ferret the coney.
But Quarlous is uneasy over his role in this part of the play, and Jonson
gives him an aphorism which tersely describes not only Quarlous' stooping to blackmail but much of the dramatic action: *Facinus quos inqui-
nat, aequat* (IV,vi,29-30). The sentence could serve as an epigraph for
the play, for few of the characters are untouched by the great leveling
accomplished at Bartholomew Fair.

The puppet show raises a difficult critical problem. At first reading, it
seems at best much too long and at worst a structurally irrelevant attack on the low tastes of the Jacobean audience. But the show serves a
number of purposes. It is an effective way of collecting the large cast for
the last scene and deftly brings in the denouement. It gives rise to excellent comedy as the simple-minded Cokes finds it "most admirable good"
and repeats with delight its crudest phrases. The debate between Rabbi Busy and a puppet is ingenious irony. But beyond the entertainment
value of the show, there is a more significant justification. Jonson has already created a social merry-go-round in which men strike each other,
rebound, and strike again in mindless confusion. Grace has been shut-
tled from Cokes to Quarlous and Winwife and then to Winwife alone.
Cokes has been tossed from Nightingale to Edgworth to Leatherhead
and then to the same man as puppeteer. The somersaults of Overdo and
Waspe have already been mentioned. The playwright is now able to en-
force his demonstration of mindless activity by placing his cast in front
of a set of puppets who curse and fight at the slightest excuse. Fair Hero
of the Bankside, who is fought over by Leander, Damon, and Pythias,
may even be a hint that the courtship of women like Grace Welborne
and Dame Purecraft is after all not much more than an obscene puppet
show. Winwife and Quarlous are close friends, like Damon and Pythias,
the "two faithful friends of the Bankside," but we recall that the two
gentlemen have been at swords' points over Grace just as Damon and
Pythias fight for Hero. In "The ancient moderne history of Hero and
Leander," a choice passage runs as follows:

> Pvp. L. *You Goat-bearded slaue!*
> Pvp. D. *You whore-master Knaue.*
> Pvp. L. *Thou art a whore-master.*
> Pvp. I.   *Whore-masters all.*
>
> [V,iv,349–52]

The audience for these lines includes a bawd, a cutpurse with a taste for
"whimsies," the temporary whores Win-the-Fight and Dame Overdo, and

the fortune-hunting gentlemen. If not whoremasters all, the spectators onstage are not far from that. The spectators in the galleries and on the ground are at liberty to draw conclusions about Jonson's opinion of them.

Like Aristophanes, Jonson was keenly aware of the values and limitations of realism. One way of limiting realism is to frame it. Jonson impaled the fluttering life under his observation and fixed it to a display board. On the other hand, as he wrote in the *Discoveries*, "The true Artificer will not run away from nature, as hee were afraid of her,"⁶ a passage consistent with the famous lines in the Induction to *Bartholomew Fair*: "If there bee neuer a *Seruant-monster* i' the *Fayre*; who can helpe it? he sayes; nor a nest of *Antiques*? Hee is loth to make Nature afraid in his *Playes*, like those that beget *Tales, Tempests*, and such like *Drolleries*, to mix his head with other mens heeles. . ." (The Induction, ll.127–31). All this would suggest that *The Tempest* was both too fanciful and too optimistic for Jonson; but the Induction continues: ". . . if the *Puppets* will please any body, they shall be intreated to come in." In this play he will give the public not exactly what it wants but what it thinks it wants; he does not reveal what uses he will put the show to. He does not say that *Hero and Leander* will make the persons at the fair seem real by contrast with the puppets and will at the same time present on a different level—that of the booth—the Jonsonian Feast of Fools. But his amused contempt will appear in the quotation from Horace on the title-page of the printed text:

> Spectaret populum attentiùs ipsis,
> Vt sibi praebentem, mimo spectacula plura.
> Scriptores autem narrare putaret asello
> Fabellam surdo.

He would watch the public more attentively than the performances themselves, since it presented more displays of mimicry, but he would think that the authors wrote their plays for deaf idiots.

If audiences are more receptive to dumb show and rant than to well-filed language designed to explicate human action, then some use can be made of this bias.

The choice of Bartholomew Cokes as spectator-in-chief was a happy stroke. The puppetlike nature of Cokes had already been described by Waspe: "I dare not let him walke alone, for feare of learning of vile tunes, which hee will sing at supper, and in the sermon-times! if hee meete but a Carman i' the streete, . . . hee will whistle him, and all his tunes ouer, at night in his sleepe!" (I,iv,76–81). As soon as he sees the puppets, he wants to be "allied to them," and during the performance he constantly repeats whole phrases and sentences of the actors. A perfect illustration of Bergson's comic character, who shows "the lifeless encrusted upon the living," he fuses the comedy of Littlewit, the puppeteer, and the comedy of Jonson.

If Cokes is perfectly cast as leading puppet, Littlewit is a daring choice as puppet-poet. Who would expect this gentle, naive, uxorious husband to be the author of a salacious entertainment? Yet from his first words—"A Pretty conceit, and worth the finding!"—he displays his envy of the professional playwright. "A poxe o' these pretenders to wit! your *Three Cranes, Miter,* and *Mermaid* men!" he says. "Not a corne of true salt, nor a graine of right mustard amongst them all" (I,i,33–36). He prides himself on his facility with conceits and quiblins, and thinks he can "giue the law to all the *Poets,* and *Poet-suckers* i' Towne" (I,i,39-40). He has therefore become the author of a "motion" which Lanthorn Leatherhead, the puppet-master, considers an excessively highbrow work of art. The atmosphere of contemptuous irony thickens as Littlewit fails to see his play acted because, in his role as uxorious husband, he is searching the fair for Win-the-Fight, while she is attending the performance in the company of Captain Whit, that *"Esquire* of Dames, *Madams,* and twelue-penny *Ladies*" (V,vi,45). When Littlewit discovers the truth, all he can say is "O my wife, my wife, my wife!" Presumably he will keep to his métier as proctor from now on and write no more plays about Bankside whores.[7]

Jonson wishes to present greater London as a greater Bedlam, but despite the insane reversals of status he depicts, he also provides a solid basis of reality by creating an extraordinary number of carefully observed people. The weighty presence of Ursula, for example, will stifle in advance any suspicion that *Bartholomew Fair* is a tour de force in which Jonson manipulates mere puppets in order to advance a message. Ursula is therefore useful to Jonson as technician. She is also a good illustration of his point that success and worth have little relation to each other. Though she is as dishonest as any other character in the play, Jonson regards her with something like affectionate contempt, for she has an indefatigable talent for living under difficult conditions. She is not only vital in herself but the cause of vitality in others. Yet she is a "failure." She is the butt of the gentlemen, the loser in many a criminal proceeding—she has been before Justice Overdo *"Punke, Pinnace* and *Bawd,* any time these two and twenty yeeres" (II,ii,73)—and even the laughing-stock of the clownish Dan Jordan Knockem. She has a great gift for invective, but the others always defeat her in wit-combat; for she is always the more worthy of an insult, this fatness of the Fair, dainty dame, and mother o' the bawds. At the end, she is apprehended by Justice Overdo. Is she included in his blanket invitation to dinner? At any rate, watching a play in which success is achieved by the cold gentlemen and the civil cutpurse, one may feel that it is better to fail with Ursula than to succeed with Quarlous. Yet it is unlikely that Jonson would agree.[8]

If the structure and the juxtaposition of the characters create a disordered society, we may expect that the language of the play will help to project the confusion. Jonson will make extensive use of parody, an art which he has long since mastered. In *Volpone*, for example, the central character gives a grotesque imitation of the pastoral lover, and the contemptible Corvino apes the rodomontade of the Elizabethan tragedy of blood. In *Bartholomew Fair*, Justice Overdo ludicrously misapplies the noble stoical sentiments that so strongly attracted the serious Elizabethan writers, Rabbi Busy misuses biblical imagery and rhetoric, and Littlewit's play completely sabotages the Greek story of Hero and Leander.

Apart from its structural significance, already discussed, the puppet play impresses the reader with the sheer obscenity of its language. To explain this obscenity, Jonson's Induction invokes the classic doctrine of decorum, a principle not very far from the realism of today. But although Jonson's world is composed of a thousand slices of life, the Jonsonian dish tastes like nothing else. He uses the real but distorts it at will. Is the stupid language of the puppet play a sop to the audience or a criticism of it—or both and more? When Jonson has Hero say, "Kisse the whore o' the arse," he is no doubt castigating vulgar audiences, but he is also indulging a taste from which the "judicious" are not exempt—indulging it safely, in this instance, since he is protected by the famous objectivity of the dramatic form. Since the line occurs in a play within a play, he is doubly protected. Insofar as the line is objective, it contributes to the writer's naturalistic scene. But the personal overtones are as inescapable as the tone which Jonson wished to and did strike. The play is, after all, by the man who wrote "The Famous Journey," a cloacal poem burlesquing the classical journey. Moreover, the "meaning" of Hero's line is partially in the no doubt perverse pleasure we get from watching a writer, renowned for his learning, genius, and high moral tone, flinging out a phrase so crude as to be incredible. When the puppeteer adds, "Now you ha' something to doe: you must kisse her o' the arse, shee sayes," he is castigating not only his audience but himself. The relentless dialogue continues:

Pvp. D. P. *So we will, so we will.*
Pvp. H. *O my hanches, O my hanches, hold, hold.*

[V,iv,342–43]

These lines surely succeeded in the theatre, but Jonson and his public had to pay for the success.

Except for the puppet play and the ballads of Nightingale, the comedy is written throughout in prose marked by an encyclopaedic vocabulary, varied rhetoric, and imagery hardly restrained by Jonson's devotion to decorum. The representation of reality has maximum density, yet the hand of the writer is everywhere apparent; we are always aware of Jonson listening, watching, searching for information, and reacting with the full weight of his temperament. At many points the representation glides into brilliant distortion. The dignified Overdo ornaments a lecture against tobacco with the argument that smoking will destroy the nose as effectively as would the pox: "Nay, the hole in the nose heere, of some tabacco-takers, or the third nostrill, (if I may so call it) which makes, that they can vent the tabacco out, like the Ace of clubs, or rather the Flower-de-lice, is caused from the tabacco, the meere tabacco! when the poore innocent pox, hauing nothing to doe there, is miserably, and most vnconscionably slander'd" (II,vi,48–54). The whole lecture is rich in scatological references. Knockem, the horse-trader, will speak out of character when he compares Ursula to Ursa Major and will begin the seduction of the young Puritan wife by this essay in declassification:

. . . is't not pitty, my delicate darke chestnut here, with the fine leane head, large fore-head, round eyes, euen mouth, sharpe eares, long necke, thinne crest, close withers, plaine backe, deepe sides, short fillets, and full flankes: with a round belly, a plumpe buttocks, large thighes, knit knees, streight legges, short pasternes, smooth hoofes, and short heeles; should lead a dull honest womans life, that might liue the life of a Lady?

[IV,v,21–28]

It is probably no accident that the description proceeds downward, from the head to the buttocks and thence to the hoofs and heels. And this magnificent physical equipment is fine enough for a great lady! Here and elsewhere the language immediately creates a topsy-turvy world.

Overdo is a particularly striking example of transvestism. In his own person, he is a learned fool. In his role as fool in a "guarded coat," he reminds his wife of Justice Overdo. Cokes agrees that the fool is like the Justice; "And 'tis, when he speakes" (II,vi,75). Overdo's effort to change his level of speech is obvious near the beginning of Act Two, as he passes from soliloquy to dialogue:

Ivs. *O Tempora! O mores!* I would not ha' lost my discouery of this one grieuance, for my place, and worship o' the *Bench,* how is the poore subiect abus'd, here! well, I will fall in with her, and with her *Moonecalfe,* and winne out wonders of enormity. By thy leaue, goodly woman, and the fatnesse of the *Fayre:* oyly as the Kings constables Lampe, and shining as his Shooing-horne! hath thy Ale vertue, or thy Beere strength? that the tongue of man may be tickled? and his palat pleas'd in the morning? let thy pretty Nephew here, goe search and see.
Vrs. What new Roarer is this?
Moo. O Lord! doe you not know him, Mistris, 'tis mad *Arthur* of *Bradley,* that makes the Orations.

[II,ii,113–25]

Although Ursula takes Overdo's speech to her as the language of a roarer, these sentences are no less oratorical—no less ornamented with rhetorical questions, alliteration, and balanced phrases—than Overdo's soliloquies. His assumed speech differs from his own idiom mainly in a greater vividness of imagery. The ironical apostrophe, "By thy leaue, goodly woman, and the fatnesse of the *Fayre,*" has at least some of the richness so brilliantly manifested in Mosca's praise of the luxurious life Voltore will lead when his chin "is borne up stiffe, with fatnesse of the floud" (*Volpone,*I,iii,72). One may feel that the orations of Mad Arthur are in fact rather beyond the foolish Overdo. In his lecture against tobacco, Arthur can say that "the lungs of the Tabacconist are rotted, the Liuer spotted, the braine smoak'd like the backside of the Pig-womans Booth. . ." (II,vi,41–43). In such speeches we are struck not so much by Overdo's decline in dignity as by his gain in imaginative force. Overdo is wiser as fool than as judge—and this is what we should expect at Bartholomew Fair. The language of Overdo's soliloquies, on the other hand, is not so much an attack on Jehovahlike severity[9] as a farcical-bitter exposé of the utter failure of bumbling justice in Jonson's mad world.

Jonson's purpose sometimes requires that he make his people speak better than they could, yet he has to avoid too obvious a violation of decorum. That Quarlous adapts an epigram of Martial is easy enough to accept; but it is not quite so easy to imagine Ursula as adapter of the Roman poet. Martial had written:

> Habere amicam nolo . . .
> quae clune nudo radat et genu pungat,
> cui serra lumbis, cuspis eminet culo.[10]

I don't wish to have a mistress . . . who rasps me with her skinny haunch and pricks me with her knee, from whose spine protrudes a saw, from whose latter end a spear. [Trans. Walter Ker]

In her flyting scene with Quarlous and Winwife, Ursula says:

Hang 'hem, rotten, roguy Cheaters, I hope to see 'hem plagu'd one day (pox'd they are already, I am sure) with leane playhouse poultry, that has the boany rumpe, sticking out like the Ace of Spades, or the point of a Partizan, that euery rib of 'hem is like the tooth of a Saw: and will so grate 'hem with their hips, & shoulders, as (take 'hem altogether) they were as good lye with a hurdle.

[II,v,104–10]

Despite his subject matter, Martial's epigram is elegantly terse. Ursula's version of the Latin passage doubles the number of images. We can attribute this prodigality to the restless yet accurate imagination of the pigwoman: the anatomical exactness of "Partizan" is impressive. Or we may prefer to credit the baroque fullness of Jonson's style: he very frequently elaborates his borrowings from the Latin. Ursula's speech is naturalistic on the surface, for if she had a superb gift for simile, this is the way she would speak. Certainly it is fitting for this vendor of roast pig to describe thin women as lean poultry. Yet because Ursula's outburst equals, in its own way, the power of Martial, it takes its place among the brilliant distortions of reality accomplished by the playwright.

The "decorum" of *Bartholomew Fair* requires that men condemn fortune hunting and then engage in it, that wisdom wear the habit of folly and therein appear wiser than itself, and that illiteracy rival the achievement of a sophisticated satirist. In all this there is much to laugh at, but the laughter is characteristically Jonsonian, ironic, and tough-minded. The controlled savagery of the representation has a peculiarly modern force. Indeed it is questionable whether the play should be called a comedy. It takes its stand on that line so difficult to plot precisely—the line separating comedy from irony and satire.

In his Induction, Jonson describes his play as "merry," and recent criticism has been agreeing with him. Introducing his edition of *Bartholomew Fair*, Edward Partridge asks where "harmless folly and idle pleasure" and the other positive feelings of comedy could go, harassed as they are in this drama by stupidity, hypocrisy, and vice. He concludes that *Bartholomew Fair* answers his question "in the only way a play can: by being itself a work of art—foolish, witty, idle, joyful."[11] But if,

as I have argued, the play is more ironic than festive, it has no obligation to rescue harmless folly and idle pleasure. As the tumultuous action moves along, one is inundated yet supported by the sheer energy
and velocity of life created and flung across the stage as punks, pimps,
thieves, watchmen, Puritans, puppeteers, vendors, madmen, and gentlemen successively demand attention, merge, disappear, and reappear,
their activities and appetites undiminished. But if one evaluates all that
has happened, the experience is sobering.

NOTES

1. Introduction to *Bartholomew Fair, Ben Jonson,* ed. C. H. Herford, Percy
Simpson, and Evelyn Simpson (Oxford, 1925–52), II, 138. Citations from *Bartholomew Fair* are to this edition.

2. Martial, *Ep.* III, xciii, 26–27; cited in Herford and Simpson.

3. Juvenal, *Sat.* i, 39–42; cited in Herford and Simpson.

4. H. R. Hays, "Satire and Identification: An Introduction to Ben Jonson,"
Kenyon Review, XIX (1957), 257–83.

5. Jonas A. Barish, "*Bartholomew Fair* and Its Puppets," *MLQ,* XX (1959),
6.

6. Herford and Simpson, VIII, 587.

7. After this chapter was substantially complete, I read Mr. Barish's excellent
essay, "*Bartholomew Fair* and Its Puppets," cited above. Mr. Barish's argument
for the structural relevance of the puppet show is much more fully developed than
mine, but my discussion supplements his at a number of points.

8. For a very different view of Ursula, see Jackson I. Cope, "*Bartholomew Fair*
as Blasphemy," in *Renaissance Drama VIII,* ed. S. Schoenbaum (Evanston, Ill.,
1965), pp. 143–46. Cope identifies the pigwoman as *Atê* or *Discordia* (p. 144)
and her booth as hell (p. 146).

9. Cope, p. 141.

10. Martial, *Ep.* XI, c.3,4; cited in Herford and Simpson.

11. Introduction, *Bartholomew Fair,* ed. Edward B. Partridge (Lincoln, Nebraska, 1964), p. xiv.

CHAPTER NINE

Tartuffe:
The Victory of Light

Molière's comedies repeatedly dramatize the attempt to rid society of lies—the lies of an ignorant medical profession, a false politesse, or an inhumane educational system. Such are the themes of *The Imaginary Invalid, The Misanthrope,* and *The School for Wives.* In *Tartuffe,* Molière struck out against the most evil lie of his time, false piety, a disease carrying with it ridiculous pride, tyrannical power, and a hypocrisy not exclusively confined to scoundrels as blatant as Tartuffe himself. The violent reaction against this play was not at all unnatural, for despite Molière's protest that he had made obvious the distinction between true and false piety, the play probably cuts everyday hypocrites more sharply than outright criminals like Tartuffe. Why should a convicted thief be shocked to hear that he has broken the law, and why should a pillar of society not be furious on being told that he is rotted within? Even the average member of the first audience might recognize in himself the latent dishonesties that Tartuffe shrewdly exploits in his dupe, Orgon.

The action of *Tartuffe* opposes light and darkness and culminates in the victory of light. The imagery of the play gives detailed support to this action. The characters can be roughly divided into the advocates of light and of darkness, though the characterization is subtler than this statement or Molière's own remarks on the play suggest. Mme. Pernelle, for example, is benighted in her opinions, but temperamentally she is so vigorous, even delightful, that her stage life refutes her deadly ideas.

The unity of the play is first of all a unity of action. Before the opening curtain Tartuffe has won the complete confidence of Orgon, the ruler of his house. The entire comedy is the attempt to expel the hypocrite and, by extension, hypocrisy from Orgon's home and from society. This action involves the effort to enlighten Mme. Pernelle, to rid the lovers, Mariane and Valère, of foolish pride, to cure the blindness of Orgon,

165

and finally to save his family from the almost irremediable consequences of his crazy devotion to Tartuffe. By the grace of the Sun King, the light of reason finally prevails over "behavior totally black" (V,vii). Valère and Mariane, who are young and relatively unspoiled, are rather easily rescued by the brilliant clarity of Dorine, one of the most admirable people in Molière. Orgon is forced to see clearly in Act Four, and his mother gets absolute proof in Act Five. But only Louis, the god from the machine, can protect the physical safety of the threatened house. In the last lines Tartuffe, the hypocrite, the boaster, the unwelcome guest, the enemy of the sane society, is expelled. The conclusion is similar to that of the *Peace*, in which Trygaeus drives the son of Lamachus, the hated warrior, from the stage. In Aristophanes, society is saved by the inspired buffoon; in Molière, reason and truth finally triumph over blindness and falsity, but reflection upon the helplessness of society deprived of the King's intervention induces misgivings close to the "tragic qualm."

The comedy begins with the angry movement of Mme. Pernelle toward the street. She cannot bear the disrespectful attitude shown Tartuffe by most of the household. "Let's go, Flipote," she says to her servant, a poor creature who pays for the errors and frustrations of her mistress.[1] "Come, deliver me from these people." Tartuffe twice parodies the Lord's Prayer in later scenes, and here, the "deliver" is an unconscious link between the hypocrite and the old woman.

Hurrying after Mme. Pernelle, Elmire, who is not feeling well, exclaims, "You walk at such a pace I can hardly keep up with you." Both Orgon and his mother have moved so rapidly into an absurd religiosity that the normal people in the play cannot keep up with it if they would. This scene, one of the most vigorous in Molière, is a series of thunderclaps from the old lady, in response to the attempts of the others to argue for moderation. As Dorine, Damis, Mariane, Elmire, and Cléante attempt in turn to speak a reasonable word, she sears them with the lightning of her glance. In the theater, each could approach her with a phrase and then be driven across the stage by her verbal power. This arrangement would recognize the solid structure of farce on which Molière built his subtle comedy. She is theatrically brilliant, but her bemused state is shown by such details as her holding up the *dead* mother of the young people as a model of behavior. Despite her energy, she is on the side of darkness and death.

As the scene develops, the fight against obscurantism gathers strength. The impulsive Damis speaks for natural instinct. He predicts that his hatred for Tartuffe will force him to break out in a great flash (*éclat*) of anger. Cléante and Dorine aid him with the abstract and concrete arguments which are the two main supports of sanity in the play. Here as elsewhere, Dorine is the more vivid. Mme. Pernelle thinks that the social life of the household has created a "shameful stir [*éclat*]" in the neighborhood. Dorine replies that neighbors like Daphne and her "little spouse"

> . . . ne manquent jamais de saisir promptement
> L'apparente lueur du moindre attachement. . . .
>
> [I,i]

> . . . never fail to seize the slightest glints
> Of friendly feeling, then they drop their hints. . . .

The actions of others, inaccurately observed, are "tinted with their colors." Dorine is magnificent on the subject of the scandalmongering Orante, whose life Mme. Pernelle thinks exemplary. In the course of a long speech, Dorine says:

> Mais l'âge dans son âme a mis ce zèle ardent,
> Et l'on sait qu'elle est prude à son corps défendant,
> Tant qu'elle a pu des coeurs attirer les hommages,
> Elle a fort bien joui de tous ses avantages;
> Mais, voyant de ses yeux tous les brillants baisser,
> Au monde, qui la quitte, elle veut renoncer,
> Et du voile pompeux d'une haute sagesse
> De ses attraits usés déguiser la faiblesse.
> Ce sont là les retours des coquettes du temps.
> Il leur est dur de voir déserter les galants.
> Dans un tel abandon, leur sombre inquiétude
> Ne voit d'autre recours que le métier de prude. . . .
>
> [I,i]

> Advancing years have made her spirit zealous;
> We know that she's a prude because she's jealous.
> When from men's hearts she could awaken homage,
> She knew how to deploy each sweet advantage.
> But time has flown, her eye's no longer bright,
> She's ready now to bid the world good-night.
> And lofty wisdom is a pompous veil
> To hide the truth that charms once strong are frail.
> Thus are transformed coquettes of yesteryear.

> It's hard to see the gallants disappear.
> In loneliness, their dark inquietude
> Sees no recourse but to become a prude.

When the eyes of Orante were bright with youth, she was a coquette; but now that she has aged, she seeks to disguise her "used up" charms —harsh insinuation!—with the "pompous veil" of supposed wisdom. But she has converted this wisdom into a métier, a profitable way of life, and after all, she is still preoccupied with her "body." This is the recourse of a woman fallen into the "somber" isolation of advancing years. The spirit of Tartuffe seems to be widespread and is manifesting itself in the play long before he himself appears.

All the deductive and inductive reasoning of Cléante and Dorine makes no impression on the old woman; she maintains that it is Dorine, not Orante, who speaks scandal. Mme. Pernelle takes the "dice" out of Dorine's hand, throws a last insult at the smiling rationalist, cuffs the innocent Flipote, and makes a triumphal exit. Oddly, this old devotee of darkness has the vigor of youth. Almost admirable, she is so entertaining that for the moment the idiocy inspired by Tartuffe does not seem a bad way of life.

In the scene following the quarrel, Dorine gives Cléante and the audience a fuller picture of the strange relationship between Orgon and Tartuffe. Orgon has made the hypocrite his god. Tartuffe directs the household, gets the best of the food and drink. Even his belching seems to be a religious occasion. But Dorine is most savage when she charges that Orgon could not have more *tendresse* (I,ii) for a mistress. In the seventeenth century, "tendresse" connoted sexual passion of the kind exhibited by Racine's tragic lovers. Molière's dramatic picture is darkening, but Dorine is so superbly healthy and sane in herself that her manner of speaking the line will protect the moment from psychopathy. We are still a long way from Genet.

Orgon, who has been away for two days, now enters with the words "Ah! good day, brother" (I,iv). The note of Tartuffery is audible. He wants to know what has gone on in his absence. As Dorine details the evidence of Elmire's illness, Orgon keeps making his famous repetition: "Et Tartuffe?" At the climax of Dorine's report she asserts that Tartuffe

> Pour réparer le sang qu'avait perdu Madame,
> But à son déjeuner quatre grands coups de vin.
>
> [I,iv]
>
> To make up for the blood Madame had lost,
> Drank down at luncheon four large cups of wine.

The lines resound unforgettably. In a play whose religious overtones profoundly shocked great men of the Church, the allusion to the Atonement and the sacrament of Communion could not fail to darken the already disquieting atmosphere. For a Bossuet or a Bourdaloue, attending such a play would be an atrocity like assisting at a Black Mass.

The dramatic movement retards in a scene between Cléante and Orgon confronting gross delusion and smiling rationalism. After revealing that the scene had been criticized as "affected, unnecessary, and irrelevant," the *Lettre sur la comédie de l'Imposteur*, probably inspired by Molière, defends it as a natural and organic part of a play in which "the Hypocrite directly or indirectly causes everything that takes place."[2] The passage may be overlong, but it is certainly neither affected nor irrelevant. In his final version of a play which had been barred from the stage by religious opposition, Molière had good reason to make Cléante carefully develop his theory of false and true piety. The controversy about the play had given additional force and meaning to the struggle for truth. If one feels that the sermons of Cléante threaten to imprison Molière in a somewhat colorless rationalism, one has only to recall that Cléante is but one character in this varied play.

Seeing that his argument has had as little effect upon Orgon as upon Mme. Pernelle, Cléante asks Orgon when he will fix the day of Valère's marriage to Orgon's daughter. Orgon's reply prepares the second act: he will do "what Heaven wishes" (I,v). He believes that Tartuffe will know God's will. In contrast with what precedes it, this section of the scene is stripped of rhetoric. Orgon has ten speeches totalling about thirty syllables. Each of his replies comes at the beginning of a line of verse, so that Cléante's speeches are a series of rhymed questions, briefly but sharply interrupted. If Cléante's argument has been overlong, Orgon's terseness is all the more striking.

Throughout the later acts, there is a careful linking of action and theme. We find that the ruses of Tartuffe drive the normally honest people into moral compromises. In order to get rid of the unwelcome guest, Elmire and Dorine, for example, must employ his dishonesty, or something approaching it.

In Act Two, Orgon orders Mariane to marry Tartuffe, Mariane begs Dorine for help, and Mariane and Valère quarrel and are reconciled. These three scenes not only result from the duping of Orgon but put in action three new examples of hypocrisy or dissembling: the ludicrously false arguments of Orgon, the pretended indifference of Dorine to Mariane's fate, and the false pride of the lovers, Mariane and Valère.

Orgon's attempt to persuade Mariane that Tartuffe will make an ideal husband is absurd but insidious, as Dorine quickly shows. When he says,

> ... vous vivrez dans vos ardeurs fidèles,
> Comme deux vrais enfants, comme deux tourterelles;
> A nul fâcheux débat jamais vous n'en viendrez,
> Et vous ferez de lui tout ce que vous voudrez,
>
> [II,ii]

> You'll be together in your faithful loves
> Just like two children or two turtle-doves.
> Living in peace, you'll make of him whatever
> You wish; no coarse debate your love will sever.

Dorine replies that Mariane will make him a fool. Married to Tartuffe, Mariane will deceive the deceiver, and his "ascendancy" will destroy the virtue of Orgon's daughter. Dorine could not more effectively shatter the debased and ambiguous idyll of Orgon's imagination. The word "ascendant" points to the sexual reality which the pastoral convention seeks to disguise.

One dishonesty leads to another. When Dorine asks Mariane why she has not answered her father frankly, Mariane pleads that Orgon has absolute power; besides, if she declared her scorn for Tartuffe, would she not reveal "a heart struck too deeply" by Valère (II,iii)? This polite sham causes Dorine to desert her usual candor. She now maintains that Tartuffe would make an excellent match, for he is well born, well made, red-cheeked, and red-eared. The irony forces the girl to drop her ladylike pretensions.

The *Lettre* points out that some of Molière's contemporaries found the lovers' quarrel (II,iv) dramatically irrelevant. The writer gives no less than six arguments in defense of the scene. His main point is that it shows the variety of principles directing different people in the same situation. But the defense omits the crucial point that Molière's variations are controlled by the theme of hypocrisy. A powerful liar can force normally honest people into protective lies.

The "natural" Damis, who has no talent for deception, opens the third act with a verbally heroic but actually laughable outburst:

> Que la foudre sur l'heure achève mes destins, ...
> S'il est aucun respect ni pouvoir qui m'arrête. ...
>
> [III,i]

> May lightning strike me down and end my days ...
> If filial respect should ever stop me. ...

A devotee of light, he thinks in terms of lightning flashes. But the cleverer Dorine forces him to hide his light in the next room, for Tartuffe will soon arrive to interview Elmire. Hiding is the inevitable way of life in a house dominated by the hypocrite. And in such a house, closets, table covers, and boxes must be used for concealment.

At last Tartuffe appears. His first couplet will be eagerly awaited. When it comes, it leaves no doubt that, for all his frightening power, he himself is a comic figure:

> Laurent, serrez ma haire avec ma discipline,
> Et priez que toujours le Ciel vous illumine.
>
> [III,ii]

> Laurent, put my hair shirt next to my whips,
> And may prayers for heavenly light be on your lips.

Next he announces that he is going with alms in hand to visit the prisons. This clumsy speech is for the benefit of Dorine, but if Tartuffe were a thoroughly polished fraud he would know that his nonsense could not deceive a normally shrewd listener. And by this time he should appreciate the clearheadedness of Dorine. Her comment—"What affectation, what impudent boasting!"—suggests, however, that he does not play his game most carefully before the servant. Tartuffe saves his best strokes for Orgon and Elmire.

Dorine announces Elmire's wish for an interview and withdraws. Elmire wants to question Tartuffe about his forthcoming marriage, but before she can do so, he has declared his love for her. His language is a subtle blend of preciosity, mysticism, liturgical rhetoric, and sexual passion. He glides imperceptibly from the eternal to the temporal. The "reflected" beauty of heaven "shines" so brightly in the flesh of Elmire that he can see and admire in her the author of nature. Here as elsewhere Molière makes frequent reference to seeing and failure to see. At first Tartuffe has supposed that his "secret ardor was only a clever surprise of the evil [*noir*] spirit" (III,iii), but in a rush of pseudo-religious inspiration he "knew" that his love was not blameworthy. He continues to speak of Elmire's "gleaming splendor," her "divine glances," and although he assures her that men like him "burn with a discreet fire," he is soon revealing "violent transports." What else can he do? He is not "blind," he is a man of flesh. His declaration comes to this: the brilliant light of heaven has ignited in him a blazing passion for his patron's wife.

Rushing from his hiding place, Damis declares that the truth must be published, the character of Tartuffe placed in "broad daylight" (III,iv). The rest of the act is Damis' unsuccessful attempt to make Orgon recognize the obvious. As Tartuffe puts it, "I see that they are trying to blacken me in the eyes of my brother" (III,vii). Orgon responds by banishing Damis from his house and announcing that Tartuffe is to be not only his son-in-law but his heir.

The powers of darkness are now in the zenith. By Act Four, Orgon has deeded his entire fortune to the impostor. One child is already banished, the other falls to her knees in an appeal for mercy. Orgon's reply is a masterpiece of horribly incongruous nonsense:

> Mortifiez vos sens avec ce mariage,
> Et ne me rompez pas la tête davantage.
>
> [IV,iii]

The advice that Mariane adopt the asceticism favored by Tartuffe is fully shown up by the trite demand which follows—that she stop driving Orgon crazy. Orgon's mind has become so deranged that all Elmire's clear thinking is necessary to avert final disaster. She will restage the seduction scene for her husband's benefit.

Masking her true feelings in order to unmask Tartuffe, Elmire now persuades him to declare his intentions while Orgon is hidden under a table covering. Very gradually Elmire "opens her heart" in words which Tartuffe finds hard to understand. We watch her delicate maneuvering in a context of farce and high melodrama—the farce supplied by the would-be cuckold, the melodrama by the dangerous antagonist. The complexity of the scene transcends conventional dramatic genres. Tartuffe is both funny and frightening as he responds to Elmire's invitations. He is too intelligent to accept at once the seeming reversal of Elmire's attitude toward him, yet his words set forth the agonized will to believe in a sensual, unsatisfied man:

> C'est sans doute, Madame, une douceur extrême
> Que d'entendre ces mots d'une bouche qu'on aime;
> Leur miel dans tous me sens fait couler à longs traits
> Une suavité qu'on ne goûta jamais.
> Le bonheur de vous plaire est ma suprême étude,
> Et mon coeur de vos voeux fait sa béatitude;
> Mais ce coeur vous demande ici la liberté
> D'oser douter un peu de sa félicité.
>
> [IV,v]

> It is a pleasure without parallel
> To hear these words from one we love so well.

> Through all my senses I feel the honey flow,
> Bringing a joy I thought I'd never know.
> To please you is for me the supreme quest;
> With your good will, I'd be among the blest.
> But I must ask you here for the liberty
> Of faintly doubting my felicity.

The anapaestic lines flow smoothly, like the honey he feels coursing through his body. Although his situation is comic, his power is too well established to let us feel that he will be easily destroyed. Elmire creates comedy by her discreet coughs, but she works almost desperately to transmit "full light" to the hidden Orgon. Tartuffe asks for some immediate proof of her availability, but Orgon still remains under the table! By this finesse Molière permits Tartuffe to develop his famous theory that evil actions can be rectified by good intentions: so long as there is no "éclat" the secret deed is innocent. When Orgon finally comes into view, he justifies his long concealment by a confession of idiocy: "I kept believing his tone would change." By pushing Orgon's blindness to the farthest limit of credibility, Molière extracted from the scene its entire potential.

In Act Five we learn that besides deeding his entire property to Tartuffe, Orgon has given him some incriminating papers. These two problems have now to be cleared up. But first Mme. Pernelle returns, whereupon we get a superb variation on the recognition scene. A half dozen attempts by Orgon to enlighten Mme. Pernelle are failures; she thinks it isn't always necessary to make decisions based on "what we see" (V,iii). Relying on blind faith, she sees the truth only when an official appears, armed with an order to quit the premises. She is speechless and "thunderstruck" ("je tombe des nues").

Two clouds remain. Tartuffe has informed the Crown of Orgon's incriminating papers and comes to occupy the house to which he holds the deed. The stage is now set for the god from the machine. If this were a masque or ballet, Louis could emerge from a cloud in the fly gallery. In fact, he speaks through the Exempt, his deputy:

> Nous vivons sous un Prince ennemi de la fraude,
> Un prince dont les yeux se *font jour* dans les coeurs.
>
> [V,vii]

A standard translation reads: "We live under the rule of a prince inimical to fraud, a monarch who can read men's hearts."[3] But the second line takes its place in the dark-and-light pattern of the play. As a whole, the speech is a hymn to the King's discernment, moderation, and vision: the imagery of light now gets its most concentrated expression. The King's insight has pierced the "folds" of Tartuffe's deception, the donation is cancelled, and Orgon's illegal act, evidenced by the mysterious papers, is forgiven. As Orgon prepares to attack Tartuffe's treachery, Cléante urges charity and humble gratitude to the King. He even hopes that Tartuffe will return to virtue on this very day! To these impeccable sentiments Orgon replies, "Well said!" For his madness is at an end.

The conclusion of the play can hardly be defended on the ground of strict dramatic logic, but comedy does not require such a defense. There has always been an element of wish-fulfillment in the comic benedictions accorded the average man, whether he be the fruit grower of Aristophanes, the lover in Shakespeare, or the citizen of Molière. In *Tartuffe*, moreover, the epiphany of Louis XIV has been prepared by the many *éclats* sighted in the text—whether false gleams or premonitory flashes—and by the clarifications accomplished by Elmire, Cléante, and Dorine. These include the significant action of Elmire in Act Four, which almost provides a solution in itself, and the steady vision of Cléante and Dorine.

Despite the victory of light over darkness, many readers think *Tartuffe* a very dark play. The insidious power of Tartuffe and the world he stands for, the vulnerability of "good" people to spreading evil, whether foreign or bred within, the obvious rage of Molière himself as he sees the frightening strength of repressive malignity—all this does mean that the play is far from resting in a safe, let alone complacent, optimism. During most of the action, the good life suffers imminent danger of strangulation. The poise of Elmire is at first seemingly unequipped to combat the antagonist, and her very decency almost condemns her to failure. The position of Dorine nearly negates the successes of her comic analysis. The sane speeches of Cléante are directed at a man who is temporarily incapable of reason, and the rhetoric of the *honnête homme* often lacks the cutting edge needed for tearing away the armor and getting at the flesh of hypocrisy. The youthful ardor of Damis, the timidity of Mariane are helpless. Only Louis XIV can save this family from disaster. To stage *Tartuffe* as a jolly comedy would be an act of sabotage.

But the emotion of the play attaches itself more tenaciously to the theme than to the characters. Molière's long struggle to put *Tartuffe* on the stage had left its mark on the play. The satire in some sense goes beyond the dramatic action—as satire often does: one feels that the dramatist is more disturbed by the famous *Cabale des dévots* than by the follies of Orgon himself. This infatuated man is not a profound study of good and evil in humanity. Nor is there any reason to treat him as an alienated man of the twentieth century for whom we feel alternate or confused emotions of sympathy and or contempt. He prefigures neither Dostoyevsky's underground man, Pirandello's Father, nor Saul Bellow's Herzog.

Although we are told that Orgon was once a sane and valuable citizen, during most of the play he is alternately besotted, violent, petty, infantile, and malicious. Sometimes he manages to be simultaneously ridiculous and disturbing. Yet he is predominantly comic. In the first act, when he tells Cléante that because of Tartuffe's instructions, he could see his whole family die without caring "as much as that" (I,v)—presumably snapping his fingers—the very extremism of the statement forbids us to place it in a fully moral universe: one feels that he doesn't know what he is saying. Similarly, when he threatens to marry Tartuffe to Mariane at once "to confound the pride of my entire family" (III,vi), the vow is not fully responsible since it develops from a paroxysm of rage. In such moments he is fully comic. But he is morally at his worst when he opens Act Two by calling the timid and obedient Mariane to him, reminding her of the love she owes him, requesting her opinion of Tartuffe, demanding that it be favorable, and when Mariane asks, "Why make me guilty of imposture?," replying, "But I wish that it be the truth." Not only must Mariane lie, but the lie must be the truth! Tyranny could go no further. In this passage Orgon is more hateful than laughable, and only the arrival of the shrewd Dorine can drive him into a comic corner.

In general, however, Molière's comic technique restrains pity and fear. The method can be illustrated by a sequence of Orgon's speeches following Damis' announcement that Tartuffe is trying to seduce Elmire. Orgon, shaken, first calls on Heaven to answer his doubts. But a single speech by Tartuffe, picturing his life as a "mass of crime and filth," is enough to sway Orgon and arouse his anger against the "traitor," Damis. Orgon now becomes incapable of anything but reaction. Every access of humility in Tartuffe, every protest by Damis, increases Orgon's rage against his son and his tenderness toward the hypocrite. In a magnificently grotesque moment Orgon raises the kneeling Tartuffe while saying, "Silence, jailbird! Eh, rise, my brother, for pity's sake!" (III,vi). What could seem a shocking inversion of natural feeling remains comic because the dupe is so obviously the victim of external stimuli, so utterly unable to analyze what he is hearing and seeing.

It is not so much Orgon as his situation and his family that give rise to distress and to concern for the plight of man. Even though the typical spectator might have to question himself from time to time as he observed Orgon, the character is so distanced as to be fixed in a series of vivid attitudes. Only his recovery changes him from a mask (or masks) to a face. This does not mean that he should be played as an outright idiot or villain. The actor should find some moments in which to suggest that he is reclaimable.

In his eagerness to prove that he was attacking false and not true piety, Molière said more than once that Tartuffe is a scoundrel. The Preface states that "he does not say one word, he does not perform one action, which fails to show the spectator the character of a wicked man. . . .[4] But as the *Lettre* says, he forgets himself in his great scenes with Elmire. There he is appalling not only because of his corrupt power but because he becomes self-deceived and so caught by the ambiguities of his own language that he apparently believes in his mission. His religious cant becomes the voice of his own emotional drives. Elmire is his hope, his peace. Through her he may attain beatitude. He is offering his heart as a sacrifice to a divinity. Others would desecrate the altar at which they present themselves by indiscreetly revealing this devotion to others, but his fire burns discreetly. There is a delicate balance between the funny and the disturbing. His unattractive exterior tends to make his pretensions ridiculous, but such verbal adroitness has often been enough to seduce. Much depends on how Elmire responds to his advances. On this issue, the text is not doubtful. After the first of the speeches I have paraphrased (III,iii), Elmire labels his discourse "galante"; after the second, her term is "rhétorique." These responses help to keep the play well within the area of comedy.

Elmire is one of the chief victims of Tartuffe, but she is too cool and poised to suffer deeply. She is also protected by her sense of humor. In her second interview with Tartuffe, the hidden Orgon allows her desperate improvisations and warning coughs to go long unanswered. She sends Tartuffe off to make sure that no spies are about, then speaks to Orgon, who has at last understood the truth and now wants to emerge. Ridiculing his blindness, she says, "What, you're joking." And there is thoroughly justified sarcasm in her "Wait till the end for absolute proof" (IV,vi). Elmire is somewhat detached in her attitude toward her husband. But to suggest that she has considered yielding to Tartuffe is silly. She not only holds him off with irony in Act Three but devises the plan which in Act Four recreates a united family. Though not a comic character herself, she strongly supports the comic ideals of sanity, health, and reason.

It is impossible to assess the tone and color of this carefully composed play without taking account of the important roles of Cléante and Dorine. From the first their mental clarity raises a hope that Tartuffery cannot long remain in power. Their attack on Orgon's delusions takes the form of abstract and rational argument from Cléante and concrete evidence from Dorine. Within the limitations of the rhymed alexandrine each point of view has its own style, but each stresses Molière's faith in the rightness of natural impulse.

In his scene with Orgon at the end of Act One, Cléante develops his thought by a series of clear and rather flatly stated contrasts:

> Hé quoi! vous ne ferez nulle distinction
> Entre l'hypocrisie et la dévotion?
> Vous les voulez traiter d'un semblable langage,
> Et rendre même honneur au masque qu'au visage. . . .
>
> [I,v]

> Good heavens! can't you master a distinction
> Between hypocrisy and true devotion?
> Can you believe they have the same sense?
> Should mask and face get equal reverence. . . .

In a long speech of which I have quoted only a few lines, he makes the same point six times. Can this be Molière's spokesman? In his effort to penetrate the obscurity of Orgon's mind, Cléante talks as if there were no difficulty in separating the true from the false—"I know . . . how to distinguish truth from falsity," he says a moment later. His repetitions testify to the difficulty of educating Orgon and men like him. It appears that the acuity of Cléante is not shared by the mass of men, who fail to attain the truly natural.

The language of the speech is mainly abstract. Even an image contrasting false and true coin is generalized. Dorine would have chosen a particular amount. After listing the general concepts that Orgon fails to recognize, Cléante moves on to his generalization about the majority of men. They think that the ranges of reason are simply "too small," and they go "too far."

This is not the raisonneur at his most pungent. Though each distinction falls on Orgon with perceptible force, there is a certain remoteness about it all. Cléante attacks insincerity, but how do we know who is insincere?

Dorine has already given the evidence for Cléante's assertions, for she has explained in detail how Tartuffe has duped Orgon:

Il l'appelle son frère et l'aime dans son âme
Cent fois plus qu'il ne fait mère, fils, fille, et femme.
C'est de tous ses secrets l'unique confident,
Et de ses actions le directeur prudent;
Il le choie, il l'embrasse, et pour une maîtresse
On ne saurait, je pense, avoir plus de tendresse;
A table, au plus haut bout il veut qu'il soit assis;
Avec joie il l'y voit manger autant que six;
Les bons morceaux de tout, il fait qu'on les lui cède;
Et s'il vient à roter, il lui dit: "Dieu vous aide!"
Enfin il en est fou; c'est son tout, son héros;
Il l'admire à tous coups, le cite à tous propos,
Ses moindres actions lui semblent des miracles,
Et tous les mots qu'il dit sont pour lui des oracles.

[I,ii]

He loves this true "brother," this dear friend for life,
A hundred times more than son, daughter, and wife,
Tartuffe is for him a father confessor,
And of all his actions the careful director.
He pets, he embraces the man, for a bride
He couldn't, I'm sure, feel more burning pride.
He wants him to sit at the head of the table,
And swallow five helpings or six, if he's able.
Choice morsels Tartuffe must receive as a prize.
If he happens to belch, "God bless you," he cries.
He's his hero, his all. He's in such a state
He will piously quote him in every debate.
To Orgon his least action looks like a miracle,
Each word that he speaks is the breath of an oracle.

At the beginning of the passage we might suppose that Tartuffe's influence is purely spiritual, for Orgon loves his director "dans son âme"; but soon the love is seen as a kind of sexual perversion, then as a theme for tough farce. Meredith's silvery laugh turns brazen as short clauses whip Orgon's insanity.

The vitality of the speech depends partially on the energy with which it moves from the spiritual to the physical. After the reference to belching, Molière added a note explaining that the speaker is a servant. For a moment we glimpse the public entertainer apologizing to the classically educated, the Cléantes, who made up Molière's best audience but (if they agreed with Boileau) underestimated the value of Molière's farce.

Cléante represents the classical and rather pastel elegance that Molière had to and did master, but in Dorine the dramatist found a character who could embody his own superb energy and penetrating observation. There is no need to suggest that Molière's comedy is an anomaly in a classical age, but it is important to see that for him "la juste nature" meant much more than a reasonable and rather obvious compromise between deplorable extremes. The light shed by *Tartuffe* aids vision, but it also burns.

NOTES

1. A *flipot* is a piece of wood used to cover a flaw in carpentry. Mme. Pernelle uses Flipote to cover her own errors.

2. *Oeuvres Complètes de Molière*, ed. Gustave Michaut (Paris, 1947), IV, 440. Much of the *Lettre* has been translated by Ruby Cohn, *TDR*, VIII (1963), 175–85.

3. *"The Misanthrope" and Other Plays*, trans. John Wood (Harmondsworth, Middlesex, England, 1959), pp. 162–63.

4. Maurice Rat, II, 682.

CHAPTER TEN

Marivaux:
The Nuances of Love and
the Balance of Comedy

Although the English-speaking world is largely ignorant of the fact, Pierre de Marivaux created a new kind of comedy during the first third of the eighteenth century. He has remained unique. Though he wrote in prose, he has been called the best French poet of the eighteenth century; though he repeatedly wrote of the "surprise of love," his amorousness never sank to the clichés of the English sentimental drama. Anticipating the poetic wit of Musset and Giraudoux, he remains unsurpassed in his ability to romanticize the loves of a highly rational people without losing his grip on the real world.

As we read Marivaux's comedies of love or watch them on the contemporary French stage, we encounter at least three related yet distinct images of the playwright: the gentle Marivaux, master of an inoffensive, graceful wit, a Watteau among playwrights; the sensual, even diabolical Marivaux, whose heroines, knowing rather than innocent, play the love game with calculating skill and suggest Boucher rather than Watteau; and the poised, quietly watchful Marivaux, not so taken by young love as to lose his head or his satirical sense. I shall analyze three plays—*The Game of Love and Chance, The Second Surprise of Love,* and *The Double Inconstancy*—each bearing one of these three images and helping to give Marivaux the high place he now holds in the French theatre.

Perhaps the most advertised picture of Marivaux is that of the somewhat overcultivated older man who idolizes the *jeune fille,* as Giraudoux would later do, and studies with scholarly affection and delicate wit every nuance in her progression from an awareness of men in general to love for one man. This is the Marivaux in whose work the tough Arlecchino became an "Arlequin poli par l'amour," the Marivaux whose plays were presented by those graceful but rather cloying Italian actors so often painted by Watteau.

Of the plays which create this image, *The Game of Love and Chance* is the most famous example. The fathers of Silvia and Dorante would like to join the two families in marriage, and Dorante will visit Silvia's home to make her acquaintance. Since she is suspicious of most men and is "not bored with being single" (I,i), Silvia asks her father if she may receive Dorante incognito: she will change places with her maid, Lisette, the better to observe this stranger who is her intended. Her father consents but does not tell his daughter that when Dorante arrives, he will have switched roles with his valet, Harlequin. Dressed as servants, Silvia and Dorante proceed to fall in love, but Silvia hides her feelings until Dorante drops his disguise. She even decides to test her power by keeping him in ignorance of her identity for another act. When Dorante proposes to Silvia-as-servant, love triumphs over chance.

As this summary indicates, the play is as romantic as it is comic. It is true that, apart from the definitely comic subplot, in which the servants fall in love while masquerading as aristocrats, Marivaux stresses the amusing discomfiture suffered by Dorante and Silvia as the result of their plans. Yet the heroine remains the unassailably sweet and charming *jeune fille*. She experiences embarrassment and temporary frustration, not because these are the appropriate wages of excessive cleverness but because she will be even more fascinating, more lovable in her distress. Even when her father describes as "insatiable vanity" (III,iv) her desire to prolong Dorante's uncertainty, the context does not allow the words their usual meaning. Marivaux refuses to push his criticism of Silvia very far. Instead of asking a place in the high court of comic justice, he prefers his role as tireless and admiring biographer of love. The play does not compete with Molière. In *The Game of Love*, there are no serious social problems, no serious conflicts between generations. Indeed, Silvia's father, Orgon, can explain his kindness to her by saying, "In this world you have to be a little too good if you want to be good enough" (I,ii). The world referred to is the world of Marivaux and not the France of 1730, in which you would be a little too good if you were good enough.

Conflict is not provided by a miserly father or a highly stratified society. Whereas the lovers in Terence or Molière are separated by social and economic barriers, the barriers are internalized here. Silvia's strong consciousness of her own position creates resistance to her growing love, and it is the gentlemanliness, the *honnêteté*, of the supposed valet that most attracts the supposed soubrette. Though the play sometimes

threatens to desert comedy for romance, we can see that the individuality of the heroine is not romantically isolated. Her soul did not come
into the world fully formed and trailing clouds of glory; it was an empty
tablet ready to take the inscriptions of a writer who knew what the
aristocratic salons of his time had to teach even though he had strong
affinities with the relatively classless society of the Italian Comedians
of the King.

The total effect of the play depends very heavily on the precise tone
of the developing love affair between Silvia and Dorante—so much so
that a proper evaluation of the comedy requires a careful study of the
love scenes. (The parallel but contrasted scenes between Harlequin and
Lisette are amusing in themselves but serve primarily to "place" the relationship between the *jeunes premiers*). As soon as he appears, the
liveried Dorante shows an inclination toward Silvia, much to the amusement of Mario (Silvia's brother) and Orgon, and much to the embarrassment of Silvia, who has already said, "As for his valet, I do not fear his
sighs. They will not dare to assail me. Something in my face will inspire
more respect than love in the rogue" (I,v). Discreetly, Dorante begins
to make love; his manner immediately illustrates that *marivaudage*—
that fondness for somewhat precious metaphysical conceits—sometimes
said to be found only in Marivaux's servants.

MARIO. Monsieur Bourguignon [Dorante's pseudonym], you have sto-
    len that gallantry somewhere.
DORANTE. You are right, Monsieur; I've found it in her eyes.
MARIO. Be quiet. I forbid you to be so witty.
SILVIA. It isn't at your expense. If he finds it in my eyes, he's welcome to
    it.

[I,vi]

Dorante is at his wittiest in his first scene alone with Silvia; later his
growing love will all but destroy his sense of humor. Silvia's wit is equal
to his first efforts. But this is the last time they will speak so light-heart-
edly.

When Silvia and Dorante meet for their second interview, the tone of
the comedy has changed. Dorante has fallen more deeply in love. According to Marcel Arland, Dorante at first speaks as a cavalier but later
learns to speak like a man. Unfortunately, the cavalier was more entertaining. Silvia has begun to detect in herself feelings she cannot ac-
knowledge, and what is worse, her family and her servant can read her
mind. Now Dorante throws himself in her way once again and declares
that his hopeless love for her has destroyed his peace of mind. Her response is as much to herself as to him:

He's sinking into fantasies! This is distressing! Come to your senses: you speak to me, I reply. That is much, too much, believe me, and if you understood the truth you'd be pleased with me. You would praise my kindness, a kindness I would blame in another. Yet I don't reproach myself, my heart tells me I'm right. What I'm doing is praiseworthy, I'm speaking to you because of my generosity. But this can't continue. This indulgence is good only for the moment, and I can't go on forever reassuring myself of the innocence of my intentions. The situation would become impossible. So let's stop, Bourguignon: no more, please. What does all this mean? It's all nonsense. This talk is over.

[II,ix]

This lyrical and beautifully modulated speech is (in French) a paradigm of dramatic writing. The monologue is really a dialogue in which Silvia plays both herself and Dorante and in addition conducts a lively debate with herself—a scene at which she herself is a deeply interested spectator. She "dramatizes," "revives" the passage in which Dorante has been appealing to her, interprets it, and places it in a vivid light. Although she cannot quite control her feelings, she is brilliantly alert to them, critical of them, and frightened. The little cross-currents of feeling are alive with dramatic action, and in the darting phrases can be seen a dance movement composed of short thrusts and half turns. At this moment Silvia has sovereign appeal. If it is possible to be comic without having a comic flaw, she achieves this rare distinction.

In a few moments Dorante is begging her to insist that she will never love him: "Destroy my dangerous passion, rescue me from it; you don't despise me, don't love me, will never love me" (II,ix). Only in Marivaux would a lover demand so careful a verbalization from the object of his love. All this she asserts, but she also admits that if he were of higher rank, she would not be averse to him. The admission prepares for the scene in which he tells her who he is.

Instead of adding her confession to his, Silvia is determined to win a marriage proposal while she is still in disguise. When he says that he is renouncing his engagement with "Silvia," the heroine replies: "A heart that would choose me in spite of my position is assuredly worth accepting, and I would gladly do so if I weren't afraid to bind it by a contract that would do it wrong." In the French the turns of phrase are as rococo as the tight curls on a wig made in 1730: "Un coeur qui m'a choisie dans la condition où je suis est assurément bien digne qu'on l'accepte, et je le paierais volontiers du mien si je ne craignais pas de le jeter dans un engagement qui lui ferait tort" (II,xii). The *marivaudage* makes itself felt in the fastidious syntax—the impersonal, the conditional, etc.—but more particularly in the persistent references to Dorante's "heart" instead of him. Silvia now has his heart, but the "servant" does not yet have his hand.

A noise offstage forces Dorante to withdraw, and Silvia has a moment in which to say: "It is certainly a good thing for me that this was Dorante" (II,xii). Presumably she is immensely relieved to learn that she has not fallen in love with a servant, since she could not marry so far below her own class. What would have been the alternative? At least one critic thinks she means that she was about to become Dorante's mistress. And there is Giraudoux's provocative assertion that there are no ingénues in Marivaux. For a twentieth-century audience Silvia becomes more interesting if she has been considering a liaison with Dorante. Undoubtedly the thought has flashed through her mind; after all, she lives in the France of the eighteenth century. Yet her strong social consciousness would force her to repress the thought quickly. So viewed, the quoted line becomes a record of a real inner struggle. And as Frédéric Deloffre says, she may be grateful that the possibility of a future yielding has been removed.[1]

To bring on a proposal of marriage from Dorante, Silvia has Mario declare his love for her as Dorante is standing by. In her role as servant she cannot say she loves Dorante unless the proposal has been made; otherwise an avowal would seem to offer a love affair. When he pleads again for "instruction," she replies: "Please, if you love me, don't question me. You fear only my indifference, and you are quite happy to have me remain silent. What do my feelings matter to you?" (III,viii). This is delicate humbug. She implies that a gentleman need not worry about the deeper emotions of a servant; for his purposes it is enough if she goes to bed with him.

DORANTE. Do they matter? Can you still doubt that I adore you?
SILVIA. No, you repeat it so often that I believe you. But why persuade me of that? What am I expected to do with that thought, Monsieur . . . ? I have scruples against saying that I love you since you're in this state of mind: the avowal of my feelings might make you act unreasonably: and you see, I do hide them from you.

[III,viii]

She has shifted her ground imperceptibly. Seeing the intensity of Dorante's emotion, she now says in effect that an avowal of love might cause Dorante to propose marriage despite the cautioning of his reason. Of course her "scruples" have exactly the right effect. "I would be ashamed if my pride resisted you," says Dorante. "My heart and my hand are yours." The reader may be surprised to learn that there was any question of "resistance" on Dorante's part. Can his elegant courtesy have masked dishonorable intentions?

Near the beginning of his extended essay *Le Cabinet du philosophe,* Marivaux has an imaginary philosopher remark that there is a vast difference between saying to a lady: "I love you, Madame; in my eyes you are a woman of a thousand charms," and speaking in these terms: "Madame, I want you very much, and you would give me great pleasure by granting me your favors." The philosopher adds, however, that the two sentences have the same meaning and that the lady knows this.[2] The passage encourages the idea that Dorante's refined dialogue disguises sexual urgency.

Though Dorante has now proposed, the end is not yet, for Silvia is a heroine of Marivaux.

SILVIA. You deserve my acceptance. I would be ungenerous to hide the pleasure you bring me. And you think this can endure?
DORANTE. Then you do love me?
SILVIA. No, no. But if you ask me again, so much the worse for you.
[III,viii]

These are the famous last words, the swan song of the *jeune fille.*

Looking back over the course Silvia has followed, we are struck by the subtle blend of spontaneity and calculation that has gone into her triumph. Her victorious progress is on the whole less comic than romantic. Her spontaneity in her predicament arouses sympathetic laughter; her calculations, on the other hand, result in a victory so personal, even selfish, that our admiration for her conquering charm is tempered by the realization that most of the world can get along very well without triumphs so complete. Dorante is delighted that he has given conclusive proofs of his love; will he some day reflect that the evidence of her love for him was not quite so convincing? That might be a moment of wry comedy.

The action takes up no more than a day or two, yet the persistence of Dorante and the delays of Silvia make the dramatic time of the play seem much longer. By contrast, the love affair of Harlequin and Lisette moves very rapidly. Silvia admits her love only after four interviews, one of which is lengthy. Harlequin, on the other hand, demands and obtains a confession of love early in Act Two, during his first scene with Lisette.

The style of the Harlequin-Lisette scenes parodies the elegance of Dorante and Silvia. In Marivaux's special language, "love," "heart," "hand," and even "head" cease to be parts or functions and take on independent existence. Silvia refers to Dorante's love as something which he throws in her path and speaks of remorselessly; and what is she expected to "do" with it? When Dorante says: "Now you can judge the suffering my heart has felt," she replies: "It isn't your heart I'm speaking to, but you" (II,xii). This style is inflated and extended in the Harlequin-Lisette scenes. At the beginning of Act Two, Lisette announces that Harlequin's heart is "accelerating." In their first dialogue Harlequin says, "A love created by you does not remain long in the cradle. Your first glance gave birth to my love, the second gave it strength, and the third made it a big boy" (II,iii). Dorante had said that he found his gallantry in Silvia's eyes; Harlequin says to Lisette, "Your beautiful eyes have stolen my reason" (II,iii). Her hand is the "dear toy" of his soul (II,iii). By Act Three Lisette is able to report to Orgon: "Monsieur, you told me a while ago you'd turn over Dorante to me and deliver his head into my hands. I've taken you at your word. . . . This head is in pretty good condition now. But what am I supposed to do with it?" Will Silvia object to Lisette's triumph? Not at all. "To put it as you do," says Silvia, "I'll never care for a heart I haven't conditioned myself" (III,v).

This last parallel briefly shows the difference between the styles of the high and low plots. Falling in with the merriment of Lisette, Silvia nevertheless alters the servant's somewhat grisly reference to the decapitated lover, though keeping the metaphor of conditioning, and incidentally points out that Lisette's style is a bit outré.

Without the contrast provided by Harlequin's ludicrous antics, the lovemaking of Dorante could easily become tedious. As it is, the main plot succeeds as romantic comedy, set off by the subplot and not undermined by it. In *The Game of Love and Chance*, Marivaux has no desire to issue a biting critique of love. Playful love is taken seriously and taken to be true.

Late in the spring of 1959, Roger Planchon brought to Paris his *Théâtre de la Cité*, a company usually performing near Lyon. Some excellent publicity preceded the increasingly famous Planchon, and his appearance in Paris was attended by a good deal of intellectual excitement. He staged the two parts of *Henry IV* and closed his engagement with Marivaux's comedy *The Second Surprise of Love*. The Marivaux production incited a new battle of the ancients and the moderns and became a rallying point for the new generation of theatre lovers. It was *Hernani* all over again.

Before Planchon reached Paris, the weekly paper, *l'Express*, printed a long and intense debate, a panel discussion broadcast by radio, on *The Second Surprise*. The production was attacked by Professor J. Deloffre of the University of Lyon and defended by the novelist Roger Vailland and by Planchon himself. Deloffre argued that the plays of Marivaux, including *The Second Surprise*, incarnate the delicacy and refined wit of the early eighteenth century and that Planchon had wrecked the comedy, particularly by introducing a scene in which the Marquise and the Count are rising from a bed of love, the Marquise in dishabille and the Count without his perruque! Marivaux's text gives no indication of the place of the action, but a natural assumption would be that it is the Marquise's salon and, perhaps, the grounds adjoining her home. Planchon's production had seven sets: the Marquise's bedroom, her salon, her garden, her laundry-yard, a corridor in her home, the salon of the Chevalier, and a fencing room, presumably in the Chevalier's stables. Deloffre accepted very few of Planchon's ideas. The debate reached a climax of excitement at this point:

DELOFFRE. What I blame you for is wasting your talent by obstinately sticking to your whims and not listening to the text.
PLANCHON. But I do listen to the text, that's exactly what I do . . .
DELOFFRE. Then if you listen to it, you don't understand it.
PLANCHON. Look, you know very well that I am a serious person, and that I work!
DELOFFRE. Aren't you getting excited?
PLANCHON. Look, pardon me, but every text I choose, I study for three or four or even six months. I can tell you that everything in the performance comes from the text. If it weren't there, I wouldn't put it there.
DELOFFRE. Yes, by a series of misconstructions.
PLANCHON. That's your interpretation![3]

Much of the argument revolved around the question: how much sensuality is there in Marivaux? Vailland maintained that the eighteenth century was more sensual than our own and that a modern producer working for an audience used to frank sex in the theatre must clarify for that audience the veiled sensuality of Marivaux. Deloffre replied that Vailland was mixing up the period of Marivaux and that of Choderlos de Laclos (he might have added the Marquis de Sade).

When the play was staged in Paris, a similar difference of opinion split two prominent newspaper critics, Robert Kemp of *le Monde* and Jacques Lemarchand of *Le Figaro littéraire*. Kemp declared that the gentle people of Marivaux were presented as neurotic, melodramatic, and as if subject to libidinous dreams. Planchon's bedroom scene would have horrified Marivaux. In an ironical reply to this protest, Lemarchand asked what would become of us if these young Brechtian rebels were allowed to violate the exquisite salons and boudoirs of Marivaux. Lemarchand approved Planchon's attempt to "lift the skin" of Marivaux's people (as in a scene for which Planchon supplied rapiers and a physiological chart) and study the veins and muscles underneath. But the critic did think that Planchon went too far in sending the Marquise to bed with the Count after the Chevalier seems to rebuff her in Act Three.

All this publicity was not in vain, and when the play was near the end of its run, the theatre was crowded with a predominantly young and intensely enthusiastic audience. Probably many of them read the thirty-page program in which Planchon and his collaborators set down their manifesto and gave the rationale of the productions.

And what is supposed to go on in Marivaux's play? The Marquise is delicately mourning the loss of her husband, who has been dead for six months. The Chevalier gently despairs of further happiness in life, for he has lost Angélique, the girl he loves. Since her father has not allowed her to marry the Chevalier, she has retired from the world. Calling on the Marquise, the Chevalier asks her to deliver his farewell letter to his lost love. He allows the Marquise to read it aloud. She is charmed by the sensitivity of his style. Soon these kindred spirits decide that they can lessen each other's grief by reading together and speaking of those they have lost. A Count is in love with the Marquise, but she is hardly willing to see him. A servant, Lisette, subtly implies that the Chevalier should court the Marquise, but he seems cool to the idea. When the Marquise hears of Lisette's suggestion and the Chevalier's response, she asks him for a clarification. In a dialogue filled with the nuances characteristic of Marivaux, she learns that the Chevalier is far from indifferent to her, and the scene ends with expressions of *amitié* but no acknowledgment of *amour*. One more misunderstanding arises. In a scene with the Chevalier, the Count asserts that the Marquise has received his courtship with kindness. The "friends" now experience a few minutes—not a night—of melancholy estrangement. But the useful servants help the hero and heroine to make at last their mutual declaration of love.

The Marquise and the rivals express themselves like eighteenth-century porcelains come to life. This is how the Chevalier says farewell to Angélique: "All I know is that I have lost you, that I wish to speak to you only to redouble the grief of my loss and pierce myself with it till I die" (I,v). The Marquise is moved and astonished, for these are the very accents of her own affliction; in the opening scene with Lisette, she had said, "I ought to sigh all my life [*Je dois soupirer toute ma vie*]."[4] Marivaux smiles at the sentimentality and self-deception of his aristocrats. It is hard to believe that these people ever raise their voices, and one is slightly shocked to read that one of the Marquise's lines is spoken with anger.

The text indicates almost no physical action. In Planchon's production, the Marquise is caressing the Chevalier's shoulder in Act Two and his thigh in Act Three—this shortly before she goes to bed with the Count because she thinks she has lost the Chevalier. The men shout at each other, and the Chevalier pricks a plywood representation of the human body with the skin removed, while his rival stands a few inches upstage of the lunging sword. As the Marquise upbraids Lisette for offering her to the Chevalier, a half-dozen invented servants skin cucumbers and hang up laundry, for this is the scene placed by the director in a laundry-yard. The reading scene, set in a grove, permits passing of books, carrying of furniture in interesting processions, and elaborate business with quilts, for the time is taken to be late autumn. The life of the servants is ingeniously developed, and by closing one scene in a gradually dimming light, the director gives the feeling of a painting by Le Nain in movement. The garden is surrounded by flats bearing sketches after Watteau, but the tone of the scene as performed is perhaps closer to Dutch realism than to French rococo.

The enclosing flats were retained through the entire play, but changes of scene were accomplished by a fascinating variety of ceilings. In a program note the designer, René Allio, explained why he decided that the Chevalier's salon should have a ceiling of outmoded design while the wealthier Marquise should have the latest thing in ceilings. The production was extremely inventive throughout.

Study of the play and the production makes two points clear. Planchon is a highly imaginative director, but he used Marivaux's play mainly as a theme on which to perform his own very numerous improvisations. Many of these were simply not true to Marivaux.

To show the special quality of the amorous manoeuvering at the heart of the play, it will be useful to analyze the important interviews in Act Two between the Marquise and the Chevalier. Lisette, who is determined to cure the Marquise's grief by finding her a new husband, has suggested to the Chevalier that he should become the Marquise's suitor. Already troubled by the Count's interest in the Marquise, the Chevalier has received Lisette's hint with embarrassment and seeming coldness. When the Marquise learns what Lisette has done and what the Che-

válier has said in reply, she is naturally upset. After saying that she does
not love the Count and has only recently become aware of his love,
she questions the Chevalier:

THE MARQUISE. . . . Did you reject Lisette's offer because you were
    piqued by the Count's love or because the offer was objectionable
    in itself? Was it jealousy? For after all, despite our agreement,
    your heart might have been affected. Or was it true disdain?
THE CHEVALIER. First of all, please reject that last idea; it is incredible.
    As for jealousy . . .
THE MARQUISE. Speak boldly.
THE CHEVALIER. What would you say if I admitted some?
THE MARQUISE. I would say . . . that you were jealous.
THE CHEVALIER. Yes. But Madame, would you pardon in me what you
    hate so much?
THE MARQUISE. Then you weren't jealous? (*She watches him.*) I under-
    stand. This is what I expected. It confirms the insult.
THE CHEVALIER. Why speak of an insult? Where is it? Are you angry
    with me?
THE MARQUISE. With you, Chevalier? Certainly not; why should I be
    angry? You don't understand me. My quarrel is with Lisette. I had
    nothing to do with the offer she made you, and I had to let you
    know this—that is all.

[II,vii]

Each is the comic victim of a struggle between self-esteem, growing
attraction, and a somewhat theoretical commitment to past loves.

A second interview takes place a few minutes later (II,ix). The Marquise takes the offensive to the extent of flattering his now hopeless
love for Angélique while saying that his *amitié* for the Marquise should
have forbidden so open a recoil from Lisette's overtures: "You don't
know," she adds, "the duties [of friendship] as I do. If someone were
to offer me your hand, for example, I would teach you the way to reply." The hint is encouraging, and in a moment the Chevalier says:
". . . if I did not love Angelique, whom I must forget, you would have
only one thing to fear from me, that my friendship might become love;
and even that would not, in reason, be something to fear either." Qualification within qualification! He *has* loved Angélique, but he *must* forget her. If he were not in love with her (perhaps he is so no longer),
the Marquise would have only one thing to fear from him, but even
that is not, in reason, to be feared. Why not? Because his love is not
frightening, because he would not be so intrusive as to love the Marquise so soon, or because he might not fall (is not falling) in love with

her? Reason would suggest that the first or the second alternative is the strongest possibility, but is it reasonable to rely on reason in a scene like this? The Marquise replies that his falling in love with her "would be too much"—a greater reparation than is necessary. They are still swimming in ambiguities.[5]

Another moment, and the Chevalier can declare that he was "outré" to see the Marquise's "attachment" to the Count contravening the friendship established in Act One. This is as close as he can come to admitting jealousy without making a declaration of love. The Countess is happy again, and Act Two can end very shortly.

The friends have found a path through a labyrinth typical of Marivaux. How openly and how quickly can they proceed from friendship to love without jeopardizing their sense of their own and each other's delicacy; on the other hand, how slowly can they proceed without injuring each other's self-esteem? Perhaps no other playwright has struggled so tenaciously with this serio-comic situation. We smile at the elaborate self-deceptions, but we admire the civilized turns and counter-turns of the dialogue.

In *Marivaux par lui-même*, Paul Gazagne stresses what he takes to be the sensuality of Marivaux's characters. Sensuality is hardly the word for the heroine of *The Game of Love*. One can sight more of this quality in the Marquise, who is certainly more *avertie* than Silvia. It is one thing, however, to recognize a normal sensuality in various characters of Marivaux, and another to see them as emblems of sensuality hypocritically disguised. Such creations as the Marquise and the Chevalier are comic not because they are amorous Tartuffes but because they are victimized by their own inhibitions and their failures to see themselves as we see them. The Marquise is more calculating than Christopher Fry's Dynamene, but she is not Petronius' Widow of Ephesus.

The Second Surprise has more depth than *The Game of Love and Chance*. The Marquise is more mature than Silvia, and her tergiversations are not so impeccably sweet. Furthermore, the refined sorrows of the Marquise and her friend are effectively satirized by Lisette and Lubin. Lubin cannot be ignorant that his deliberately inflated griefs are a reduction to absurdity of the fine postures taken by his "betters." Like his master, he has lost a mistress, and as the Chevalier languishes for Angélique, Lubin bemoans the loss of Marton; but he makes less of his own deprivation than of his master's. When he first announces the coming of the Chevalier, he cannot refrain from a sympathetic sob or two. He adds that if it weren't for his *honnêteté* or good manners, he would weep still louder: a sly reference to the tasteful grief of the Chevalier. But as Lubin soon explains to Lisette, who immediately attracts him, "my master sighs because he has lost a mistress; and since I am the most kind-hearted fellow in the world, I start acting like him to distract him and I go around weeping without being sad, as a compliment to him" (I,iii). Which of the two men is the more ridiculous at such a point? Without attempting a revolutionary appraisal of the class system, Marivaux uses Lubin in the way Shakespeare sometimes uses his clowns—as critics whose attack is valid without necessarily constituting proof of their own superiority to the object of satire. Lubin toughens the play and helps to preserve it from excessive delicacy.

  The Double Inconstancy is the earliest of the three plays chosen for discussion, yet it is in one respect the most subtle and the most mature. If The Game of Love is a romantic and essentially innocent comedy, if The Second Surprise is a comedy of controlled sensuality mingled with self-deception, The Double Inconstancy is marked above all by a quiet yet firm irony, a double-edged irony at the expense of courtly society on the one hand and deflected innocence on the other.

  The double inconstancy is the result of a double seduction. A recent critic has found the subject frightful, and in The Rehearsal, Anouilh has one of his characters say: "The Twofold Inconstancy is a grim play, I beg you to remember that," and the "little universe" of the play is "corrupt and cynical and tittering under its silks and plumes and winking gems."[6] Although this description fits Anouilh's play better than Marivaux's, it is significant as a twentieth-century response to a comedy written in 1723.

  Two simple villagers, Silvia and Harlequin, are deeply in love. But the Prince of the realm, who has been hunting near their village, happens upon Silvia outside her home. Pretending that he is merely an officer of the court, he visits her five or six times. He cannot shake her love for Harlequin. In this imaginary kingdom a law requires the Prince to marry one of his subjects after obtaining her free consent. At the beginning of the play Silvia has been carried by force to the Prince's palace, but she has not yet seen him there. The entire court, including the officious Trivelin, the coquettish Lisette, and the subtle Flaminia, is vainly attempting to persuade Silvia to abandon her love for Harlequin and accept the Prince in marriage. Flaminia, who is a fine lady of the court, suggests to the Prince that Harlequin be permitted to see Silvia again but that the two lovers be surprised into new affections, Silvia by the "officer" and Harlequin by Lisette or Flaminia herself. The action of the play is the execution of this plan. By flattery, insinuation, lies, and discreet lovemaking, Flaminia and the still incognito Prince gradually destroy the village love-affair. Silvia will marry the Prince and Harlequin will take Flaminia off to a country life. Because of their services to the Prince, Flaminia and Harlequin need never fear for the future.

In outline the play appears unreal and even silly. The pretty laws of the realm, the Prince's prolonged disguise, the notion that a sophisticated court lady could wish to marry a country fellow who is also a black-face comedian—all this would succeed better, one would think, in a Russian ballet than as a basis for a social comedy. Yet the story of a Prince who carries off attractive girls would not seem too remote in a France ruled by the dissolute Duke of Orléans. (The actor who played the Prince was at the unromantic age of 49, exactly the Duke's age.) Furthermore, Marivaux derives several advantages from his seemingly stultifying and unreal premises. For example, since the village lovers are both naive and direct in their thinking, they can make some devastating comments on the artificialities and absurdities of court life. And although they frequently moralize, the amusing simplicity of their characters preserves the commentary from the pitfalls of the sentimental drama. In addition, the very gaps between the court and village, which for most playwrights would be impassable, inspires Marivaux to a brilliantly managed, gradual conversion of Silvia and Harlequin from one state of mind and heart to another. At first indifferent to courtly lovemaking, Silvia comes to appreciate her royal lover fully; in the process a simple country girl becomes as conscious as any Marquise of her attractions. Despising coquetries, Harlequin falls prey to the higher blandishments of Flaminia; and along the way, the laughably humble lover becomes a complacent fellow willing to set up a *ménage à trois*.

The poise of *The Double Inconstancy* rests on its intricate ironies. No one is immune from them. The play is a balancing act which could be imaged by that famous tumbler, the traditional Arlecchino—his torso thrown slightly to the right, his left thigh rather far to the left, the rest of his body contributing to his vitality and stability. The oppositions within the play are like the bodily oppositions of the dancer. Silvia has been carried off from her home, but she has been offered no other violence, but does this excuse the gentle Prince? He himself speaks quietly and pleasantly, but he is surrounded by a servile court. He is perfectly *honnête*, yet his wishes are advanced by the officious Trivelin as well as the suave Lord whom the unpolished Harlequin easily confutes in a passage of dialectic. Is the Prince's love for the unspoiled Silvia a sign

of his essential humanity or a hint that the sated ruler must stimulate
his jaded appetite with new sauces? The glittering court girl Lisette is
put to shame by the unaffected Silvia, who will shortly become as vain
as Lisette. We cannot help asking how long the Prince will continue to
believe that "Silvia's love alone is truly love" (III,i). Flaminia, who sets
out to trap Harlequin, is by Act Three both conqueror and conquered.
In a moment alone she says: "In truth, the Prince is right. These little
people make love in a manner that can't be resisted" (III,viii). A sincere
exclamation; but is there something decadent about the phrasing?

There is no need to exaggerate the bite of the irony. Marivaux's social
criticism is not fortissimo. Fully aware of the falsities inherent in an
aristocratic society, he also sees the insincerities ready to manifest themselves in the soul of the peasant, superficially so remote from the creature of the court. An aristocratic society has no monopoly on lies. "What
are these people?" asks the still constant Silvia. "Where do they come
from? What stuff are they made of?" (II,i). Of the same flesh and blood
as her own. A "natural" self can deceive itself as easily as one with a peri-
wig. And Marivaux refuses to say that his charming villagers, who are
as winning as the lovers in his other plays, have any patent on attractiveness and good will.

In the first act the court tries to undermine Silvia's love and then
Harlequin's, failing to shake either. The lovers have a touching reunion
as Flaminia stands by, warmly sympathetic. But when Silvia is called
off to see her mother, Flaminia remains behind with Harlequin. She
will join him at dinner. The seduction of Harlequin by food and sympathy has already begun. Silvia seems as yet untainted, but her impul-
siveness, vivacity, and wit are facets of a nature in which coquetry is
not far beneath the surface.

Silvia's opening lines in Act One are almost too pert for one in her
classically pathetic plight.

TRIVELIN. But Madame, listen to me.
SILVIA. You bore me.
TRIVELIN. Shouldn't we be reasonable?
SILVIA. No, we shouldn't, and I won't be.
TRIVELIN. However . . .
SILVIA (angered). "However," I want no "reason" . . .

[I,i]

When reproached for eating too little, she replies that she "hates health"
and is "content to be ill." If Trivelin wishes her to lose her mind, he
has only to recommend that she be "reasonable." The Prince wishes to

give her his hand, but "what does he want me to do with that hand, since I have no desire to take it in mine?" (I,i). This is the higher *marivaudage*. What is it doing in the mouth of an artless country girl?

Though Trivelin thinks the girl a prodigy of fidelity, Flaminia finds the notion laughable. To the Prince she says: "Oh my lord, don't listen to him and his 'prodigies.' Prodigies are found only in fairy tales. I know my sex: there is nothing prodigious about us but our coquetry. Silvia is not vulnerable on the side of ambition; but she has a heart and there-fore vanity. So I will know how to bring her down to her duty as a woman" (I,ii). In a sentimental play, Flaminia would be proved wrong. In this play she is right.

Her shrewd analysis is in striking contrast with Harlequin's descrip-tion of how Silvia fell in love with him: "You should have seen how she withdrew from me during the first days; and then she withdrew more sweetly; and then, little by little, not at all; next she looked at me se-cretly; and then she was ashamed that I saw her do so, and then, seeing her shame—that was the pleasure of a king; next I caught her hand and she let me take it . . ." (I,vi). This panegyric comes a few pages after Flaminia's ironic prediction, and there is yet little evidence that Harle-quin's Silvia is not the only Silvia. Harlequin had said, "That's what I call a girl!" (I,vi). She will still deserve this praise at the end of Act One. But in Act Two she will fall in love with the "officer" just as grace-fully as with Harlequin.

When the village lovers meet again in Act Two, they are already giddy, distracted by the flattering attentions they have been getting. Alone with Flaminia, Silvia can compare Harlequin unfavorably with her new admirer and even apologize for having loved Harlequin. The stage is set for the reentrance of the "officer" and Silvia's virtual admis-sion that she loves him.

Ironic cross-references crowd the first two acts. The first meeting of Harlequin and Silvia is *appassionato*, the second almost cool. Harle-quin's picture of Silvia falling in love is tender; in Act Two her version of the story comes as a shock: "Put yourself in my place. He was the most acceptable boy in our district; he is merry, I am good-humored; he sometimes made me laugh; he followed me everywhere, he loved me; I was used to seeing him, and out of habit I loved him for lack of some-one better; but I always noticed that he was fond of eating and drink-ing" (II,xi). The ironies include many parallels. By Act Two Harlequin is boasting that courtiers now beg his pardon for slight impertinences, and Silvia is expecting an apology from Lisette because that girl had not found her beautiful. In Act Two, Scene Three Silvia regrets that she met Harlequin before the officer; in Act Two, Scene Four Harlequin responds to the overtures of Flaminia by saying: "It's unfortunate that I love Silvia." It now appears that if the "little" people have lived innocently, it is because they have been ignorant of the ways of self-indulgence.

If Racine's Nero is a *monstre naissant*, Silvia and Harlequin are *sensualistes naissants*. To put it solemnly, we see them about to become as corrupt as we are. And yet, there is almost no bitterness in the laughter aroused by the play. By a tour de force, the little accessions of feeling in the two extend the histrionic time of the play without destroying the first image of innocence. Silvia in particular awakens to sentience, and we can see each discovery as it comes to her, each step she takes toward the tree of knowledge. In Act Two, Scene Eleven she says of Harlequin, "I love him; it is really necessary." A page later, "I ought to love Harlequin." And a moment later, "If Harlequin should marry another girl, fine! I should have the right to say: 'You have left me, I leave you, I'm taking my revenge.'" As a Lord has recently explained to Harlequin, courtiers hope to acquire the Prince's favor so that they will have the power to take revenge on those who have injured them. Silvia's growing love for the officer is teaching her the language and thought processes of the Prince's creatures. Marivaux's women ordinarily become more appealing as their love grows. Silvia's development cannot be described so simply.

By the end of Act Two she has arrived at a love that she cannot quite assert, unless we say that characters in Marivaux do not love until they use the word. At any rate, the struggle to speak it is as important as the coming of the emotion which the word names. As Stanislavsky might have said, "to love" as Marivaux understands the infinitive is not an action, but to name the feeling is. In Act Two, Scene Twelve, after saying that the Prince "asks for my heart," Silvia tells the officer: "you . . . would deserve it [*mériteriez*]." This is the very grammar of her motives.

Her soul is certainly not yet lost. But Act Three completes the emotional revolution which is the subject of the play; it also shows that as she attains her greatest happiness, she is beginning to divest herself of the qualities that attract the Prince, though he is unaware of what is happening to her.

Holding the stage for most of Act Three, Harlequin reaches a definite understanding with Flaminia. Silvia enters late in the act. Confessing to Flaminia that she no longer loves Harlequin, she asserts that she is not to blame. When Flaminia "almost" agrees, Silvia turns on her friend: "What do you mean by 'almost'? Kindly think just as I do, because I'm right. These people of mine who can't make up their minds!" (III,viii). The village girl has assumed the tone of the spoiled noblewoman. She does ask what she should do about Harlequin, but she adds, "Don't make me feel too scrupulous." With quiet irony Flaminia hints that Harlequin will perhaps be appeased. Then Harlequin can forget her so easily? Every word of Flaminia irritates the new Silvia, who is exactly fulfilling the early predictions of the court lady. But the Prince enters, and the courting can be completed. When Harlequin reappears, there is nothing more about scruples. But he has received consolation in advance.

Harlequin and Flaminia will live in the country. This is the right decision. Harlequin's native wit has cut through the shams and deadening malice of court life, and Flaminia is keenly aware of the man she is getting. Their departure will balance Silvia's decision to become a princess.

Confronted by the religion of love, comedy is neither a devout worshipper nor a complete infidel. Love exists and is often true, often corresponds to the image which the lover makes of it. The comedies of Marivaux, which end happily, neither assert nor deny that love can be eternal. The comedy which most interests him is the comedy of falling in love, and occasionally this comedy expires in devotion. But in such a play as *The Double Inconstancy* there are, as Gustave Lanson wrote, pleasures for one who is "disabused without being bitter, who is no longer the dupe of love, but who has not lost his fondness for it."[7]

NOTES

1. *Marivaux et le marivaudage* (Paris, 1955), p. 194.

2. *Oeuvres Complètes de M. de Marivaux*, 12 vols. (Paris, 1781), IX, 537-38.

3. *L'Express*, April 2, 1959, pp. 29–30.

4. J. B. Ratermanis writes, "The obligation replaces the fact one does not discuss" (*Étude sur le comique dans le théâtre de Marivaux* [Geneva and Paris, 1961], p. 215).

5. Ratermanis, p. 224.

6. *The Rehearsal*, trans. Lucienne Hill, I,ii, in *Jean Anouilh (Five Plays)*, (New York, 1958), pp. 208–9.

7. *Nivelle de la chaussée et la comédie larmoyante* (Paris, 1903), p. 36.

CHAPTER ELEVEN

Shaw's Comedy and Major Barbara

Shaw once remarked that if he tried to explain his plays to his confused public, they would be ten times more confused. Of course he did explain them, often with misleading effect. If his plays were as intellectually haughty and uncompromising as his prefaces, essays, and statements to the press, he would be remembered primarily as a satirist, not as a comic dramatist. Despite the trumpet blasts introducing his comedy, the plays themselves, no mere expositions of his contempt for error and folly, prove that he was continually seduced by the absurdity of the human spectacle.

In 1897, Shaw reviewed George Meredith's *Essay on Comedy* when it appeared in book form, twenty years after the lecture on which it was based. The occasion was rich in ironic comedy. What would the impossible Irishman, the socialist author of a half-dozen plays including *Mrs. Warren's Profession* and *The Devil's Disciple*, have to say about this refined presentation of comedy as an essentially conservative art reflecting the common sense of a civilized society? What would he think of Meredith's Comic Spirit poised over the heads of congregated ladies and gentlemen, instructing them so nicely about vanity and affectation that they are ready, on signal, to smile with unequalled politeness or break into silvery laughter? Shaw's response was disingenuous in the extreme. The *Essay* is "perfectly straightforward and accurate," as one would expect from "perhaps the highest living authority" on the subject. It is "excellent," "superfine." Yes, but in thinking that the English are capable of appreciating comedy, Mr. Meredith shows that he is as ill-informed about the English public as he is well-informed about comedy. In Shaw's view, English habits, morals, and society completely lack Meredith's common sense. And after twenty years the high authority might perhaps admit that the purpose of comedy is "nothing less than the destruction of old-established morals."[1] Almost fifty years later in *Everybody's Political What's What?* Shaw would say during the course of an argument against universal suffrage that mankind is permanently divided into the average, the superaverage, and the subaverage. In the review, only the elite have common sense.

Shaw's revolutionary view of comedy carries over into the *Prefaces.* His high-powered polemics over *Arms and the Man* (1894) might lead one to suppose that the play was as shocking as Ibsen's *Ghosts.* The Preface to *Plays Pleasant* (1898) declares that Shaw has been "making war" on the majority of the theatregoing public. A "general onslaught on idealism . . . is implicit, and indeed explicit, in *Arms and the Man* and the naturalist plays of the modern school." The author can no longer accept a morality "shedding fictitious glory on robbery, starvation, disease, crime, drink, war," etc., etc.[2] From such intonations one would think that the witty and genial farce of Raina and Bluntschli must be closer to *The Weavers* than to *The Importance of Being Earnest.* Actually, Wilde's play has more satiric thrust than Shaw's. Satire rarely exorcises the evils it uncovers, but in *Arms and the Man*, Raina and Sergius see through their own romantic sins long before the play is over. Shaw is writing light comedy.

His plays of the new century are, of course, far more serious than *Arms and the Man.* His statement in the review of Meredith that comedy is "the fine art of disillusion,"[3] begins to mean not only that comedy supplants childish dreams with mature awareness but that this awareness contains an element of stoic and perhaps ineradicable sadness. Between 1901 and 1905 Shaw wrote *Man and Superman, John Bull's Other Island*, and *Major Barbara.* Each play treats folly and illusion in a distinctive way. Despite its length and its panoply of biological and sociological argument, *Man and Superman* is the most cheerful, even youthful, of the three plays. Yet it reveals increasing maturity in that the archetypal Shavian, John Tanner, instead of carrying everything before him with his cascading speeches, convinces no one, except of his brilliance, repeatedly looks very foolish, and is victimized by a heroine without a single aim beyond that of trapping the man of her choice. In his weaker plays, Shaw sometimes gives the impression that to live the good life, the one thing required is to put your enthymemes in order; but not so here. If Tanner attains a happy ending, it is not because his intelligence has made the right choices but because someone else knows what is right for him.

The play is subtitled "A Comedy and a Philosophy." Apart from the Epistle Dedicatory and the appended Revolutionist's Handbook, the philosophy appears mainly in Tanner's dream during Act Three. Although this dream is usually omitted in performance and makes an excellent dialogue in itself, it has important structural significance; for Tanner is suspiciously though entertainingly glib in his waking hours, but in his dream he triumphantly refutes the devil himself in speeches which not only eulogize but seem to embody "the philosophic man: he who seeks in contemplation to discover the inner will of the world, in invention to discover the means of fulfilling that will, and in action to do that will by the so-discovered means" (pp. 379–80). The Doña Ana of his dreams is utterly convinced that such a man must be brought to life; the Ann Whitefield of his waking hours, hearing his final essay in comic desperation, tells him to "go on talking" (p. 405). Only in his dreams is this Shavian hero the stepping-stone to definitely higher things.

Like Larry Doyle in *John Bull's Other Island*, Tanner is both foolish and clever—a good prescription for a comic hero. But there are no heroes in *John Bull*. Neither a comedy nor a tragicomedy nor even a satire, though abundantly satiric, it is a deeply ironic work, perhaps the most bitter and melancholy play Shaw ever wrote. It explores a fundamentally hopeless situation, the relationship of England and Ireland in the early twentieth century. Both countries are to blame for the poverty of Ireland—or rather, two kinds of character are at fault, here the English and the Irish. Although there is a plot, it has little importance. Shaw develops his theme chiefly by means of three characters arranged in hierarchical order. Tom Broadbent, the Gladstonized Englishman, earnest, moral, putting his morality at the service of his interests but completely without hypocrisy, "clever in [his] foolishness" (p. 451), will exploit the Irish with the best will in the world. He will lend them more money on their properties than they are worth, then foreclose his mortgages and appropriate the land for the syndicate he represents. As if this were not enough, he wins an Irish girl with a small fortune and is certain to be elected as an Irish member of the British Parliament, for as a Liberal he favors Home Rule. In his lack of Shaw's "completer consciousness," he is farcical, but ultimately the joke is on Ireland and the poor. His business partner and friend, Larry Doyle, Anglicized Irishman, far more conscious than Broadbent but bitter, cynical, ambivalent in his feelings toward his country because of his tortured wish to escape Irish poverty and footlessness, "foolish in his cleverness" (p. 451), will satirize his friend's blindness but join with him in taking the profits from the land, hating himself for doing so. Mr. Keegan, saint and unfrocked priest under the influence of Oriental philosophy, neither foolish nor merely clever, clearly sees the condition of Ireland, understands what is ruining her, arraigns her betrayers, and dreams of a religious Utopia.

The Broadbents and the Doyles control Ireland for the present, but, if Keegan is right, "the day may come when these islands shall live by the quality of their men rather than by the abundance of their minerals" (p. 450). This tentative statement comes closer to hope than any other in the play. In the powerful final scene Keegan's vision of Ireland merges with the heaven he would substitute for the hell of modern life. When Broadbent asks what this heaven is like, Keegan answers that it is a commonwealth in which Church, State, and people are one. "It is a temple in which the priest is the worshipper and the worshipper the worshipped: three in one and one in three. It is a godhead in which all life is human and all humanity divine: three in one and one in three. It is, in short, the dream of a madman" (p. 452). The dream is clearly related to the vitalist aspirations of Shaw, but here it is the vision of a mystic whom everyone tolerates but ignores. Compared with Tanner's dreams, Keegan's are utterly lacking in cocksureness and so far more moving. In comedy the divine average is triumphant. One measure of the distance between comedy and *John Bull* is that in Shaw's play this triumph seems very far away, so distant as to be almost inconceivable.

The follies and illusions at which Shaw laughs are the subject matter of his comedies. Sometimes these follies and illusions are eradicable, as in *Arms and the Man*, sometimes not, as in *Getting Married*, which presents marriage as absurd but unavoidable and finally tolerable. But there are follies which he regards as disastrous. Characteristically, he does not treat these as the errors of tragic heroes; despite *Saint Joan*, perhaps the tragic hero is the one paradox in which he did not believe. "Tragic" error is social, not personal, as one may see in *John Bull* and *Heartbreak House*. In the Irish play, the men selected to represent Ireland's destroyers are ridiculous or pitiful, and the only man with the brains and the desire to save her is helpless. In *Heartbreak House* Captain Shotover, who speaks for Shaw, inveighs against the generations who have followed him, but their representatives onstage are delightful or amusing or both. Shaw's darker plays tend to be ironic rather than tragic or tragicomic.

In *John Bull*, the gap between Broadbent and the meaning of what he is doing threatens to scatter the play into fragments. In *Major Barbara*, a more dramatic play, there is a strong tension between the comedy of its people and what Shaw takes to be the intolerable state of modern society, but the strain is not excessive. The total effect is that of problem comedy. If Barbara and Cusins had rejected Undershaft's invitation to join the firm of Undershaft and Lazarus and had lapsed into hopelessness, the play would have been predominantly ironic. As concluded, it offers a hopeful, though hypothetical, solution to the problem posed.

Major Barbara contains a plot within an allegory. The central question of the plot is this: who shall succeed Andrew Undershaft as director of Undershaft and Lazarus, munitions makers? Symbolically considered, the question means: what shall replace the ruinous state of modern civilization, in which men have to choose among poverty, crime, and prosperity built on war and legalized theft?

Lady Britomart Undershaft, daughter of the Earl of Stevenage, naturally thinks that her son Stephen (crown) should inherit his father's industrial empire, which is so powerful that its products are purchased by foreign nations through loans floated by the British government. Like Spenser's Britomart, she is clad in unassailable virtue—"ne euill thing she fear'd, ne euill thing she ment."[4] But Undershaft is determined to follow the tradition of his firm that a foundling always inherits the business. Besides, Stephen is incompetent. Though Shaw was an aristocratic socialist who demanded equal distribution of wealth while denying the ability of many or most men to choose their leaders intelligently, he obviously thought that the ruling classes in England had failed. Leaders might emerge from any class. The Liberal aristocrats are as bad as the Conservatives, if not worse. One recalls that the ridiculous Broadbent in *John Bull's Other Island* was a fervent Liberal. Lady Brit is proud of her Whig background and, like Roebuck Ramsden in *Man and Superman*, has a library from which advanced books are not excluded. At one point Stephen picks up a copy of a Liberal weekly. But Liberalism is not enough.

Undershaft becomes strongly attracted to his vital daughter, Major Barbara of the Salvation Army, and decides to convert her to his own religion, which he first announces as money and gunpowder but later reveals as vitalist, with at least a touch of the Dionysian. He is also drawn to Barbara's fiancé, Adolphus Cusins, a Greek professor and collector of religions, including the Dionysian.[5] Cusins' first name means "noble wolf," and Shaw said he had chosen the character's name carefully. His family name is a function of the plot, for when he learns that only a foundling can inherit the firm, he reveals that his mother was his father's deceased wife's sister—which in Lady Brit's interpretation makes him his own cousin. This farcical development illustrates Shaw's method of placing in comic perspective ideas about which he felt the deepest concern. It is as if he needed to keep them at a distance, so strongly did they shake him.

Undershaft is a realist-mystic; Cusins and Barbara are humanitarian idealists, both ignorant of economic and political realities. Their education or conversion is necessary to the happy ending. And conversion of superior people like them is necessary to the Utopia envisioned by Shaw. But the full meaning of this conversion can be understood only by consideration of the play in some detail.

Each of the four divisions of the play opens with deceptively amusing dialogue and moves toward more overtly serious conflict. If the tone of the opening scene in Lady Brit's library had been preserved throughout the comedy, the work could bear Wilde's ironic subtitle for *The Importance of Being Earnest*—"A Trivial Comedy for Serious People." Just as Wilde's criticism of private property, private charity, the Church, and the press, as voiced in "The Soul of Man Under Socialism" (1891), reappears in *The Importance of Being Earnest*, so Shaw's themes emerge in his first act, though wearing the guise of drawing-room comedy. The scene is masterful both as exposition and for its characterization of Lady Britomart, at once so strong-minded and so immersed in the illusions that she and her class know what is right and who should rule the world. The presentation of these illusions adumbrates Shaw's attempt, in later scenes, at transvaluation of values, his demand for a new concept of crime and punishment, and his call for a new aristocracy.

As the play proceeds, Lady Brit quickly loses her dominating position. Unlike Lady Bracknell, Wilde's social juggernaut, Lady Brit has been adjusted to a dramatic world in which real conflicts and hesitations are possible. She can easily control Sarah Undershaft and her clownish fiancé, Lomax—tag ends of the aristocratic tradition. But the immature Stephen insists on growing up. Barbara and Cusins are stronger than she and hopeful symbols for the future of England. Their poise can be seen in such small details as Cusins' ironic statement to Lady Brit, "You have my unhesitating support in everything you do" (p. 465), and even in Barbara's cool way of responding to a belligerent question from her mother by sitting on a table and whistling "Onward, Christian Soldiers."

Soon after the family assembles, Undershaft arrives in response to Lady Brit's summons, for she has some requests to make of her estranged husband. At his entrance, Undershaft is described as "on the surface" an easygoing man, kindly, patient, and simple. "His gentleness is partly that of a strong man who has learned by experience that his natural grip hurts ordinary people . . ." (p. 466). Although Shaw's characters do not always live up to their advance billing, this sentence should be remembered while Undershaft is making the sensational speeches that seem to exhibit utter indifference to suffering and death. It is essential to the effect of the play that he should postpone as long as possible any admission of humane sentiments, for a main point of the comedy is that these feelings will have to be shelved if the world is to emerge from the inferno of the twentieth century.

In 1905, Japan defeated Russia in the Far East, and the Revolution of 1905 was the first major blow to absolute monarchy in Russia. This revolution is on Shaw's mind when he writes in his Preface: "I am and always have been, and shall now always be, a revolutionary writer. . . . Our natural safety from the cheap and devastating explosives which every Russian student can make, and every Russian grenadier has learnt to handle in Manchuria, lies in the fact that brave and resolute men, when they are rascals, will not risk their skins for the good of humanity, and, when they are not, are sympathetic enough to care for humanity, abhorring murder, and never committing it until their consciences are outraged beyond endurance."[6] Brave and resolute men had not shrunk from murder in Russia.[7] How long would they continue to do so in England?

Undershaft is not a Communist. He is a business man who blows up soldiers through intermediaries, and at a huge profit. In the first act, after some preliminary farce which establishes him as likably prone to mistaking identities, he announces his first position on the morality of war production. The greater the success his engineers have in increasing the destructiveness of his weapons, the more "amiable" he becomes. So he says, and no one, except Lomax, begs leave to find a justification for this good humor. Far from being ashamed of his business, far from salving his conscience by huge gifts to charity, he wishes to be distinguished from rivals "who keep their morals and their business in watertight compartments" (p. 468). His morality is a function of his work, and for him the moral course is to put back into his industry what others sacrifice to charity.

But even in the first act, the audience may become suspicious of so much villainy in so pleasant a man. What are his real motives? He gives no evidence of wanting great wealth or power for himself. To say that he merely enjoys shocking conventional people is no answer; he has something else on his mind. The more shamelessly he plays out—and plays up—his role as ruthless capitalist, the more shameful modern capitalism appears. The capitalists are the power-structure, and Undershaft admires power. But when placed beside his object-lesson in shamelessness, this admiration leads to the thought that power is in the wrong hands. Can Undershaft be holding power as trustee for a beneficiary that has not yet appeared? Who is the foundling to be?

The Barbara-theme is sounded next. When Stephen divides humanity into honest men and scoundrels, Barbara replies that all are sinners but none are scoundrels. Salvation by faith awaits them all. Undershaft wants to know if even a maker of cannons may be saved. The question leads to a contract. If he will come to her Salvation Army shelter, she will visit his cannon works. Each will attempt to "save" the other.[8] Now the bargain will be sealed by a religious service. As all reject Lady Brit's demand for Anglican prayers, her power begins to crumble.

Act Two, in the West Ham shelter, puts in action the vigorous, devoted, but misapplied leadership of Barbara in the struggle to raise the depressed classes. The act succeeds in being both an entertaining genre picture and a comprehensive attack on current social conditions. The recipients of charity show far greater knowledge of the world than do the naive Salvation Army workers. The system drags down men with brains and ability, and for all its good will, the Army cannot accomplish much. An intelligent object of charity almost sums up the act when he says to Barbara: "Ah! it's a pity you never was trained to use your reason, miss. Youd have been a very taking lecturer on Secularism" (p. 476). Barbara is at her strongest in her battle for the soul of Bill Walker, a brute who has just struck a Salvation Army girl in the face. Barbara's friendly, courageous manner awakens in him the remorse that she hopes will lead him to God. But Undershaft arrives at the shelter.

In an important scene between Undershaft and Cusins, the two men agree that the spirit of God is more important than his name. Convinced that this spirit is within Barbara—a handsome example of what the evolutionary process can accomplish—Undershaft resolves to turn her propagation of faith from God to gunpowder. Excited by his idea, he declares, "I shall hand on my torch to my daughter. She shall make my converts and preach my gospel—" (p. 479). At the moment of utterance, this prediction sounds like mere perversity or madness, but as the scene moves on, the inner meaning of this Dionysus-Machiavelli becomes clearer. To Cusins he says with ostentatious harshness, "What have we three to do with the common mob of slaves and idolaters?" (p. 479). The Shaw-Undershaft mind is so rapt in a vision not yet defined that the speaker can coolly ignore the poor souls at his feet. And it is helpful to remember that much of Shaw's life was devoted to improving the lot of people for whom, as individuals, he had a low regard. He will not love the common people until they have been made uncommon by present standards. In a major speech attacking poverty Undershaft says, "We three must stand together above the common people: how else can we help their children to climb up beside us?" (p. 480). If the older generation is already beyond salvation, the men of the future are not.

The way must be prepared by shattering Barbara's faith in the God of charity and passivity. Undershaft will accomplish this feat by showing her that the Army must depend on the contributions of those whose lives are devoted to destroying its ideals.

When Cusins points out that the Army makes men sober, honest, unselfish, and spiritual, his mentor replies that these qualities are safeguards against socialism and revolution and therefore pleasing to him as an industrialist. Taken literally, his argument here is inconsistent with the higher motives he elsewhere intimates. But for the moment he is speaking not as himself but as The Capitalist, and giving Cusins an elementary lesson in political economy.

In the last section of this act, Barbara almost succeeds in her fight for Bill Walker. She will not allow him to pay for his blow by inviting another or by giving money. Baffled, he seems ready to accept religion and repentance. But word comes that a prominent distiller is offering £ 5,000 to the Salvation Army. Despite Barbara's horror, the Army will gratefully accept. Bill relapses into cynicism with his memorable question, "Wot prawce selvytion nah?" (p. 486). Barbara's occupation is gone.

Shaw did not like to be dismissed as brilliant, but apart from some brilliant light comedy, the first scene in Act Three is mainly an opportunity for a big speech by Undershaft instructing the fatuous Stephen that capital, not Parliament, rules the country. The government recognizes capital's needs as national needs and is ready to call out the police when private enterprise is threatened. This is one of Undershaft's more ruthless moments, for there is no point in his explaining to Stephen what is really on his mind. Even if Undershaft unmasked, Stephen could not understand him.

The final scene takes place at Perivale St. Andrews, on a height looking down on the beautiful community built by Undershaft. The name of the place, its elevation, and its beauty help to give Andrew Undershaft the religious status he asserts in tones not merely ironical. Manufacturing death, the workers live a good life. The chief question of the scene is whether Cusins, greatly tempted by the place, can bridge the moral abyss between himself and Undershaft. He does so by a process of reasoning largely supplied by Undershaft. As if to show how difficult the decision to join him will be, Undershaft quickly reasserts his ruthlessness: he takes pleasure in the destructiveness of his weapons but remains indifferent to the identity of the victor in the wars of the time. He will sell arms to anyone who will pay for them. But in his oblique way, he reveals two justifications for this policy. First, it has enabled him to build a town which a sane society could study with profit. Secondly, his amorality is a goad applied to the flanks of the timid. Poverty and slavery, he says, can be destroyed by bullets. "If you good people prefer preaching and shirking to buying my weapons and fighting the rascals, dont blame me" (p. 497). Money and power are prerequisite to good deeds. And as Cusins still wavers, Shaw's Machiavelli speaks more pointedly: "Whatever can blow men up can blow society up" (p. 499).

Cusins is moving to the acknowledgment that power is the basis of social change for good or evil. But he clings to the Christian virtues of love and pity. He is in the dilemma of the Fabian socialist torn between "gradualness" and violent revolution. When he says that he hates war, Undershaft replies, "Hatred is the coward's revenge for being intimidated. Dare you make war on war?" (p. 501). He can go no further without destroying his persona as war profiteer.

Alone with Barbara, Cusins announces his decision to accept Undershaft's dare—for that is what it is. Undershaft has offered power. Cusins will ultimately use it not indifferently but for the common good. Intellectual, imaginative, and religious power, he now declares, have served the few against the many; his guns will create a counter-force. He has already said that he will choose his clients, though Undershaft has forbidden such a course. Adolphus can one day become the "noble wolf" suggested by his name. By such a course he would "cozen" the forces of darkness. The audience may wonder just how Cusins will be able to use his factory for the common people, but Shaw cannot answer that question within the play without acts or plans instituting revolution. This would jeopardize the comedy.

The Greeks considered all who did not speak their language "barbarians," Gentiles outside the law. Barbara ceases to be a barbarian. She too is converted by her tour of Perivale St. Andrews and by her indoctrination in the "Gospel of St. Andrew Undershaft." "Transfigured," she says, "I have got rid of the bribe of bread. I have got rid of the bribe of heaven." She will help to unveil "an eternal light in the Valley of the Shadow" (p. 503). We are to believe that the *élan vital* of the daughter is not less than that of her "mystic" father. She will place her spiritual gift at the service of men not irretrievably shackled by poverty but free to advance in human godliness.

The ironic method of Undershaft has educated Cusins and Barbara. The other members of the family group are beyond "salvation" and remain variously foolish. Lomax is at the bottom of the hierarchy, though like certain Restoration fools, he at one point stumbles on the "truth" as he says: "The fact is, you know, there's a certain amount of tosh about this notion of wickedness. It doesnt work. . . . You see, all sorts of chaps are always doing all sorts of things; and we have to fit them in somehow, dont you know" (p. 500). Sarah has nothing on her mind. Stephen begins with a perfectly conventional horror of Undershaft. He learns to admire his father's business acumen but is incapable of learning much more than that. He will continue to suffer from the illusions of the unthinking members of his class. Lady Brit, for all her absurd narrowness, wins respect for her formidable strong-mindedness. She proves that Shaw can clearly distinguish between illusion and the illuded but attractive personality.

The decision to cure Barbara of her illusions and to give her a credible faith was daring, but it did not succeed. She is the great disappointment of the play. Shaw could not find the vocabulary for her new religion. In the early scenes it is piquant that so charming and lively a girl should be speaking the naive language of the Salvation Army. Her verve seems to justify her simple notions, though what she actually says can command little more than smiling sympathy. But from the moment of her disillusionment and defeat at the West Ham shelter, Shaw does not quite know what to do with her. At the first production in 1905, some reviewers were scandalized by the moment in which, "almost delirious," she cries, "My God: why hast thou forsaken me?" (p. 485). The line is objectionable not because it is blasphemous but because it is out of key with the character and the context. Inevitably, the words suggest either that Barbara is of very great stature or that her conception of her own role is vastly inflated. Yet she is neither a tragic heroine nor a fool.

In the third act, her decision to save the souls of the well-fed and complacent residents of Perivale St. Andrews is accompanied by grandiose rhetoric. To Cusins she exclaims, "Oh! did you think my courage would never come back? did you believe that I was a deserter? that I, who have stood in the streets, and taken my people to my heart, and talked of the holiest and greatest things with them, could ever turn back and chatter foolishly to fashionable people about nothing in a drawing room?" (p. 503). It is not at all clear that Undershaft's employees will need to be taken to her heart. And when she adds, "Oh! and I have my dear little Dolly boy still" (p. 503), one would expect the Greek professor to be slightly embarrassed. Barbara sounds more foolish after salvation than before. One may conclude that she has exchanged one illusion for another.

Cusins makes his transitions more successfully, in part because he has not been committed to an untenable position. In Act Two Undershaft stuns him by demolishing standard and comforting ideas; in the third act the professor begins to think for himself. He has been called the protagonist of the play, but this is to make too much of conclusions almost put in his mouth by Undershaft. Near the beginning of the last scene he says that if he had been interested in power he would not have come to the munitions plant, yet at the close he wants to accept power for all. Alone with Barbara, he says, "I love the common people," opposing the stated scorn of Undershaft. "I want to arm them against the lawyers, the doctors, the priests, the literary men, the professors, the artists, and the politicians, who, once in authority, are more disastrous and tyrannical than all the fools, rascals, and impostors" (p. 502). This dazzling Shavian hyperbole makes Cusins sound like Undershaft even as he propounds ideas that Undershaft could not explicitly accept. Cusins is walking a logical tightrope, taking suggestions from his teacher and pushing them to previously unexpressed conclusions. There may be some doubt whether he would say all this to Undershaft, but even if the passage is not fully adjusted to the context, it is morally and theatrically plausible.

Most of the minor characters show no strain between life and idea. Lady Brit, for example, is wholly consistent and delightfully real. Barbara and Cusins have to struggle with Shaw's plans for them. But Undershaft is the great achievement of the play. Like John Tanner he is a prodigious talker, but whereas Tanner is transparent, Undershaft has about him the mystery of a poetic creation. He seems to be all compact of oratory, but as we listen to him moving from brutal advocacy of warmaking to his last significant question, "Dare you make war on war?" we begin to attribute to him an inner conflict which is not presented psychologically. He remains a mask, but increasingly we are aware of the face beneath. He is a character whose whereabouts can be plotted though it is not seen by the naked eye.

Ultimately we realize that he regards himself as custodian of power held ready for one who will use it rightly—though his profession forbids him to use that adverb. One hint of his inner meaning is contained in the aphorism he assigns to the Undershaft who preceded him: "NOTHING IS EVER DONE IN THIS WORLD UNTIL MEN ARE PREPARED TO KILL ONE ANOTHER IF IT IS NOT DONE" (p. 497). Scoundrels have no objection to violence, but the point is that the victims of oppression must prepare to turn on their oppressors. Undershaft's "realism" does not exclude Shaw's intense moral feeling. In addition to being a Dionysus and a Machiavelli, he is also a Moses who cannot enter the Promised Land.

His complex passion is projected in speeches which, at first restrained, rise to torrential force. When Mrs. Baines tells him that although the

Army fights drunkenness, the distiller Saxmunden is making a large gift to the Army, Undershaft tears out the check he has just signed and says to her:

I also, Mrs. Baines, may claim a little disinterestedness. Think of my business! think of the widows and orphans! the men and lads torn to pieces with shrapnel and poisoned with lyddite! [*Mrs. Baines shrinks; but he goes on remorselessly*] the oceans of blood, not one drop of which is shed in a really just cause! the ravaged crops! the peaceful peasants forced, women and men, to till their fields under the fire of opposing armies on pain of starvation! the bad blood of the fierce little cowards at home who egg on others to fight for the gratification of their national vanity! All this makes money for me: I am never richer, never busier than when the papers are full of it. Well, it is your work to preach peace on earth and goodwill to men. [*Mrs. Baines's face lights up again*]. Every convert you make is a vote against war. [*Her lips move in prayer*]. Yet I give you this money to help you to hasten my own commercial ruin [*He gives her the cheque*].

[p. 484]

One purpose of the speech is to prove to Cusins the thesis that the Army can be bought. A second purpose is to separate Barbara from her faith and work, for Undershaft has already decided that she must preach his gospel. But coming from one who grows rich on war, the words are ignited by irony. They condemn charity from millionaires and, more important, uncover the speaker's conviction that up to 1905, no modern war has been fought for a justifiable reason. We notice that the only kind of war mentioned pits nation against nation. While not abandoning his doctrine of power, the speech reveals through its violent indirection an intense though unspecified desire for revolutionary change. Undershaft means more than he says. Only Cusins has a chance of understanding him.

The speech begins in ominous quiet, rises to a climax of horror, and falls back into the irony with which it began. The long series is a very marked characteristic of Shaw's prose.[9] The series beginning with "my business" contains seven members, not an unusually large number for Shaw in his non-dramatic writing. Undershaft talks much as Shaw writes. As elsewhere in Undershaft's use of series, the members grow progressively longer, flooding the listener with the weight of the speaker's conviction. Only the fifth member interrupts the expansion. The iron-willed force of the speech is increased by another stylistic trait of Shaw, his proneness to total assertions and denials. "Not one" drop of blood has been shed in a just cause. "All this" enriches Undershaft. He is "never" richer or busier than when the newspapers are "full" of war. The horrors are, of course, specific enough; they strike harder through alliteration and balanced phrases. The entire speech resounds with powerful but directed emotion.

In *Major Barbara*, the comic form just succeeds in containing impulses toward violence. Scorn, wrath, Nietzschean contempt for the virtues of forbearance and pity join with a radicalism grown fiercely impatient and encounter a faith in life supported by a quite normal liking for people. The shock of battle is there; a state of high tension persists to the final curtain. For now, comedy holds the stage, but there is no assurance that Shaw will not soon drive it into the wings.

Actually, he was not about to do so. Perhaps his faith in the power of life to raise even the "subaverage" to ever higher levels of consciousness ultimately gripped him more strongly than his long and intense preoccupation with the question: what can now be made of the crooked stick of man? Shaw the Utopian supported Shaw the comic dramatist. His plays extended the boundaries of comedy and were, he must have hoped, a significant moment in the evolution of mankind, for as he made his Father Keegan say in the last scene of *John Bull's Other Island*, "Every jest is an earnest in the womb of Time" (p. 452).

NOTES

1. "Meredith on Comedy," *Our Theatres in the Nineties*, rev. ed. (London, 1948), III, 83, 87.

2. *Prefaces* (London, 1934), p. 702.

3. "Meredith on Comedy," p. 85.

4. *The Faerie Queene*, III,i,19.

5. As is well known, Cusins is based on Professor Gilbert Murray. In 1905, Murray and other Cambridge scholars were developing the theory, already hinted by Nietzsche, that tragedy and comedy were not only Dionysian in origin but fundamentally concerned with the myth of the Year Spirit.

6. *Prefaces*, pp. 135–36.

7. On "Bloody Sunday," January 22, 1905, Russian police fired on a workers' demonstration. "The summer of 1905 witnessed new strikes, mass peasant uprisings in many provinces, active opposition and revolutionary movements among national minorities, and even occasional rebellions in the armed forces . . ." (Nicholas Riasonovsky, *A History of Russia* [New York, 1963], pp. 451–52). *Major Barbara* was first presented on November 28, 1905. Shaw himself had participated in a Bloody Sunday, November 13, 1887. See his *Essays in Fabian Socialism* (London, 1932), pp. 130–35.

8.   In an excellent study of *Major Barbara*, Joseph Frank interprets the play as a parable of sin, repentance, and salvation. The salvation is, of course, that envisioned by Undershaft. See "*Major Barbara*—Shaw's Divine Comedy," *PMLA*, LXXII (1956), 61–74.

9.   On the characteristics of Shaw's prose, see Richard M. Ohmann's detailed investigation, *Shaw: The Style and the Man* (Middletown, Conn., 1962).

Postscript

In our time serious writers, however striking their comic gifts, have usually found it impossible or undesirable to remain long within the area of comedy, partially, perhaps, because their contemplation of current social forms depresses them and partially because they fear to be looked on as mere entertainers or, worse yet, optimists. It is hard to think of a recent American playwright whose comic successes do not make him an object of suspicion among intellectuals—witness the decline of Thornton Wilder's reputation as his commitment to comedy became more pronounced. In his delightful play *The Matchmaker*, the central character says, "There comes a moment in everybody's life when he must decide whether he'll live among human beings or not—a fool among fools or a fool alone." She is making a shrewd statement of the comedy of life and the life of comedy. But what if readers and spectators have become convinced that all men are fools alone and that even the crowd is lonely?

Since 1945 the most impressive comic achievements have been fragmentary effects in what can hardly be classed as comedy. The comic dialogue in Williams' *A Streetcar Named Desire* or Osborne's *The Entertainer* far surpasses what can be heard in a typical Broadway comedy. After turning to the drama, Beckett and Ionesco quickly revealed that comic effects can reach maximum brilliance when set in a context of mystery and fear. Ionesco's *Victims of Duty* (1952) is a handsome illustration of the method.

Ionesco calls his play a "pseudo-drama." The term might easily be taken to mean "comedy," since a false claim to dramatic power is ludicrous. The play itself approaches comedy from a number of directions. Although the basic action is a young detective's ruthless interrogation of a timid bourgeois, Choubert, the play includes wry comments on the drama of the past, alludes to the importance of Ionesco, and parodies assorted dramatic and literary styles. Characters suddenly appear, demanding the spectator's sympathy, and as suddenly disappear. Part of the play is a performance on a little stage by Choubert, who pursues his search for answers as the detective-spectator watches from a chair and throws out new questions. Whether or not the episode parodies the psychoanalytic process, it is strange and strangely funny. Choubert's shrewish wife, Madeleine, frequently interrupts the performance with contemptuous remarks, for she is now a demanding theatre patron, a transposition of her character into another key. The constant oscillation between realism and fantasy produces astonishment, laughter, and a mingling of the two. The total effect is breathtaking, theatrical in the best sense.

The greatest achievement of the play is the scene in which the young detective suddenly becomes Choubert's father. Within a few sentences Ionesco creates a tortured, lonely, defeated man pouring out his love for his son and his anguish at his inability to reach him. The power of the episode is a product of an imperious rhetoric rapidly forcing the moment from the intense to the ridiculous and back, multiplied by the sheer daring of transforming the cold young interrogator into a suffering, middle-aged man. When well played, the passage has an extraordinary force whether or not the audience senses a parallel between paternalistic government and the superego. Laughter and a somewhat troubled wonderment revolve dizzily without the aid of any clear explanation of what it all means.

Victims of Duty realizes Ionesco's "dream of finding theatrical projects in their pure state." Comedy and other genres are employed as material for bravura effects. The content of drama—wit, irony, pity, and fear—has become its medium.

At present, "theatrical projects," whether pure or stirred with meaning, exercise a hypnotic power over the stage. Comedy is often a perspective adopted and then displaced, a hypothesis entertained, made much of, and then set aside by the speculative mind. In Tom Stoppard's brilliant *Rosencrantz and Guildenstern are Dead* (1967), for example, the leading men, whose very prominence is a joke, are attractive fools caught up in a world of laughable chances which takes on the nature of compulsion—part of the compulsion being the plot of Shakespeare's *Hamlet*. But these innocents, who become less innocent as the play proceeds, learn that Hamlet is to be treacherously slain. Offered an opportunity to save him, they fail to seize it, and the play is no longer a comedy.

When Saul Bellow was writing his provocative play *The Last Analysis* (1965), he may have been tempted to turn comedy into "infinite sadness salted with jokes," in the phrase of Bummidge, the suffering clown of the work. Instead Bellow explored new comic terrain. He has said that the play is about the mind's comic struggle for survival in the midst of Ideas. But since the mind in question is that of a famous comic cursed with such a severe case of the "Pagliacci gangrene" that he can no longer bear to see, hear, or smell the audiences he once set laughing, the play also concerns comedy itself.

Once wealthy and adored, Bummidge has been excluded from stage and television because of his increasing intellectuality. Relatives, mistresses, and friends had gouged him while he was rich, and still hope to do so again. Now he plans to act out his troubled psychological history on closed circuit television for an audience of analysts and others gathered at the Waldorf. Through no efforts of his own, executives from the entertainment media will also be watching the show. A huge success, the performance brings a million dollars in business offers. Bummidge not only rejects them but banishes all his greedy associates. He will establish the Bummidge Institute of Nonsense, where he will train disciples in his newly developed comic therapy.

Bummidge has obviously been reading not only in abnormal psychology itself but in up-to-date psychoanalytic theories of laughter and comedy. Consequently, he now talks about comedy as if it were a pretty dark affair. The text is sprinkled with observations like these:

Have you ever watched audiences laughing? You should see how monstrous it looks; you should listen from my side of the footlights.

Farce follows horror into darkness. Deeper, deeper.

Not surprisingly, therefore, Bummidge thinks that the new comedy must be built on the conflicts of Ego and Superego. As assistants read from his notes on comedy and the state of man, he himself has collapsed under the stress of "humanitis," the disease of being human. But he will recover in time for the end of the play.

A clown "driven to thought," Bummidge treats ideas clownishly but often felicitously. Actually, his thoughts on comedy are darker than the play in which he appears. For one thing, he himself is a lively buffoon, a symbol of the regenerative powers of man, as his revival near the end of the play demonstrates. For another, his absurdity and vitality contradict the darkness of his theory; indeed they make it look laughably solemn. Further, in an important passage late in the play, his thoughts, quoted while he is in collapse, stress the idea that for all our sickness, fumbling, and vice, the human comedy must ultimately rest on the recognition of manhood and the individual. By the end of the play, Bum-

midge's, and Bellow's, theory of comedy has come through as percep-
tibly sanguine, not nihilistic.

The old zany has more than a touch of the Aristophanic clown about
him—the Trygaeus who digs up the buried corpse of Peace, the Dicaeopolis who, disenchanted with the war policies of Athens, makes a private peace with Sparta, which he celebrates with wine, women, and
song. But Bummidge's victory is much shakier than that of the Greek
clowns; it is funny but also sad, and it is not what he thinks it is. And it
is not the social triumph associated for many centuries with the conclusion of comedy. It is a small, almost pitiful, perhaps temporary, advance he makes against his personal demons and a charming, ludicrous
hope that his success can be passed on to others. The divine average
embraced by Whitman and pursued by the Utopian Shaw is a long stalk
from Bummidge, but he sights the game in the distance. The play is
new comedy sustained by the old.

In the New York theatre of the nineteen sixties one became aware of
a sharp cleavage between traditional drama in which it was relatively
safe to invest and the experiments and advances of off-Broadway. Standard drama attracted the mature, although their guilt feelings sometimes caused them to punish themselves by attending in large numbers
such a play as *Who's Afraid of Virginia Woolf?* Downtown theatre
drew the young but was directed against their elders. Broadway could
be stimulating but tended to confirm the educated and middle-aged
in their own values, whereas drama in the lower reaches of Manhattan
sought to shake and bewilder their often timid liberalism. Actually,
self-congratulation was manifesting itself both on Broadway and in
the Village. By making a choice between Forty-Second Street and Wash-
ington Square, one could hear the songs he delighted to hear.

For Broadway, Neil Simon wrote a series of immensely successful
comedies. His *Plaza Suite* (1968), a group of three short plays, makes
plain the reason for his success, for as one reads, one can hear the audience exploding with laughter at regular intervals. The last and best of
the group, however, voices a persisting comic theme in the very process
of gracefully acknowledging that the rising generation in America is
better than the old. A girl about to be married has locked herself in the
bathroom of her parents' hotel suite and refuses to emerge. The parents, who dominate the play, argue, plead, demand that she come out,
and attempt to break down the door, but everything fails. She remains
inaccessible and silent. The prospective bride, we finally learn, fears
that marriage will turn her into someone like her parents. At the end

of the play, however, the groom arrives, has only to say, "Cool it," and the holdout is over. The marriage will proceed.

The parents are funny, benighted, almost contemptible, but not unlikable. By implication the girl has all the sensitivity they lack. Like the comedy of the past, this play chooses beauty before age. The norm is to be found not in what is called the Establishment (the very word is by now disestablishing) but with those who will shortly replace it. Yet to say this of a play written in the late sixties is not quite the same as remarking that *A Midsummer-Night's Dream* favors Hermia over Egeus. In a society essentially stable, an affectionate glance toward the young does not imply any stern dismissal of the old—Egeus simply fades away; but in a time when public communications emphasize and consequently intensify the conflicts of the generations, a smile in one directon all but guarantees a frown in the other. At present the comic theme of renewal has taken on a note of exacerbation threatening comedy itself. In the third play of *Plaza Suite*, which avoids hysteria, the point is made in comic terms but with a certain seriousness. To defend Simon against the charge of triviality, it is unnecessary to argue that he presents life as a steady ache made tolerable by perception of the ludicrous.

If Neil Simon represents the prosperous comedy of the sixties, Rosalyn Drexler and Terrence McNally illustrate two aspects of the new comedy or paracomedy. Winner of an Obie award and named by Clive Barnes in 1968 as the queen of the underground drama, Mrs. Drexler has been praised for her "highly serious" farces. Her *Hot Buttered Roll*, fairly typical of her work, might be roughly described as Ben Jonson reduced to one act and translated into East Village camp.

A rich and lecherous old invalid, Corrupt Savage, spends his time devouring girlie magazines, speaking in parody of their ads and correspondence columns, taping conversations on a concealed recorder, and wetting his bed. His outsized nurse, a call girl, and a pimp plot to get his money, but the old buffoon turns out to be cleverer than they and sends them on a fool's errand. The plans to excite and break down Corrupt are as fantastic as the writer can make them, as at the point where the call girl enters in a rubber outfit for deep-sea diving but gets no response from Corrupt's "sex-o-meter." The play's claim, if any, to seriousness must rest on its language. The dialogue is filled with pornographic joking kept furiously going by all the characters. If Corrupt recalls the supposed invalid Volpone, Drexler's comic talks more like a liberated Groucho Marx than Jonson's scoundrel. When Volpone leaps from his bed and makes for Celia, he sings, "Come, my Celia." But as

Corrupt's nurse carries him to bed, he says, "Nice. So nice to be pressed against your genuine heavy equipment; it's really ringside, isn't it?" Whereas Jonson's attitude toward Volpone fuses condemnation, laughter, and an appreciation of ingenuity, however appalling, Drexler's characters exist for the sake of the raffish jests that, except for a number of deliberately outrageous or repellent phrases, move laughter but no serious reflection. The play is new comedy only to the extent that its language attacks the gentility of an imagined audience—one probably out of earshot. In the main, the play is a fairly good-natured put-on. And if we compare Corrupt with the people around him, we can say that virtue if not normality triumphs.

In the late sixties, Terrence McNally came to prominence with a number of short plays including *Sweet Eros* and *Next*. *Sweet Eros* is sophisticated Grand Guignol. *Next* begins as an ominous but funny satire on American militarism and ends in a long monologue of free fantasy combining sympathy for the sorry protagonist with troubling implications about the dismal drift of our society. The writer is unquestionably talented. His sketch is the kind of drama reviewers now constantly describe as riotous and terrifying comedy. It is not comedy, but for the present, theatre critics will go on using the term to label plays they find both "screamingly funny" and frighteningly indicative of our corruption. The objection to the classification is not, of course, that *Next* and comparable plays "fall short" of comedy; but the supposition that writing about current disorientation must be more profound *and* somehow more comic than comedy as understood, say, through Molière, Shaw, and Giraudoux illustrates two confusions at once: the failure to distinguish grim drama exciting an often nervous laughter from an art form with a long history and a degree of stability, and the notion that by contradicting a noun with an adjective we arrive at a brilliant paradox—black comedy.

In his "Problems of the Theatre," Friedrich Dürrenmatt addresses himself to questions about the relation between genre and epoch. Like most intellectuals, Dürrenmatt is depressed, almost hopeless, about our world, in which "there are no more guilty and also, no responsible men." Tragedy, he thinks, is therefore unsuitable for us. But comedy is not. Though the world is now senseless, grotesque, apocalyptic—a landscape Hieronymus Bosch might have painted—the comic writer himself need not despair; he may choose endurance and courage. And though tragedy seems no longer possible, "the tragic" may arise as a frightening moment within an already threatened comic world.

Recognizing that art cannot repeat itself, Dürrenmatt attempts to accommodate genre to epoch. Others would engulf art form in the flight of time. It is one thing to argue that comedy is irrelevant to the year 1970; although the proposition is false, it is not self-contradictory. It is quite another thing to proclaim that "black comedy" is our mode. For of course black comedy is an impossibility. Although comedies vary in mood, any play presenting human life as pitiful surrender and grotesque cruelty, no matter how often hilarious, absolutely inverts the meaning of comedy. Pathological laughter, however expressive of a well-publicized moment in time, is not comic laughter.

Two full-length plays by the English playwright Joe Orton have recently been assigned to the supposed genre, black comedy. Orton's *Loot* is a farce involving numerous manipulations of a corpse, the casket of which is used to conceal money stolen from a bank. The stage business could be grisly, but in at least one production the action, instead of being frightening, was merry to the point of silliness. In the much superior *Entertaining Mr. Sloane*, a middle-aged woman and her brother agree to conceal a murder committed by a seventeen-year-old boy in return for his favors, to be shared on a seasonal basis. The arrangement is a debased version, perhaps, of the story of Proserpine, Ceres, and Pluto. The play is strongly, even deeply, ironic and far more chilling than *Loot*. The understated and at first mysterious dialogue, somewhat reminiscent of Harold Pinter, creates a vision of evil both horrid and credible. Though sometimes provocative of laughter, the play, far from being a comedy, illustrates Northrop Frye's thesis that criticism needs to increase the number of generic terms in common usage. Frye's "irony" applies very well to *Sloane*. Whereas Saul Bellow, in *The Last Analysis*, appears to consider the idea that "farce follows horror" but implicitly rejects the thesis in the play he writes, Orton enters horror but allows laughter when the less evil and more stupid is duped by the more cleverly vile. *The Last Analysis* is comedy; *Sloane* is not.

For the time being, playwrights with comic gifts have a number of options. Ignoring fashionable preoccupations, they can write traditional comedy. They can use traditional comedy as a thread in a pattern. They can abandon the form. Or attending to the revolution on the borders of comedy, they can reexamine its presuppositions, as Bellow has done, and where necessary modify them. For although comedy cannot become precisely what it is not, this social art will inevitably be affected by the mood of the particular society in which it appears, and at present this means that comedy, like tragedy, will be attacked by fear, disgust, and cynicism and threatened with dismemberment. Fortunately, the idea of comedy is itself a persisting social influence.

Selected Bibliography

PLAYS

Anouilh, Jean. *The Rehearsal* [*La Répétition*]. Translated by Lucienne Hill. In *Jean Anouilh (Five Plays)*. A Mermaid Dramabook. New York: Hill and Wang, 1958.

Aristophanes. *The Acharnians of Aristophanes*. Edited by W. J. M. Starkie. London: Macmillan and Co., Limited, 1909.

———. *The Birds of Aristophanes*. Edited by Benjamin B. Rogers. London: G. Bell and Sons, 1906.

———. *Ladies' Day* [*Thesmophoriazusae*]. Translated by Dudley Fitts. New York: Harcourt, Brace, and Co., 1959.

Beaumarchais, Pierre-Augustin de. *Le Barbier de Séville*. Edited by E. J. Arnould. Oxford: Oxford University Press, 1963.

Bellow, Saul. *The Last Analysis*. New York: The Viking Press, 1965.

Congreve, William. *William Congreve (Complete Plays)*. Edited by Alexander C. Ewald. A Mermaid Dramabook. New York: Hill and Wang, 1956.

Drexler, Rosalyn. *"The Line of Least Existence" and Other Plays*. New York: Random House, 1967.

Etherege, Sir George. *The Man of Mode*. Edited by Bernard F. Dukore. San Francisco: Chandler Publishing Company, 1962.

Feydeau, Georges. *Keep an Eye on Amélie* [*Occupe-toi d'Amélie*]. In *"Let's Get a Divorce!" and Other Plays*. Edited by Eric Bentley. A Mermaid Dramabook. New York: Hill and Wang, 1958.

Fry, Christopher. *A Phoenix Too Frequent*. London: Oxford University Press, 1953.

Jonson, Ben. *The Alchemist*. In *Elizabethan and Jacobean Comedy*. Edited by Robert Ornstein and Hazelton Spencer. Boston: D. C. Heath and Company, 1964.

———. *Ben Jonson*. Edited by C. H. Herford, Percy Simpson, and Evelyn Simpson. 11 vols. Oxford: The Clarendon Press, 1925–52.

————. *Volpone*. In *Elizabethan and Stuart Plays*. Edited by Charles Read Baskervill et al. New York: Holt, Rinehart, and Winston, 1934.

Marivaux, Pierre Carlet de. *Théâtre Complet*. Edited by Marcel Arland. Bibliothèque de la Pléiade, No. 79. N. p.: Librairie Gallimard, 1949.

Middleton, Thomas. *A Trick to Catch the Old One*. In *Elizabethan and Stuart Plays*. Edited by Charles Read Baskervill et al. New York: Holt, Rinehart, and Winston, 1934.

Molière. *Oeuvres Complètes*. Edited by Maurice Rat. Bibliothèque de la Pléiade, Nos. 8 and 9. 2 vols. N. p.: Librairie Gallimard, 1956.

Musset, Alfred de. *Il ne faut jurer de rien*. Edited by Jacques Nathan. Classiques Larousse. Paris: Librairie Larousse, 1941.

Shakespeare, William. *The Complete Plays and Poems of William Shakespeare*. Edited by William Allan Neilson and Charles Jarvis Hill. New Cambridge Edition. Boston: Houghton Mifflin Company, 1942.

————. *Much Ado About Nothing*. Edited by David L. Stevenson. The Signet Classic Shakespeare. New York: The New American Library, 1964.

Shaw, George Bernard. *The Complete Plays of Bernard Shaw*. London: Odhams Press, Limited, 1934.

Wilde, Oscar. *The Importance of Being Earnest*. 6th ed. London: Methuen & Co., 1912.

Wilder, Thornton. *Three Plays: "Our Town," "The Skin of Our Teeth," "The Matchmaker."* New York: Harper & Row, Publishers, 1962.

THEORY AND CRITICISM

Adams, Henry H., and Baxter Hathaway, eds. *Dramatic Essays of the Neoclassic Age*. New York: Columbia University Press, 1950.

Addison, Joseph. *The Spectator*, No. 249. In *Eighteenth-Century Critical Essays*. Edited by Scott Elledge. Vol. I. Ithaca, N. Y.: Cornell University Press, 1961.

Barish, Jonas A. "*Bartholomew Fair* and Its Puppets," *MLQ*, XX (1959), 3–17.

Bentley, Eric. *The Life of the Drama*. New York: Atheneum, 1964.

Bergler, Edmund. *Laughter and the Sense of Humor*. New York: Intercontinental Medical Book Corp., 1956.

Bergson, Henri. *Laughter*. [Translated by Cloudesley Brereton and Fred Rothwell.] In *Comedy*. Edited by Wylie Sypher. Anchor Books. Garden City, N.Y.: Doubleday & Company, Inc., 1956.

Blaiklock, E. M. "Walking Away from the News," *Greece and Rome*, Second Series, I (1954), 98–111.

Brown, John Russell. *Shakespeare and His Comedies*. 2d ed. London: Methuen & Co., 1962.

Butcher, S. H. *Aristotle's Theory of Poetry and Fine Art, with a Critical Text and Translation of the Poetics*. 4th ed. London: Macmillan and Company, Limited, 1932.

Cahiers de la Compagnie Madeleine Renaud–Jean-Louis Barrault, XV (Jan., 1956). (Essays on Georges Feydeau.)

Cassirer, Ernst. *An Essay on Man*. Anchor Books. Garden City, N.Y.: Doubleday & Company, Inc., 1953.

Collingwood, R. G. *The Principles of Art*. A Galaxy Book. Oxford: Oxford University Press, 1955.

Cook, Albert. *The Dark Voyage and the Golden Mean: A Philosophy of Comedy*. Cambridge: Harvard University Press, 1949.

Cope, Jackson I. "*Bartholomew Fair* as Blasphemy." In *Renaissance Drama VIII*. Edited by Samuel Schoenbaum. Evanston, Ill.: Northwestern University Press, 1965.

Cornford, Francis M. *The Origin of Attic Comedy*. London: E. Arnold, 1914.

Crane, William G. *Wit and Rhetoric in the Renaissance*. New York: Columbia University Press, 1937.

Deloffre, Frédéric. *Marivaux et le marivaudage*. Paris: Société d'édition Les Belles Lettres, 1955.

Dürrenmatt, Friedrich. Preface: "Problems of the Theatre." *Four Plays: 1957–62*. Translated by Gerhard Nellhaus. London: Jonathan Cape, n.d.

Ehrenberg, Victor. *The People of Aristophanes*. 2d ed. Cambridge: Harvard University Press, 1951.

Eidelberg, Ludwig. "A Contribution to the Study of Wit," *Psychoanalytic Review*, XXXII (1945), 33–61.

Else, Gerald F. *Aristotle's Poetics: The Argument*. Cambridge: Harvard University Press, 1957.

Empson, William. *The Structure of Complex Words*. London: Chatto & Windus, 1951.

Feibleman, James K. *In Praise of Comedy*. New York: Russell & Russell, 1962.

Fielding, Henry. Preface. *Joseph Andrews*. Signet Classics. New York: The New American Library, 1961.

Frank, Joseph. "*Major Barbara*–Shaw's Divine Comedy," *PMLA*, LXXII (1956), 61–74.

Fredrick, Edna C. *The Plot and Its Construction in Eighteenth-Century Criticism of French Comedy.* Bryn Mawr, Pa., 1934.

Freud, Sigmund. *Jokes and Their Relation to the Unconscious.* Translated by James Strachey. New York: W. W. Norton & Company, Inc., 1960.

Frye, Northrop. *Anatomy of Criticism.* Princeton: Princeton University Press, 1957.

Fujimara, Thomas. *The Restoration Comedy of Wit.* Princeton: Princeton University Press, 1952.

Goddard, Harold C. *The Meaning of Shakespeare.* Chicago: The University of Chicago Press, 1951.

Gomme, A. W. "Aristophanes and Politics," *Classical Review,* LII (1938), 97–109.

Gregory, J. C. *The Nature of Laughter.* London: K. Paul, Trench, Trübner and Co., Ltd., 1924.

Hays, H. R. "Satire and Identification: An Introduction to Ben Jonson," *Kenyon Review,* XIX (1957), 257–83.

Hegel, Georg W. F. *Hegel on Tragedy.* Edited by Anne and Henry Paolucci. Anchor Books. Garden City, N. Y.: Doubleday & Company, Inc., 1962.

Ionesco, Eugène. "Notes on My Theatre," translated by Leonard C. Pronko, *TDR,* VII (1963), 127–59.

Jaeger, Werner. *Paideia: The Ideals of Greek Culture.* Translated by Gilbert Highet. 3 vols. New York: Oxford University Press, 1939–44.

Jenkins, Harold. "Shakespeare's *Twelfth Night,*" *Rice Institute Pamphlets,* XLV (1959). In *Shakespeare: The Comedies.* Edited by Kenneth Muir. Englewood Cliffs, N. J.: Prentice-Hall, Inc., 1965.

Kerr, Walter. *Tragedy and Comedy.* New York: Simon & Schuster, 1967.

Knights, L. C. *Explorations.* New York: George W. Stewart, Inc., 1947.

Koestler, Arthur. *The Act of Creation.* New York: The Macmillan Company, 1964.

Lamb, Charles. *The Complete Works and Letters of Charles Lamb.* New York: The Modern Library, 1935.

Langer, Susanne K. *Feeling and Form: A Theory of Art. . . .* New York: Charles Scribner's Sons, 1953.

Lanson, Gustave. *Nivelle de la chaussée et la comédie larmoyante.* Paris: Librairie Hachette, 1903.

L'Express. April 2, 1959. Pp. 29–30. (Symposium on Marivaux.)

Mahood, Molly M. *Shakespeare's Wordplay.* London: Methuen & Co., 1957.

Martinovitch, N. N. *The Turkish Theatre*. New York: Theatre Arts, Inc., 1933.

Mazon, Paul. *Essai sur le composition des comédies d'Aristophane*. Paris: Librairie Hachette, 1904.

Moore, Will G. *Molière: A New Criticism*. Anchor Books. Garden City, N. Y.: Doubleday & Company, Inc., 1962.

Murray, Gilbert. *Aristophanes: A Study*. New York: Oxford University Press, 1933.

Norwood, Gilbert. *Greek Comedy*. Boston: John W. Luce and Co., 1932.

Ohmann, Richard M. *Shaw: The Style and the Man*. Middletown, Conn.: Wesleyan University Press, 1962.

Partridge, Edward B. *The Broken Compass: A Study of the Major Comedies of Ben Jonson*. London: Chatto & Windus, 1958.

————. Introduction. *Bartholomew Fair*. By Ben Jonson. Regents Renaissance Drama Series. Lincoln: University of Nebraska Press, 1964.

Pickard-Cambridge, A. W. *Dithyramb, Tragedy, and Comedy*. Oxford: Oxford University Press, 1927; 2d ed., revised by T. B. L. Webster. Oxford: Oxford University Press, 1962.

Ratermanis, Janis B. *Étude sur le comique dans le théâtre de Marivaux*. Geneva and Paris: E. Droz, 1961.

Richards, I. A. *The Philosophy of Rhetoric*. New York: Oxford University Press, 1936.

Schérer, Jacques. *La Dramaturgie de Beaumarchais*. Paris: Librairie Nizet, 1954.

Schopenhauer, Arthur. *The World as Will and Idea*. Translated by R. B. Haldane and J. Kemp. Vol. III. London: K. Paul, Trench, Trübner, and Co., Ltd., 1891.

Shaw, George Bernard. "Meredith on Comedy." In *Our Theatres in the Nineties*. Rev. ed. Vol. III. London: Constable and Company, Limited, 1948.

————. *Prefaces*. London: Constable and Company, Limited, 1934.

Simon, Alfred. *Molière par lui-même*. "Écrivains de toujours." N.p.: Éditions du Seuil, n.d.

Smith, James. "*Much Ado About Nothing*," *Scrutiny*, XIII (1946), 242–57.

Stevenson, David L., ed. Introduction. *Much Ado About Nothing*. The Signet Classic Shakespeare. New York: The New American Library, 1964.

Styan, John L. *The Dark Comedy*. New York: Cambridge University Press, 1962.

Swabey, Marie C. *Comic Laughter*. New Haven: Yale University Press, 1961.

Thibaudet, Albert. "Le Rire de Molière," *Revue de Paris*, XXIX (1922), 312–33.

Welsford, Enid. *The Fool: His Social and Literary History*. Anchor Books. Garden City, N. Y.: Doubleday & Company, Inc., 1961.

Whitman, Cedric H. *Aristophanes and the Comic Hero*. Cambridge: Harvard University Press, 1964.

Index

Action, 15, 19, 196; and thematic imagery in *Tartuffe*, 165–74; and theme in *Much Ado*, 140, 149
Aeschylus, *Agamemnon*, 69
Agroikos (boor), 77, 78
Alazôn (boaster), 71, 77, 78
Albee, Edward, *Who's Afraid of Virginia Woolf?*, 216
Allio, René, 189
Anouilh, Jean, 43, 45; on Marivaux, 192
Arden, John, 73
Aristophanes, 7, 16, 38, 65, 73, 76, 82, 83, 88, 118, 216
    The Acharnians, 65–72, 126
    The Birds, 65, 125–38
    The Clouds, 39, 65, 130–31, 133
    The Frogs, 49
    The Knights, 78, 126
    Lysistrata, 82
    Peace, 65, 126, 166
    The Wasps, 88
    The Women of the Ecclesia (*Ecclesiazusae*), 82
    The Women of Thesmophoria (*Thesmophoriazusae*), 11–13, 82
Aristotle, 21, 77, 107
Arland, Marcel, 182
Arlecchino, 180, 193
Arrabal, Fernando, 50

Beaumarchais, Pierre-Augustin de
    The Barber of Seville, 59–74
    The Marriage of Figaro, 62
Beaumont, Sir Francis, 5, 45
Beckett, Samuel, 5, 213
    Waiting for Godot, 45
Bellow, Saul, 175
    The Last Analysis, 214–16, 219

Bentley, Eric, 32–33
Bergler, Edmund, 32
Bergson, Henri, 8, 16, 56, 83, 87, 88, 145, 159
Boileau-Despréaux, Nicolas, 179
Bômolochos (buffoon), 77, 78
Bosch, Hieronymus, 218
Bossuet, Jacques-Bénigne, 169
Boucher, François, 180
Bourdaloue, Louis, 169
Brecht, Bertolt, 73, 188
Brown, John Russell, 140

Cabale des dévots, 174
Cassirer, Ernst, 8
Catullus, 115
Cervantes, Miguel de, 9
Chance, 19, 21, 22–23, 52–59, 83; and fate, 57
Chaucer, Geoffrey, 9
Chekhov, Anton, 43–44
Collingwood, R. G., 6
Comedy: as amusing action, 8–10; catharsis in, 18; chance in 19, 21, 22–23, 52–59, 83; conservative and liberal, 9; definition of, 7; discontinuity in, 11–16, 28–29, 68–69, 130–32; the divine average in, 18, 19–20; the festive in, 41–42, 75, 88, 118; inevitability in, 19, 28; of intrigue, 52–53; and irony, 38; laughter in, 31–36; and other forms, 44–46; realism in, 21; reduction of consciousness in, 16, 29; and romance, 45; and satire, 24, 49; social success and failure in, 16, 17–20, 26, 30, 154–55; and tragicomedy, 45–46

Comic hero, 82–87; Dicaeopolis as, 135–36; and the tragic hero, 87
Comic poetry: in *The Acharnians*, 70–72; in *The Alchemist*, 113–22; in *The Birds*, 130–32; in Fry, 105–7; and prose, 101–3; in *Twelfth Night*, 102–5
Congreve, William, 8, 43, 44
  The Double Dealer, 52
  Love for Love, 108–13
  The Way of the World, 37, 59, 111
Cook, Albert, 83
Corneille, Pierre de, 5–6
  Polyeucte, 57
Cornford, F. M., 65, 78, 80, 127
Courteline, Georges, 59
Croiset, Maurice, 125

Dark comedy, 42–43, 174–76, 215, 218–19
Decorum, 107, 110, 112, 142; in *Bartholomew Fair*, 160–61, 162, 163; Congreve on, 112; Jonson on, 114
Deloffre, Frédéric, 184
Deloffe, J., 187
Descartes, René, 39
Dicaeopolis, 135–36
Divine average, the, 18, 19–20, 25, 39, 87, 201, 216
Donneau de Visé, 41
Drame, le, 62–63
Drexler, Rosalyn, *Hot Buttered Roll*, 217–18
Dryden, John, *The Spanish Friar*, 45
Dürrenmatt, Friedrich, 218–19

Eidelberg, Ludwig, 34–36
Eirôn, 69, 77, 78
Empson, William, 29, 139, 144
Erasmus, Desiderius, 38, 148
Etherege, Sir George, *The Man of Mode*, 42, 107, 108

Falstaff, 7, 25, 36, 58, 78–82
Farce, 6, 11, 42, 215; *Sganarelle*, 52–59; in *Tartuffe*, 165, 172, 178–79
Farce du Cuvier, 42
Feibleman, James K., 131

Fernandez, Ramon, 19
Feydeau, Georges, *Keep an Eye on Amélie!* (*Occupe-toi d'Amélie*), 59
Fielding, Henry, *Joseph Andrews*, 87
Fletcher, John, 5, 45
  The Faithful Shepherdess, 45
Folly, 22, 75–78, 87, 162; in *As You Like It*, 22–24, 28; and the divine average, 19–20; and foolishness, 38; the language of, 119–22; and wit, 24, 108, 113, 140–51, 163
Freud, Sigmund, 32
  Jokes and Their Relation to the Unconscious, 10, 88–89, 144, 146, 147, 149
Fry, Christopher, 97
  A Phoenix Too Frequent, 105–7
Frye, Northrop, 44–45, 219

Gautier, Théophile, 14, 86
Gazagne, Paul, 191
Ghelderode, Michel de, 5, 38
Giraudoux, Jean, 8, 9, 180, 184
  The Enchanted (*Intermezzo*), 17–18
Goddard, H. C., 80
Gogol, Nikolai, 146
  The Inspector General, 83
Goldsmith, Oliver, 31, 43
Gomme, A. W., 126
Gordon, George, 22
Gorgias, 136–37
Gregory, J. C., 32
Guarini, Giovanni, 45

Herford, C. H., 153
Hobbes, Thomas, 32
Horace, 158

Ibsen, Henrik
  An Enemy of the People, 156
  Ghosts, 156, 199
Imagery: in *The Acharnians*, 70–72; in *The Alchemist*, 114-21; in *Love for Love*, 112–13; in *A Phoenix Too Frequent*, 105–7; in *Tartuffe*, 165 ff.
Ionesco, Eugène, 7
  Victims of Duty, 13, 213–14

Irony, 36; and comedy, 38, 49–50,
    163–64; in *The Double Incon-
    stancy*, 193–96; as a dramatic form,
    44–46; *Entertaining Mr. Sloane* as,
    219; *John Bull's Other Island* as,
    200–201.

Jaeger, Werner, 126
Jenkins, Harold, 104
Jonson, Ben, 16, 24, 44, 59, 75, 76, 77
    The Alchemist, 114–22
    Bartholomew Fair, 153–64
    Epicoene, 78
    Every Man out of His Humour, 156
    "The Famous Journey," 160
    Timber; or, Discoveries, 114, 158
    Volpone, 17, 42, 52, 94–95, 155–56,
        160, 217–18
Journal Encyclopédique, 60, 63
Juvenal, 153, 154

Kemp, Robert 187–88
Knights, L. C., vii, 112
Koestler, Arthur, 32

Labiche, Eugène, 59
Laclos, Choderlos de, 187
Lamb, Charles, 16
Langer, Susanne, 32, 78, 140
Language: and action, 97–107; in
    Congreve, 108–13; in Fry, 105–7;
    in Jonson, 113–22; in Molière,
    98–99; in Shakespeare, 101–5; in
    Shaw, 99–101, 209–11; and the
    speaker, 107–22
Lanson, Gustave, 197
La Rochefoucauld, François duc de,
    146, 147
Laughter, 31–36, 215
Lemarchand, Jacques, 187–88
Lettre sur la comédie de l'Imposteur,
    169, 170, 176
L'Express, 186–87
Louis XIV, 166, 173, 174

Macchiavelli, Niccolò, *Mandragola*, 50
McNally, Terrence, 217
    Next, 218
    Sweet Eros, 218
Mahood, M. M., 139

Marivaudage, 182, 183–84, 185–86, 195
Marivaux, Pierre de, 9
    Arlequin (*Arlequin poli par l'Amour*),
        46–48
    Le Cabinet du philosophe, 185
    The Double Inconstancy (*La Double
        Inconstance*), 47, 192–97
    The Game of Love and Chance (*Le
        Jeu de l'Amour et du Hasard*),
        180–86
    The Second Surprise of Love (*La
        Seconde Surprise de l'Amour*),
        186–92
    The Surprise of Love (*La Surprise de
        l'Amour*), 13–15
Martial, 153, 154, 162–63
Martinovitch, N. N., 78
Marx, Groucho, 217
Maugham, W. Somerset, 17
    The Circle, 97–98
Mazon, Paul, 66
Melodrama, 6
Meredith, George, 41, 113, 178, 198
Middleton, Thomas, 46
    A Trick to Catch the Old One, 49–50
Molière, 7, 8, 22, 43, 75, 76, 77, 82, 83,
        97, 99, 154, 181
    The Bourgeois Gentleman (*Le
        Bourgeois gentilhomme*), 65
    The Cheats of Scapin (*Les Fourberies
        de Scapin*), 83, 94–95
    The Doctor in Spite of Himself (*Le
        Médecin malgré lui*), 98–99
    Doctor Love (*L'Amour médicin*), 92
    Don Juan, 59
    The Forced Marriage (*Le Mariage
        forcé*), 9
    George Dandin, 77
    The Imaginary Invalid (*Le Malade
        imaginaire*), 17, 65, 89–94, 165
    The Learned Ladies (*Les Femmes
        savantes*), 38–42
    The Misanthrope, 7, 9, 20, 43, 93,
        94, 165
    The Miser (*L'Avare*), 93
    Monsieur de Pourceaugnac, 75
    The School for Wives (*L'École des
        Femmes*), 10–11, 58, 165

Sganarelle, 54–59
Tartuffe, 9, 92, 165–79
Moore, W. G., 91–92
Murray, Gilbert, 65
Musset, Alfred de, 9, 180
　　Don't Swear to It (*Il ne faut jurer de rien*), 84–86

Norwood, Gilbert, 66

Orton, Joe
　　Entertaining Mr. Sloane, 219
　　Loot, 219
Oxford Classical Dictionary: on Aristophanes, 66

Partridge, Edward B., 163
Petronius, 153
Picnic to Ialova, A, 78
Pinter, Harold, 219
Pirandello, Luigi, 43, 155
　　Henry IV, 117
Planchon, Roger, 186–89
Plato, 125
Plautus, 94
Ponêria (comic villainy), 94, 118, 134–35

Racine, Jean, 62, 196
Restoration comedy, 42, 82, 108
Ritualists, 33
Rogers, Benjamin, 131
Romance, 45, 182

Satire, 24, 49
Shaw, G. B., 7, 8, 75, 83, 97, 99, 216
　　Androcles and the Lion, 83
　　Arms and the Man, 199
　　The Devil's Disciple, 198
　　Everybody's Political What's What, 199
　　Getting Married, 65, 201
　　Heartbreak House, 201
　　John Bull's Other Island, 199–201
　　Major Barbara, 49, 198–212
　　Man and Superman, 199–200
　　The Man of Destiny, 52–54
　　Mrs. Warren's Profession, 198
　　On the Rocks, 100–101

Saint Joan, 201
　　Too True to Be Good, 100
Schérer, Jacques, 62
Schopenhauer, Arthur, 32, 33
Sellers, Peter, 52
Shakespeare, William, 7, 9, 17, 22, 72, 75, 76, 83, 88, 106, 107
　　All's Well That Ends Well, 84
　　As You Like It, 22–30, 42, 82
　　Henry IV, 18, 78–82, 150
　　Henry V, 82
　　Love's Labour's Lost, 9, 65, 75
　　A Midsummer Night's Dream, 217
　　Much Ado About Nothing, 21, 85, 139–52
　　Richard III, 83
　　Sonnets, 151
　　The Taming of the Shrew, 88
　　The Tempest, 146
　　Troilus and Cressida, 44–45
　　Twelfth Night, 42, 83, 101–5, 139
　　Two Gentlemen of Verona, 101–2
　　The Winter's Tale, 46
Sheridan, Richard B., 43, 44
　　The School for Scandal, 85
Sidney, Sir Philip, 8
Simon, Alfred, 95
Simon, Neil, *Plaza Suite*, 216–17
Smith, James, 140
Stanislavsky, Constantin, 44, 90, 149, 196
Starkie, W. J. M., 68
Stevenson, David L., 148
Stoppard, Tom, *Rosencrantz and Guildenstern Are Dead*, 214
Styan, J. L., 43
Subplots, 28–29
Swabey, Marie, 32

Tasso, Torquato, *Aminta*, 45
Terence, 94, 181
Thibaudet, Albert, 94
Thucydides, 127
Tractatus Coislinianus, 77–78
Tragedy, 6, 44–45; and comedy, 8, 11, 15, 29, 33, 52, 57; consciousness in, 15–16
Tragicomedy, 5–6; kinds of, 45–46

Vitalism, 202, 207
Voltaire, François Marie Arouet de, 9

Watteau, Antoine, 180, 181, 189
Welles, Orson, 34
Welsford, Enid, 80
West, Mae, 34–36
Whitman, Cedric, 70, 71, 118, 134–35, 136
Whitman, Walt, 19–20, 87, 216
Wilde, Oscar, 43, 44

The Importance of Being Earnest, 8, 36–37, 54, 108, 203
"The Soul of Man Under Socialism," 203
Wilder, Thornton, *The Matchmaker*, 213
Wit: dimensions of, 144–47; in *Love for Love*, 108–13; in Marivaux, 181, 182, 183–86; in *Much Ado About Nothing*, 139–52
Wycherley, William, 85
The Country Wife, 42, 59